IMAGES
of America

TAYLOR

On the Cover: Moffat Coal Company. In its heyday the Moffat Coal Company employed nearly 800 men in its mines and breakers. It was capable of producing 6,000 tons of coal per day. By 1966, the Moffat ceased operations; in the 1970s, when this photograph was taken, it had become a playground for vandals. Eventually, it was deemed an eyesore by the community and finally demolished in 1983. (Author's collection.)

IMAGES
of America

TAYLOR

Margo L. Azzarelli

ARCADIA
PUBLISHING

ISBN 978-0-7385-7256-7

Published by Arcadia Publishing
Charleston, South Carolina

Printed in the United States of America

Library of Congress Control Number: 2009936161

For all general information, please contact Arcadia Publishing:
Telephone 843-853-2070
Fax 843-853-0044
E-mail sales@arcadiapublishing.com
For customer service and orders:
Toll-Free 1-888-313-2665

Visit us on the Internet at www.arcadiapublishing.com

To my dad, Thomas Crispino, I know you are reading this up in heaven, but I wish you were here. Love, the Kid.

Contents

ACKNOWLEDGMENTS

I would like to thank all the wonderful people of Taylor who shared their memories and bits and pieces of its past with me, especially Marie Eskra, Mrs. Catarini, Doug Kneis, Bud Seever, and the senior citizens at the community center. I am extremely grateful to Dale Malecki for sharing his extraordinary photograph collection of the "Patch"; Nancy and Bob Thomas; Jacob Davis Funeral Home; Lenny and Joanie Green; the Taylor Community Library, especially director Jeanie Sluck; Kathy and Dennis Gawel; Banks Ries, my favorite coal miner; Mary Ann Moran Savakinus (the all powerful "OZ") and the Lackawanna Historical Society; Barbara Powell for all her help; Shawn Murphy for his extraordinary knowledge of Taylor and his willingness to share it with me; and Erin Vosgien, my very patient and kind editor.

I have a few special "thank yous," for without these people in my life this book would still be an idea in my head. First and foremost, my daughter, Marnie, for contributing all her computer talents, spending hours scanning photographs, and providing me with those much-needed cups of tea; my husband, Dominick, for his constant offers of help and a week's worth of suppers I didn't have to cook in order to reach my deadline; my mother, Donna, for her wisdom and the strength she gave me to finish the book (I only wish I were half the talented writer you are—it's time for you to share that talent with the rest of the world!); my grandparents, Susanna and Quinto Rossi, for always being there; my muse, "The GaGa"; and to my three special friends who I cannot imagine my life without: Christine Schaefer, my strong arm and soul sister; Monica Osborne, my sister and dearest friend (you are my comfort, just hearing your voice always makes me feel better); and Cheryl Kashuba, my inspiration (your faith in me is never ending). I love all of you.

INTRODUCTION

Taylor is known for being the first white settlement in the Lackawanna Valley. Until the mid-1700s, Taylor was nothing more than a mere wilderness. That changed with the arrival of three excavators from Connecticut sent by the Susquehanna Company. Timothy Keyes, Soloman Hocksey, and Andrew Hickman built the first cabin on the west bank of Keyser Creek. A decade later, those same three men would be brutally scalped by Native Americans shortly after the Wyoming Massacre, July 3, 1778. Mrs. Hickman and child were also violently murdered; she was one of the first women to come to the valley. What family members remained fled for their own safety.

In the early 1780s, Cornelius Atherton, a blacksmith and tailor by trade, and his family permanently settled in Taylor. Cornelius purchased 500 acres of land and proclaimed it "Ye Settlement of Lackawanna." As a young man, he was the superintendent of an armory owned by Samuel Adams. Besides serving our country in the Revolutionary War, he also invented clothier shears used by tailors in America. Cornelius's first wife died before coming to Lackawanna Valley, and he eventually remarried; between the two marriages, he fathered 14 children.

Two of Atherton's sons, Eleazer and John, often referred to as the founding fathers of Taylor, farmed the land, as did some of Taylor's other early families, such as the Coons, Bieseckers, and Gordons. During this time, Taylor's chief industry was agriculture; land was inexpensive because the value of coal had not yet been realized. By the early 1800s, much of the land sold for as little as a nickel an acre or for the exchange of whiskey. Once the value of the "black stuff" was discovered, the price of land soared to $10 and $20 an acre.

In 1856, the Union Coal Company built a breaker and sunk a shaft for mining. In order to accommodate its employees, the coal company built houses on the hill. The mining community became known as "the Union." This group of company houses covered the distance of one block on Union, Middle, and High Streets.

With the growth of the coal industry, many New York financiers jumped on the bandwagon, so as not to miss a financial opportunity. The Delaware, Lackawanna and Western Railroad gained ownership of the Union breaker. Its chief investor, Moses Taylor, president of City Bank (New York's most prominent financial institution), purchased most of the valuable coal land for an estimated $50 an acre. In 1882, Moses Taylor gave, in trust, the sum of $250,000 to the presidents of the Lackawanna Iron and Coal Company and the Delaware, Lackawanna and Western Railroad, making it clear the money be used to build a hospital for the care of coal miners and railroad workers. Moses Taylor Hospital is still in operation today. After much research, I found only one source—*A Century of Caring, 1892–1992, Moses Taylor Hospital*, by Rev. Charles P. Conner, Ph.D.—that makes mention of Moses Taylor visiting this area on a few occasions for a short period of time, despite how much his generosity helped the community. The Union breaker was renamed "the Taylor," and the Town of Union became known as "Taylorville" in his honor. The post office would later shorten it to "Taylor."

Church and faith have always been an important part of life to the people of Taylor. In the pioneer days, the gospel was preached in barns several times a year by a traveling preacher who obeyed the command "As ye go preach." Cornelius Atherton played a significant role in organizing weekly prayer meetings. Before regular church services were established, Cornelius would often call the people together on the Sabbath for prayers and to read excerpts from printed sermons.

Right in the middle of Taylor stands its oldest and most prominent landmarks, the original Mother Presbyterian Church of Lackawanna Valley and the Taylor Memorial Cemetery. The church was built in 1848; however, due to lack of records, no one knows the actual age of the cemetery. Its land was part of a farm used by its owners for family members' burials. In January 1855, the cemetery was purchased for $100, and the cost for building the church totaled $400. For quite a number of years, the Presbyterian church served as the meeting place on alternate Sabbaths for both Baptists and Presbyterians. Later they were joined by the Methodists, and the trio became the Pioneer Church of Taylor.

Buried in the surrounding cemetery are 24 soldiers from the Revolutionary, Civil, and Spanish American Wars. Among its best-known historical residents are Parley Hughes, a veteran of the Revolutionary War, and Eliza Pulver, a teacher who taught Pres. Grover Cleveland.

In 1905, the Women's Christian Temperance Union raised money to replace the dilapidated 1,000-foot wooden fence surrounding the church and cemetery with a new iron fence, which still guards its inhabitants some 104 years later. The church celebrated its last service in the 1950s.

Shortly after the Civil War, a new wave of Welsh immigrants settled in Taylor(ville). Many of them resided in Feltsville, better known as the "Patch," its name derived from the surname of Isaac Felts, meaning lord of the manor. This northern section of Taylor was built on Felts's farm, and his mansion stood regally in the center. Due to mine subsidences, all the original homes and buildings were condemned, and today, sadly, nothing remains of the Patch except memories.

Not all people who resided in Taylor worked underground. The first store in town was kept by James Gordon in 1816. By 1880, Taylor had six churches, nine stores, six taverns, two liveries, an undertaker, a barbershop, a drugstore, and a school. South Main Street was considered the heart of Taylor, and it served primarily as its business district. Past businesses—Friedman's Department Store, Taylorville Furniture House, Taylor Discount and Deposit Bank, and many more—have adorned its sidewalks throughout the centuries. Taylor's industry also included three silk mills and a cigar factory.

The Taylor wooden breaker had to be replaced due to its deterioration in 1871 and again in 1909—but this time, the wooden breaker was replaced with a first-of-its-kind concrete breaker. In 1944, W. Y. Moffat purchased the Taylor, and the Moffat Coal Company continued operations until 1966, at which time all remaining coal mining in the county came to a halt because water levels in the mines made it impossible to continue. For many years, the Moffat's empty shell stood as a reminder of Taylor's grand anthracite past. Some people did not respect it, and the structure became a victim of arsonists on several occasions. In 1983, what was left of it was torn down completely, taking with it a large part of Taylor's past. Still today, many residents I spoke to wish it remained.

I would like to conclude with a quote taken from *A Brief Historical Sketch of Taylor*: "We are a favored town, we not only have age, being the oldest county settlement, but we have history within our gates. At almost every entrance leading into Taylor one may turn upon a page of an honorable past."

One

From Agriculture to Anthracite Coal

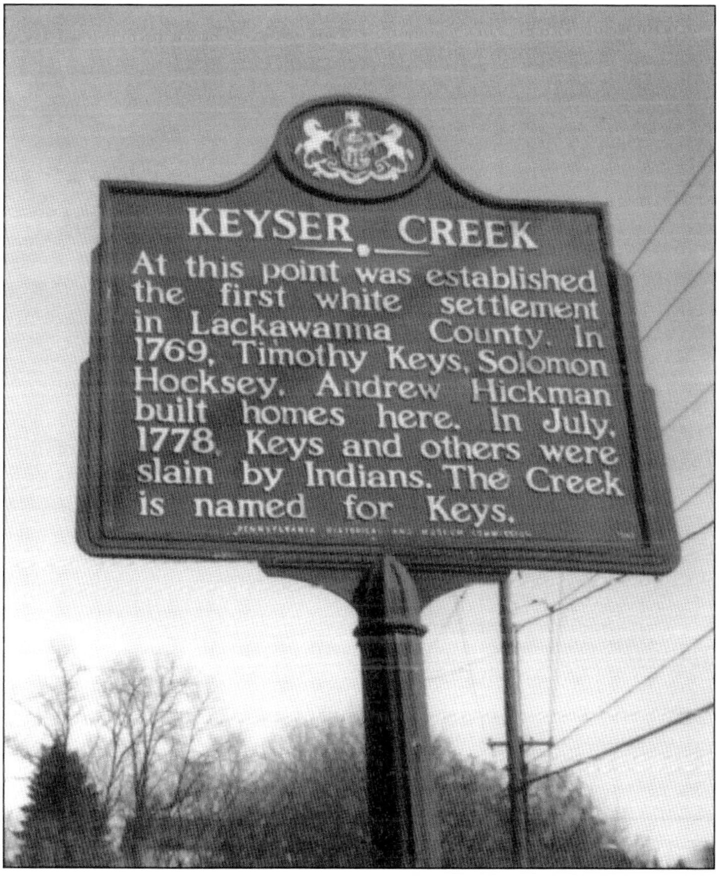

Keyser Creek. In 1769, Timothy Keys, Soloman Hocksey, and Andrew Hickman built a log cabin, establishing the first white settlement in the Lackawanna Valley. Shortly after the Wyoming Massacre of 1778, the three men along with Mrs. Hickman and child were brutally murdered by Native Americans. The creek is named in honor of Timothy Keys. The Pennsylvania Historical and Museum Commission (PHMC) Historical Marker was erected in 1948. (Author's collection.)

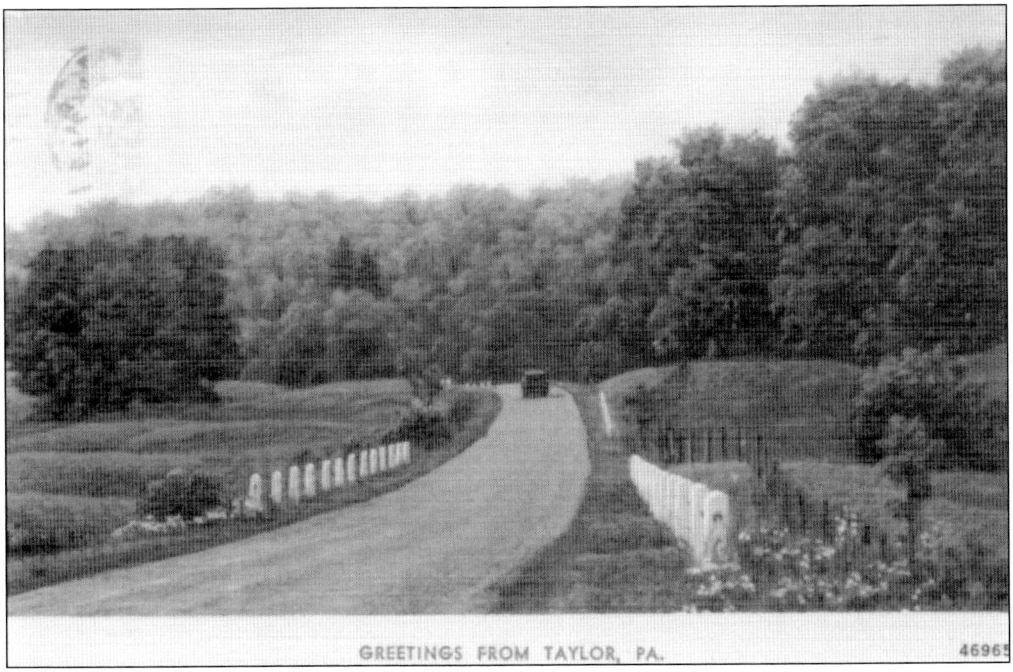

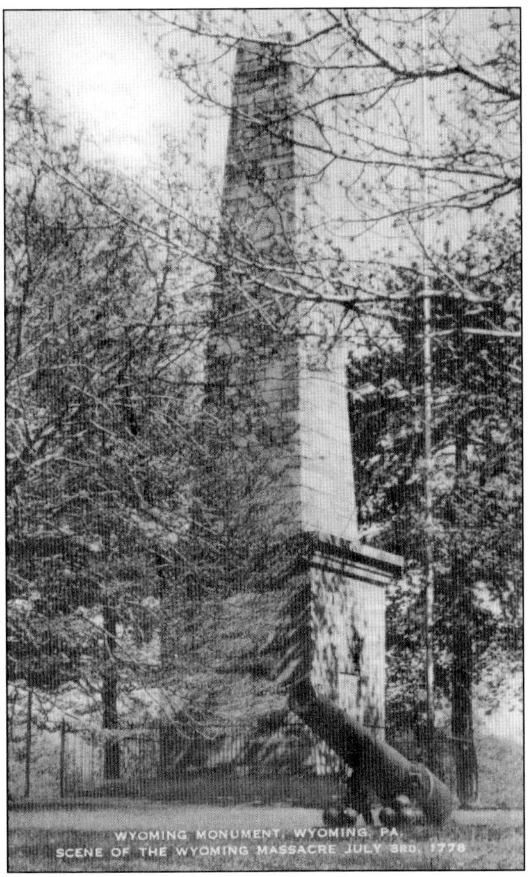

THE ATHERTONS. In the early 1780s, Cornelius Atherton purchased 500 acres of land and erected a house near the Taylor depot, on the brow of the hill overlooking the river. He proclaimed it "ye settlement of Lackawanna." Two of his sons, John and Eleazer, are often referred to as the founding fathers of Taylor. (Author's collection.)

THE WYOMING MASSACRE, JULY 3, 1778. Jabez Atherton, the eldest son of Cornelius, fell in the Battle of Wyoming at the age of 17. Cornelius had been drafted to the battle, but Jabez took his place. For if his father fell, what would become of his mother and younger siblings? Sadly, his body was among those found horribly mutilated near Queen Esther's Rock. His name heads the list on the Wyoming Monument. (Author's collection.)

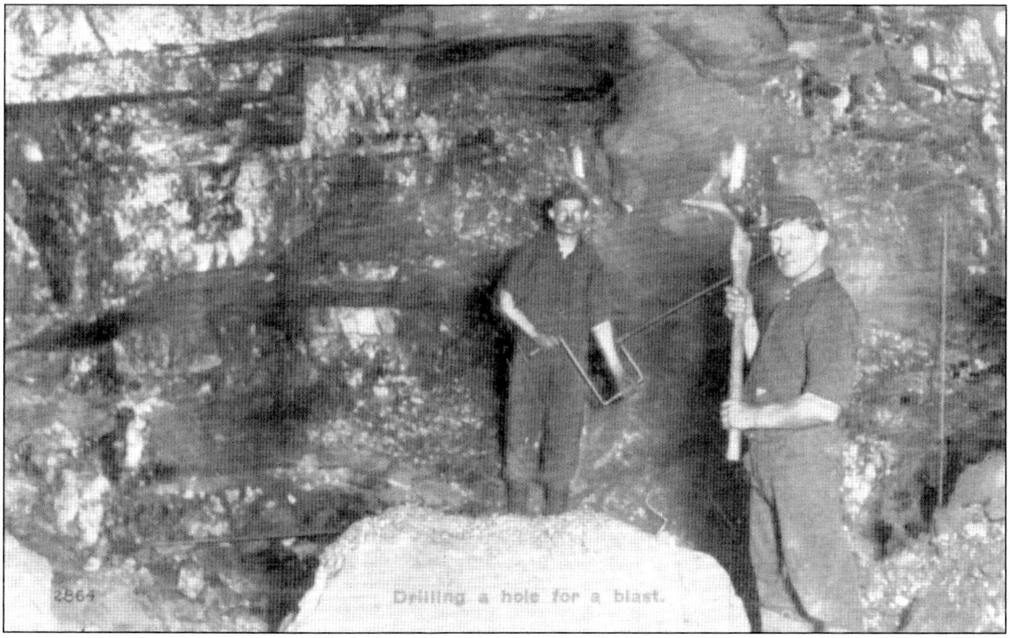

Discovery of Black Diamond. In 1856, a breaker was built for Taylor's first coal company. The Union Coal Company employed many of Taylor's residents, and it built company houses spanning the distance of one block. This little hamlet became known as "the Union." (Author's collection.)

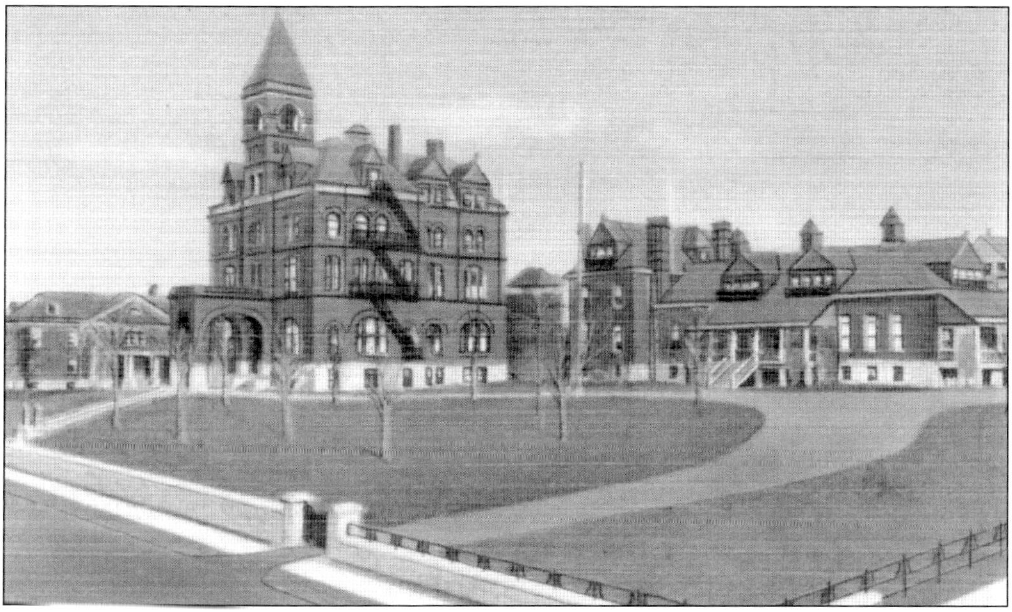

Moses Taylor. By the late 1860s, the Union Coal Company had gone bankrupt. Anthracite coal was still in great demand, which peaked the interest of New York City financiers such as Moses Taylor, chief stockholder in the Delaware, Lackawanna and Western Railroad and Coal Company. He purchased the defunct Union Coal Company and put money in a trust to build a hospital, seen in the photograph, for the care of coal miners and railroad workers. In his honor, the Union became "the Taylor," and the town was renamed Taylorville. (Author's collection.)

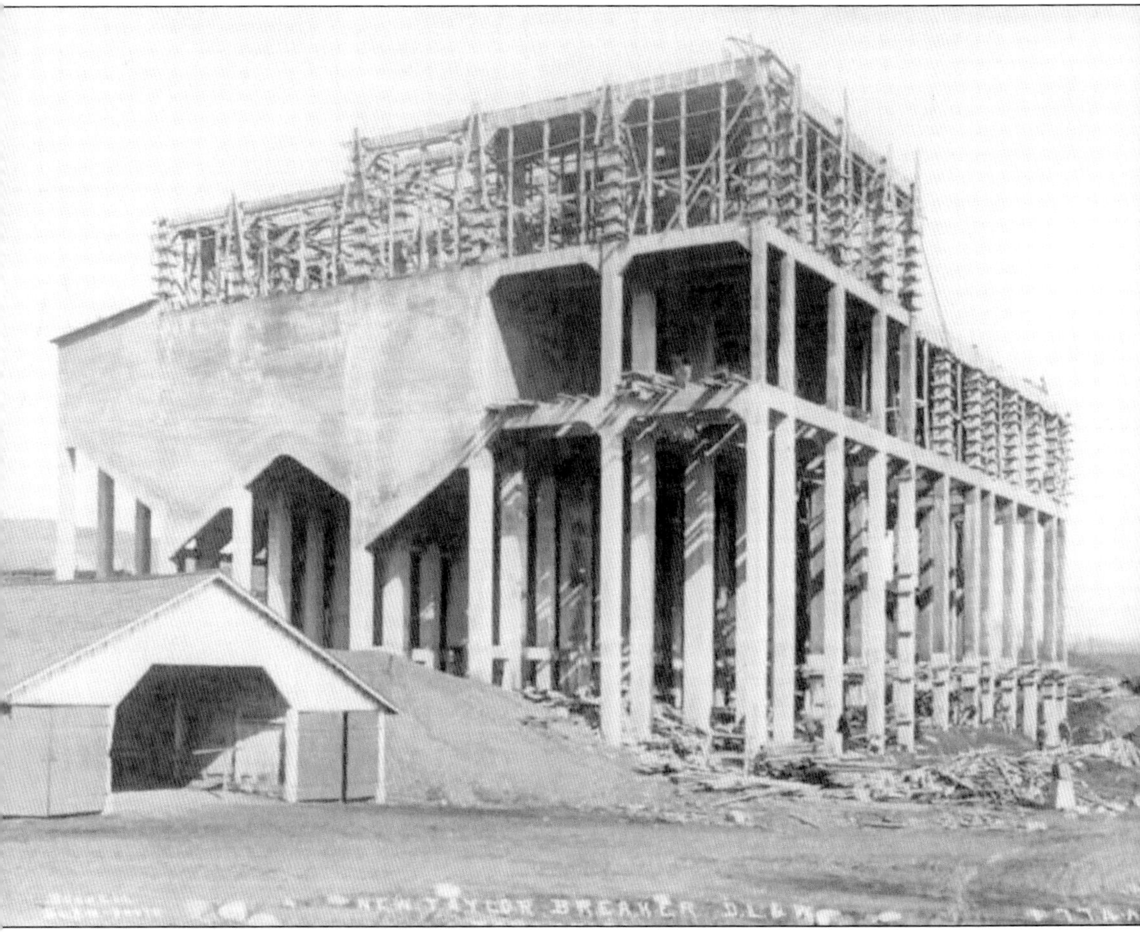

Taylor Breaker. In 1868, the breaker was acquired by the Delaware, Lackawanna and Western Railroad and Coal Company. In 1911, a state-of-the-art breaker was constructed out of concrete. Col. R. A. Phillips was the superintendent of the Delaware, Lackawanna and Western mining department at the time of construction. Bradford Samson was the designer. The breaker was built of reinforced concrete mixed on site and discharged upward by an automatic dumping bucket then conveyed to the forms by carts and wheelbarrows. The structure stood 107 feet wide, 133 feet long, and 167 feet high from the foundation to the highest point of the roof. The concrete was made of one part Portland cement, two parts sand, and four parts crushed stone. All outside walls were 5 feet thick. It cost $200,000 to build and was capable of producing 6,000 tons of coal per day. (Courtesy of Dan Zeleniak and Shawn Murphy.)

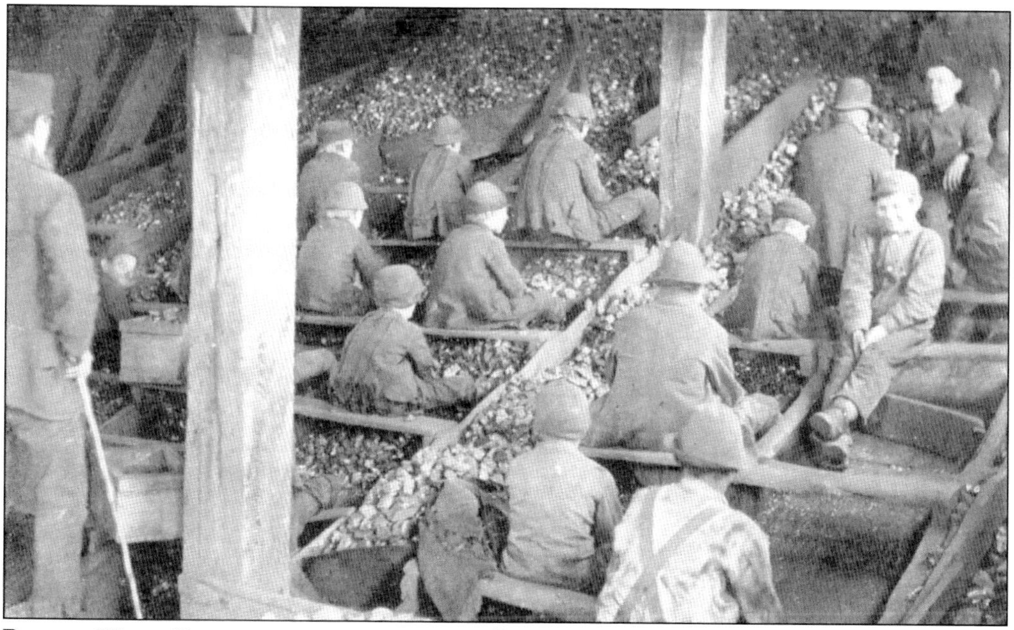

Boys at Work. Boys as young as seven went off to work in the Taylor coal mines to help support their families; breaker boys, as seen in the photograph, spent 12-hour shifts, six days a week, picking the slate and rock from the coal for very meager pay. (Author's collection.)

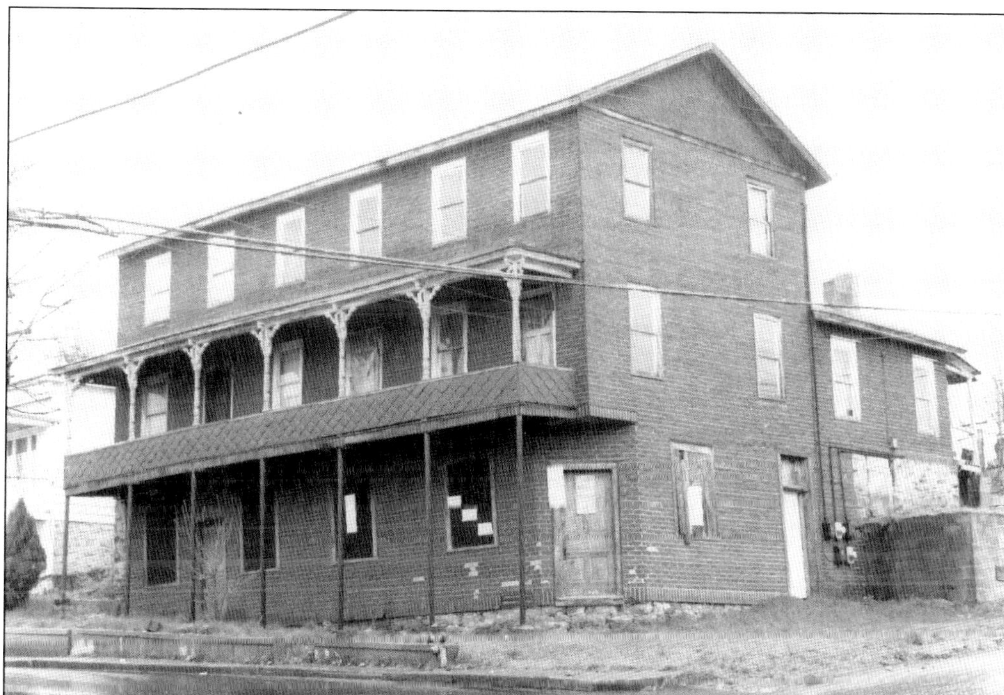

Miner Housing. This is an apartment building that at one time was occupied by miners and their families. This particular one was located in "the Patch" section. (Courtesy of Dale Malecki.)

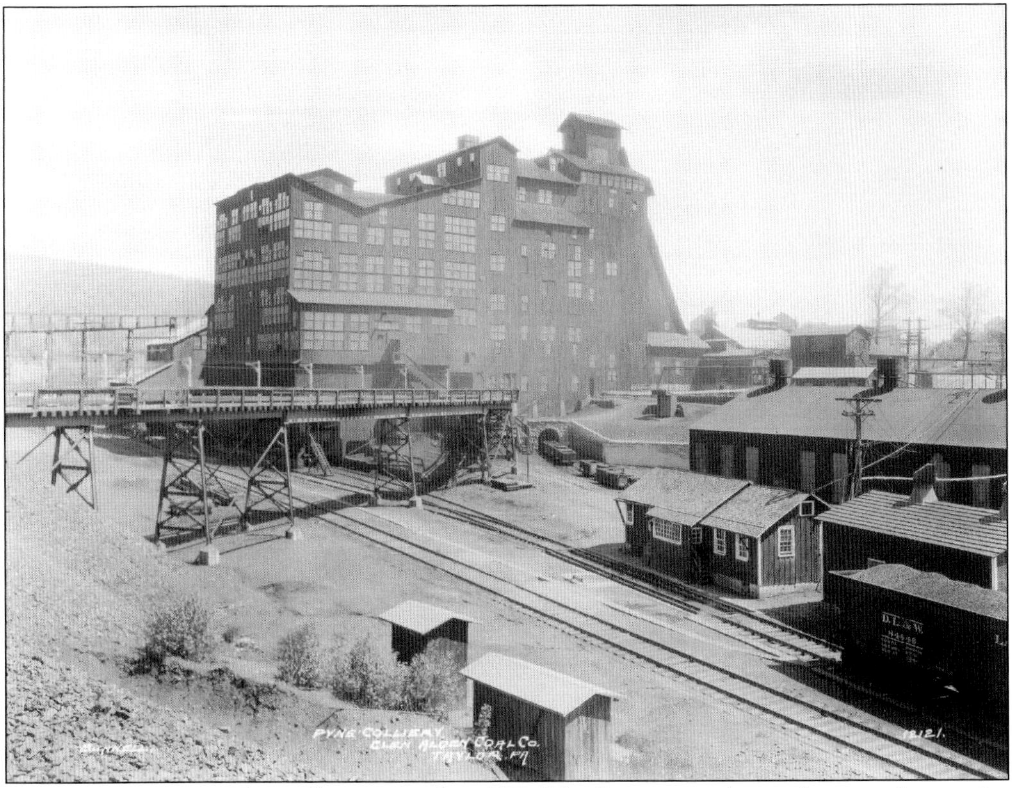

THE PYNE COLLIERY. This colliery opened in 1870. John Lewis served as its foreman; he was the stepfather of Taylor druggist, Joseph Davis. It is believed the colliery was named for Moses Taylor's grandson, Percy Pyne. The present location of the colliery is the 286 Corporation, an automotive dealership on Keyser Avenue. (Courtesy of the Lackawanna Historical Society.)

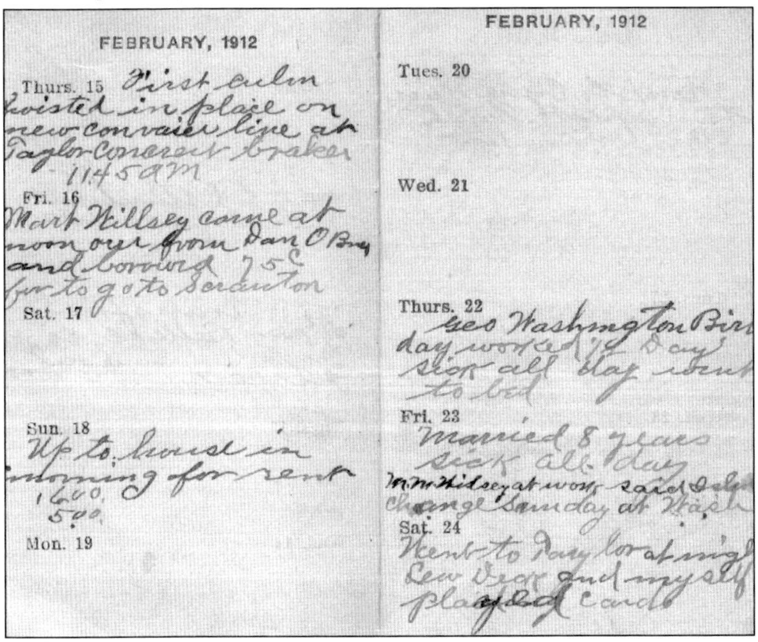

FEBRUARY, 1912

Thurs. 15 First culm hoisted in place on new convaier line at Taylor Concreet braker 11.45 AM

Fri. 16 Mart Hillsey came at noon over from Dan O'Brey and borrowd 75c for to go to Scranton

Sat. 17

Sun. 18 Up to house in morning for rent 16.00 5.00

Mon. 19

FEBRUARY, 1912

Tues. 20

Wed. 21

Thurs. 22 Geo Washington Birthday worked 1/4 Day sick all day went to bed

Fri. 23 married 8 years sick all day M.M. Hilsey at work said [illegible] change Sunday at Wash

Sat. 24 Went to Taylor at night Lew Dear and myself played cards

A TAYLOR MINER'S JOURNAL, C. 1912. Adolph Ureveider is the owner of the journal. An entry dated July 15, 1912, "started the concrete breaker," refers to the Taylor Breaker. There is also an entry on July 4, 1912, of the Gibson Train Wreck, where 41 people were killed, 5 of the 41 dead were from Scranton and surrounding area. (Courtesy of Shawn Murphy and the Taylor Community Library.)

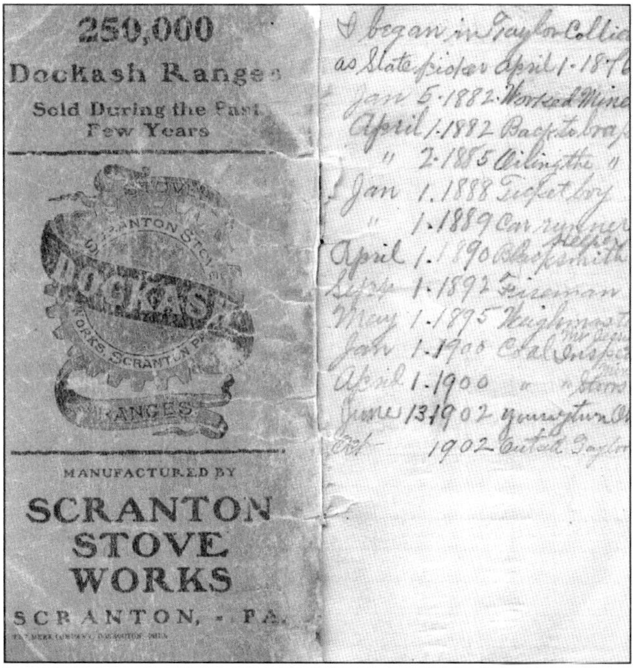

A MINER'S TIMELINE. The owner's name was A. D. ? from North Scranton. The notebook describes a miner's job duties. This miner began in the Taylor colliery as a slate picker on April 1, 1876, and by January 1, 1900, had been promoted to coal inspector. (Courtesy of Shawn Murphy and the Taylor Community Library.)

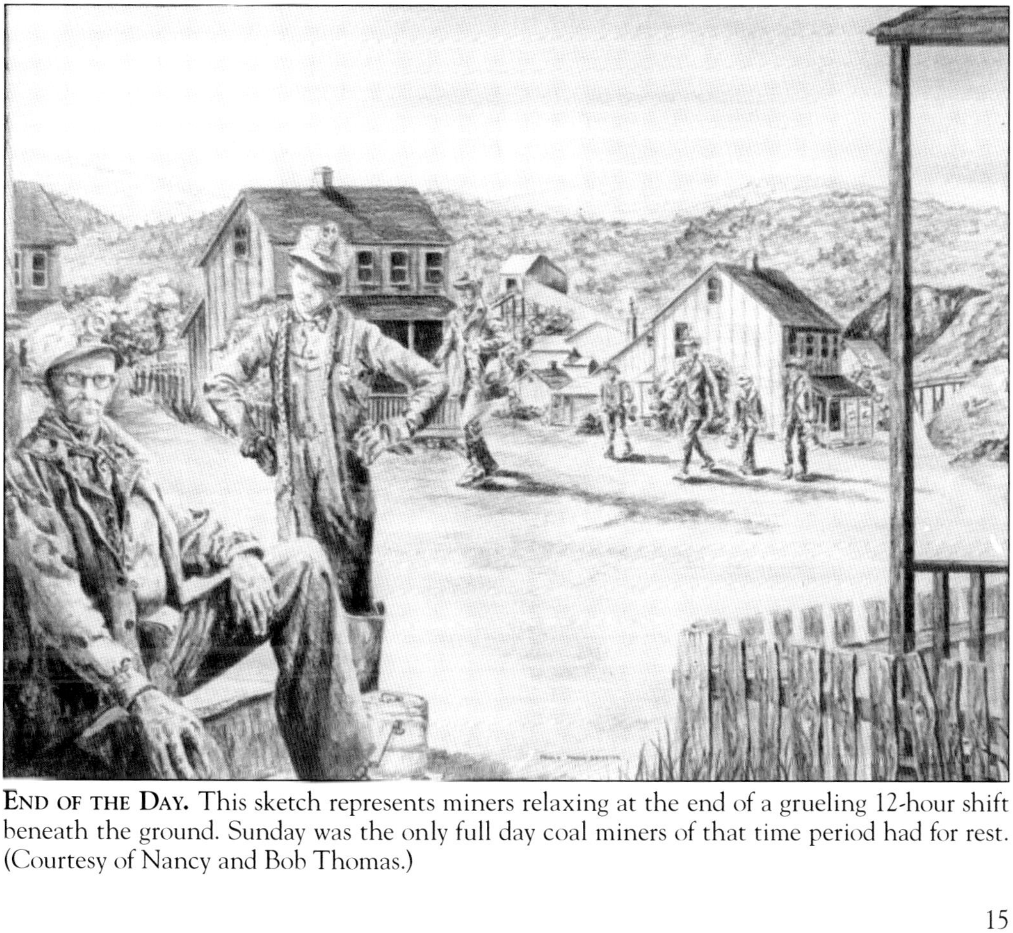

END OF THE DAY. This sketch represents miners relaxing at the end of a grueling 12-hour shift beneath the ground. Sunday was the only full day coal miners of that time period had for rest. (Courtesy of Nancy and Bob Thomas.)

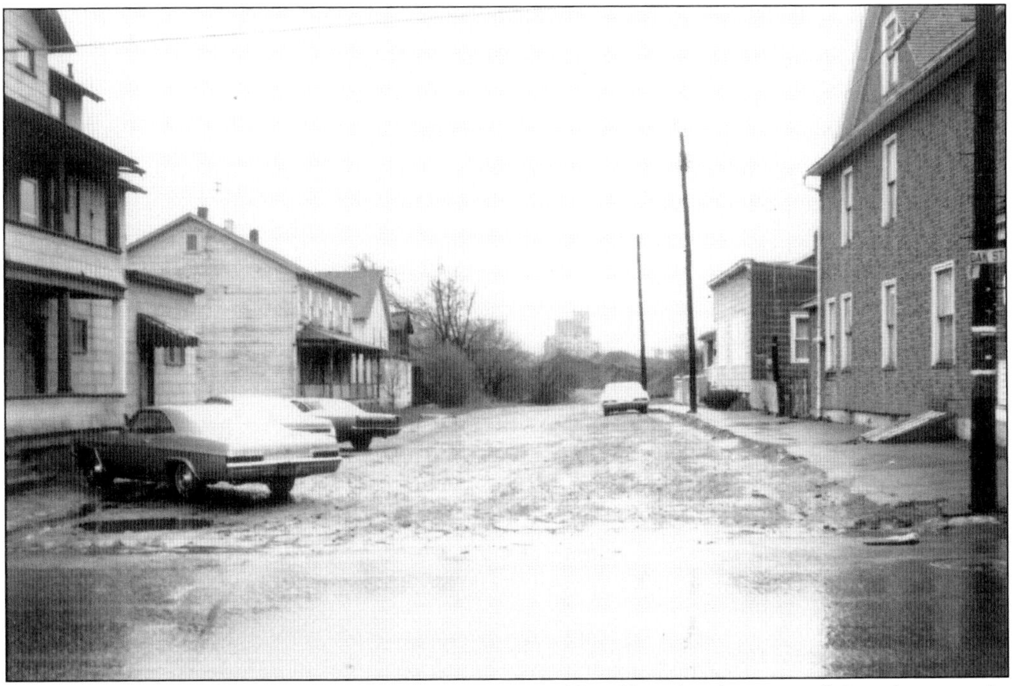

IN THE DISTANCE. The Moffat Coal Company is visible off in the distance of this photograph. From whatever direction you entered into Taylor you could feel the impact it had on the coal mining community. This photograph was taken from the Patch. (Courtesy of Dale Malecki.)

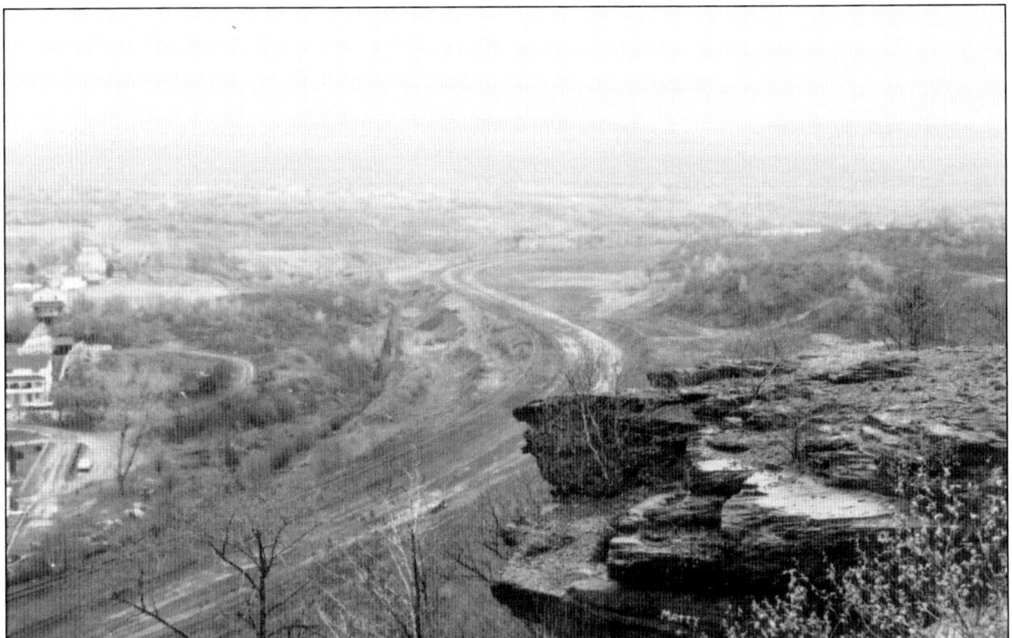

RAILWAY SYSTEM. A portion of Felt's Patch is shown on the left and the infamous hanging rocks on the right. Nestled between both is the all-important railway system used for the shipment of coal. It was rare for a mining company to have the tracks so near to its facility. (Courtesy of Dale Malecki.)

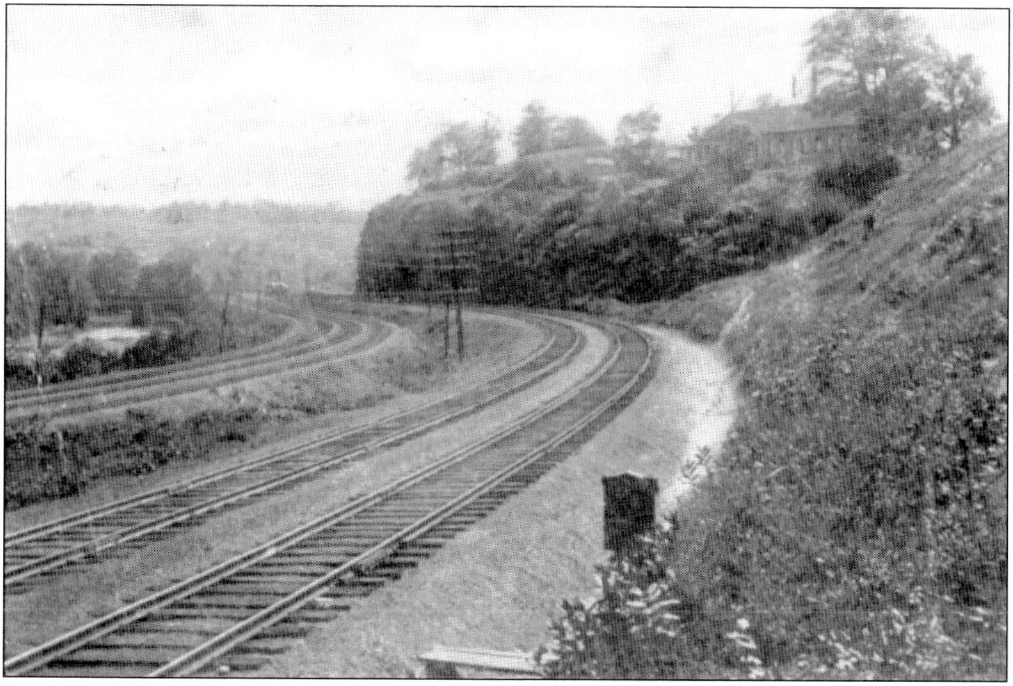

FIRST RAILROAD. The first railroad contracted through Taylor dates back to the 1850s. This photograph is of the tracks used by the Delaware, Lackawanna and Western Railroad. (Author's collection.)

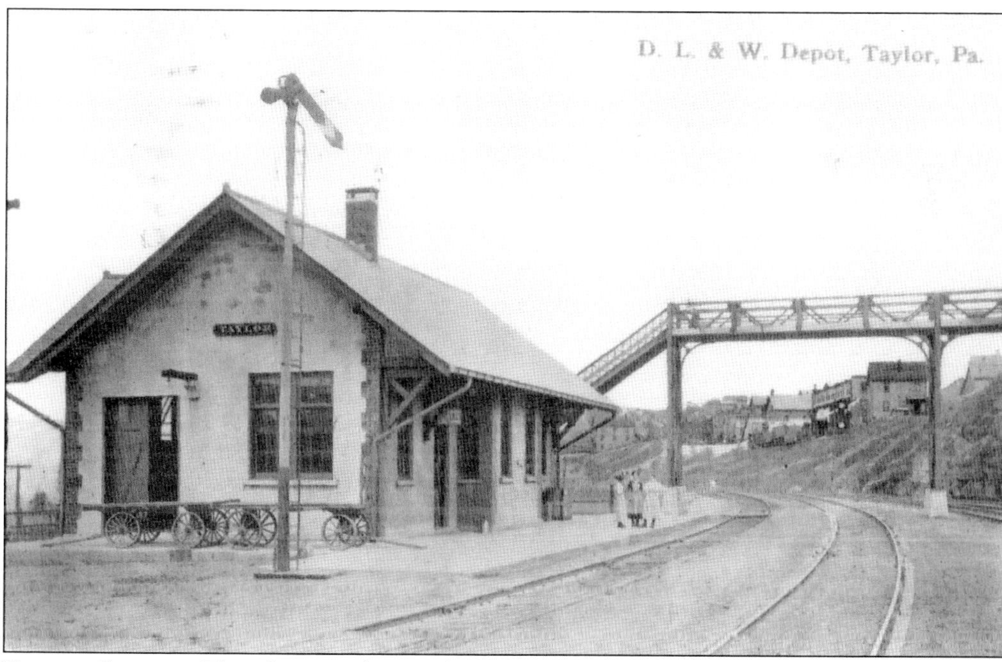

FREIGHT STATION. This photograph was taken in the late 1800s of the New Jersey Central freight station, Taylor yard. Trains were essential for the transportation of anthracite coal to other parts of the country. (Courtesy of Shawn Murphy.)

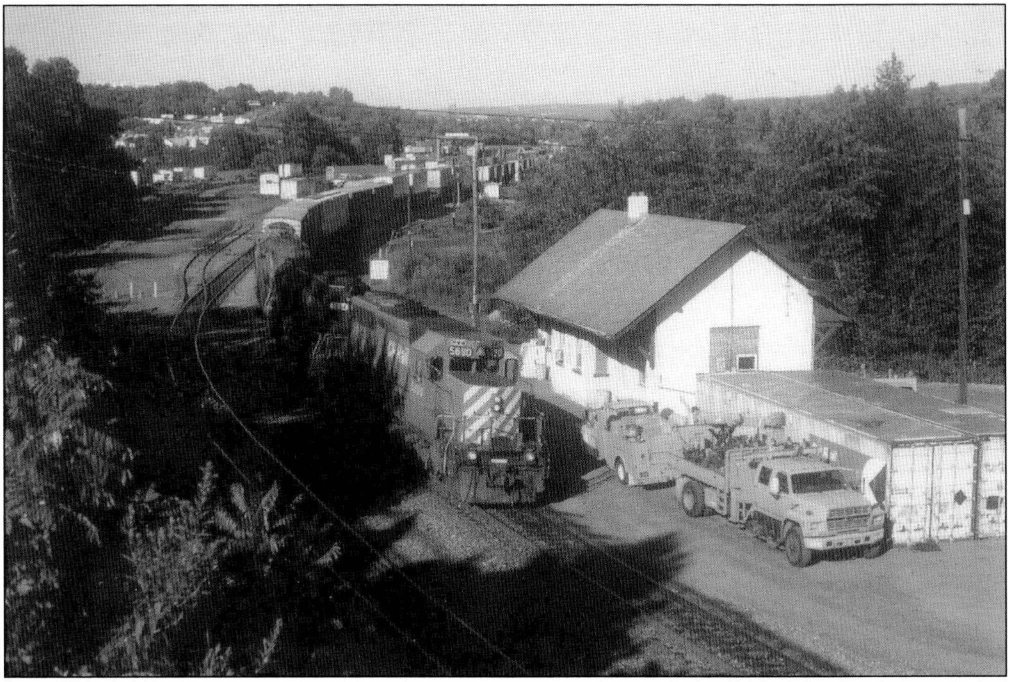

Taylor Station. This station was used by the Delaware and Hudson Railroad. An estimated five different railroads came through Taylor at the height of the coal boom. Mainly the trains were used for the shipment of coal and did not carry passengers. (Author's collection.)

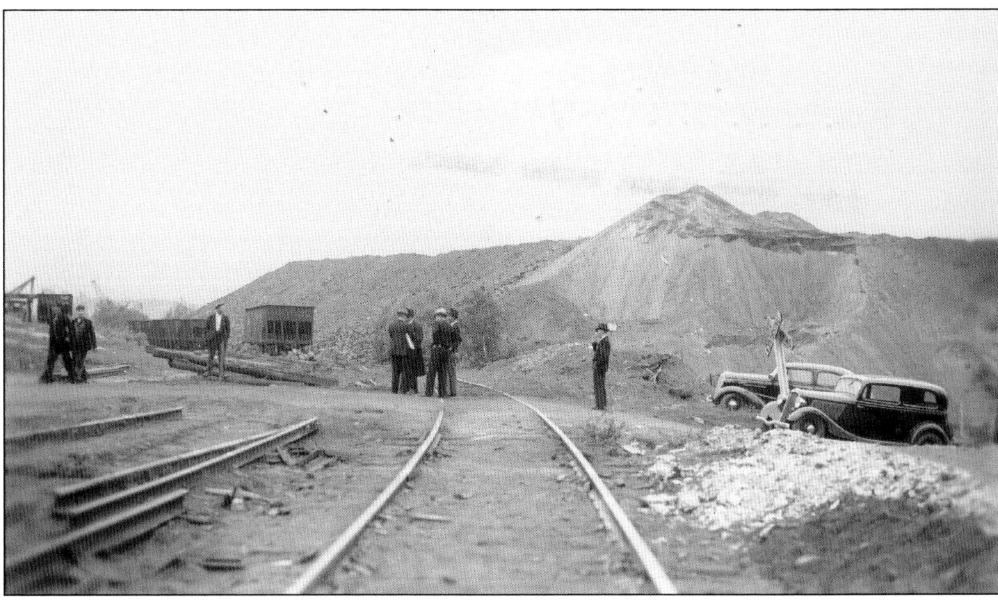

Delaware, Lackawanna and Western Railroad Crossing. This *c.* 1938 view is looking south along the tracks toward the crossing from a point of 75-degree distance. This was officially Lackawanna County Route 35049 in Taylor Borough. (Courtesy of Lackawanna Historical Society.)

Two

THE PATCH

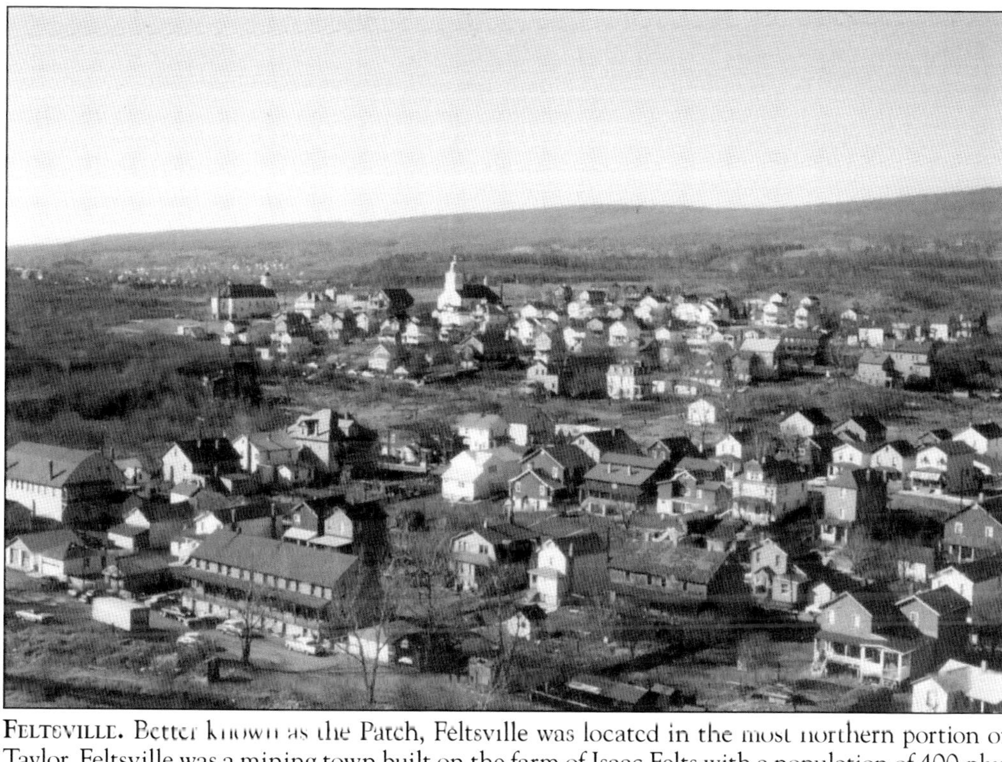

FELTSVILLE. Better known as the Patch, Feltsville was located in the most northern portion of Taylor. Feltsville was a mining town built on the farm of Isaac Felts with a population of 400-plus people. Many Welsh families settled there and found work in the nearby coal mines. It was the First Ward of Taylor. (Courtesy of Chester Lewandowski.)

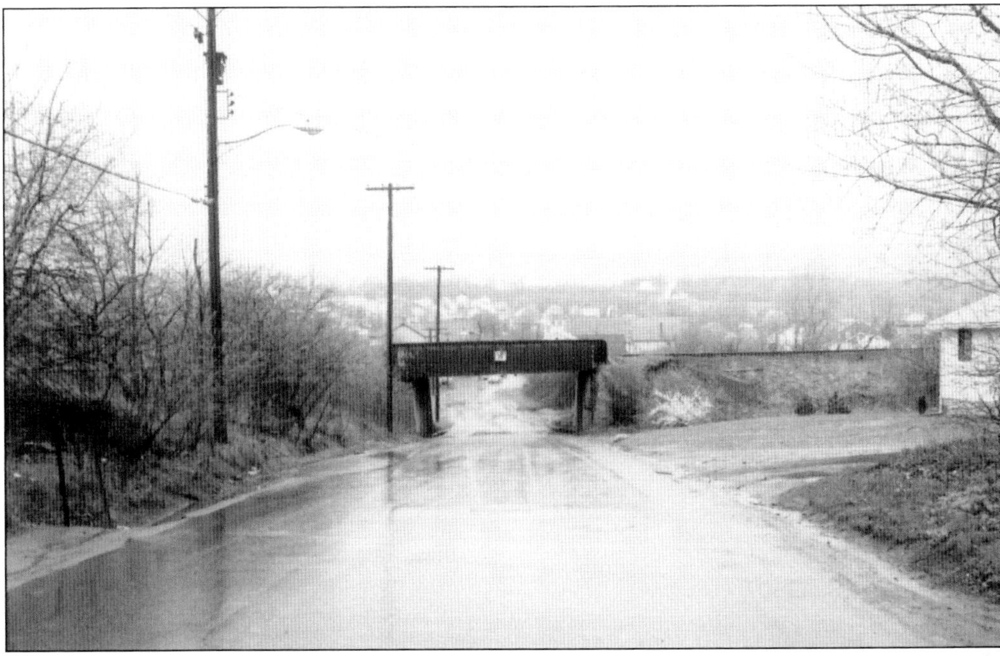

GATEWAY TO THE PATCH. The black bridge on Oak Street, shown here, was the entrance to the Patch. Feltsville ran from First to Sixth Streets. Over the years, there have been many tractor trailers stuck under the bridge due to the drivers ignoring the posted height restrictions. (Courtesy of Dale Malecki.)

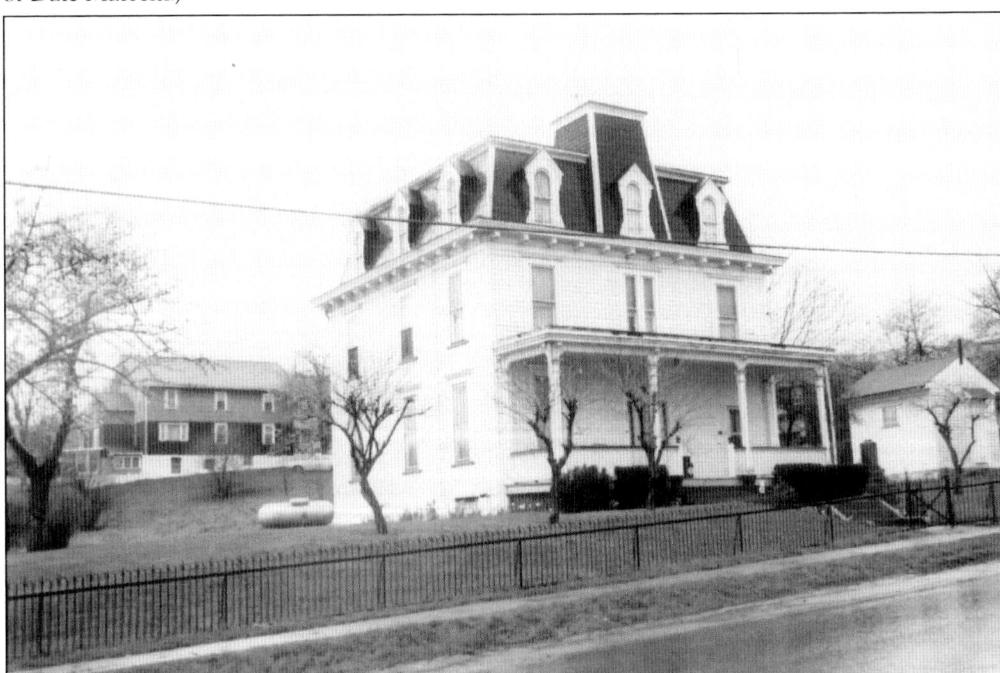

ISAAC FELT'S MANSION. An 1864 map indicates Isaac Felt's farm, but the village had not yet come into existence. In later years, it became St. George's Rectory and the residence of Monsignor and Martha Zeleniak. Note the summer kitchen next to the house. (Courtesy of Dale Malecki.)

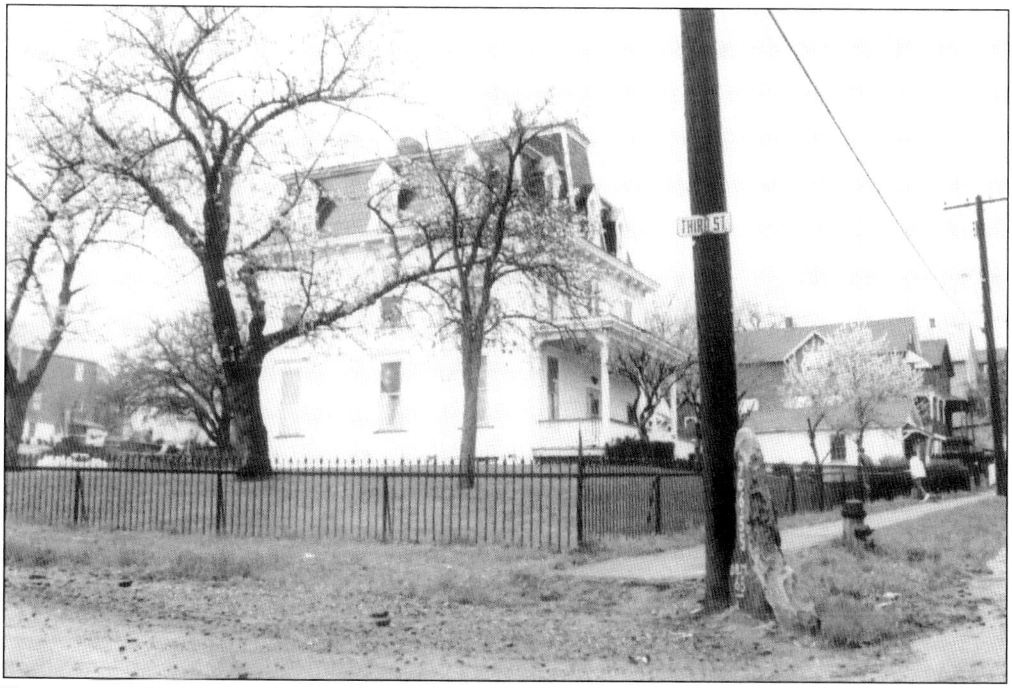

Feltsville Marker. In the forefront of the photograph is the original survey marker (stone near pole) for Feltsville. It was situated at the corner of Third and Oak Streets. (Courtesy of Dale Malecki.)

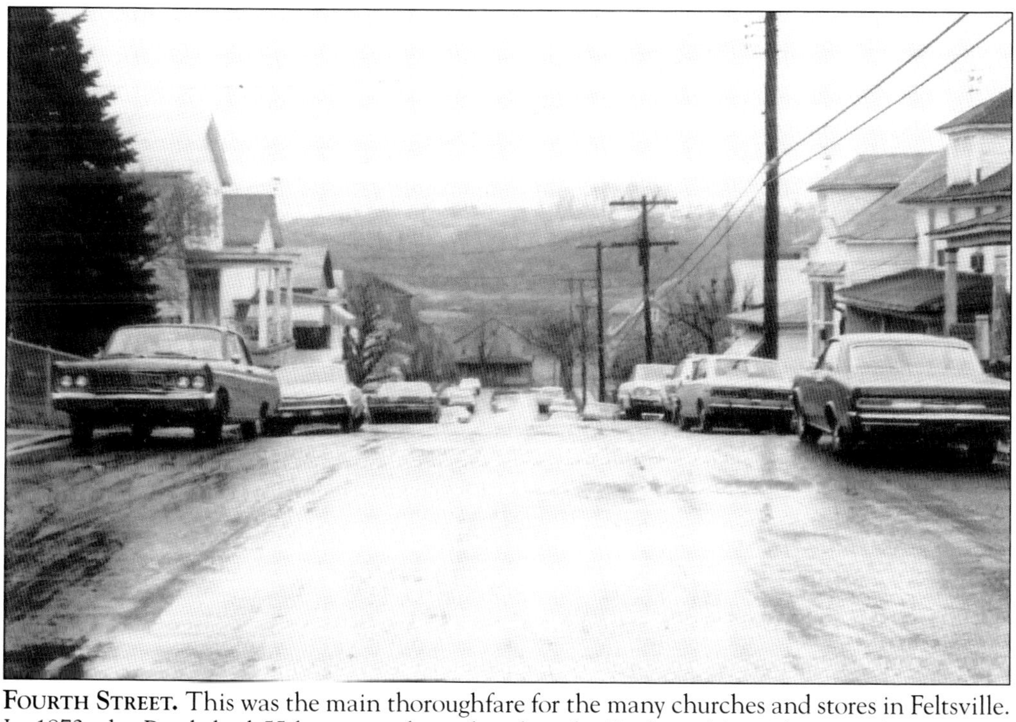

Fourth Street. This was the main thoroughfare for the many churches and stores in Feltsville. In 1873, the Patch had 55 homes and two hotels—the Eagle and Mt. Pleasant. (Courtesy of Dale Malecki.)

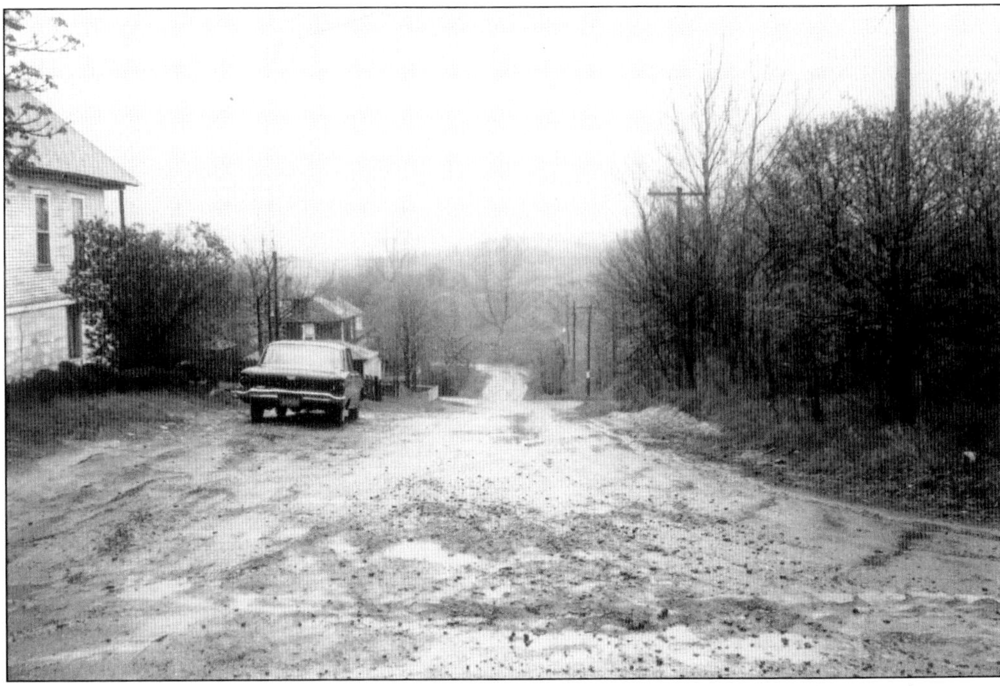

Dog Hole. A renegade mine pit opening was found here, and the section became known as "Dog Hole." The Butch and Homadick families both resided in this neighborhood. (Courtesy of Dale Malecki.)

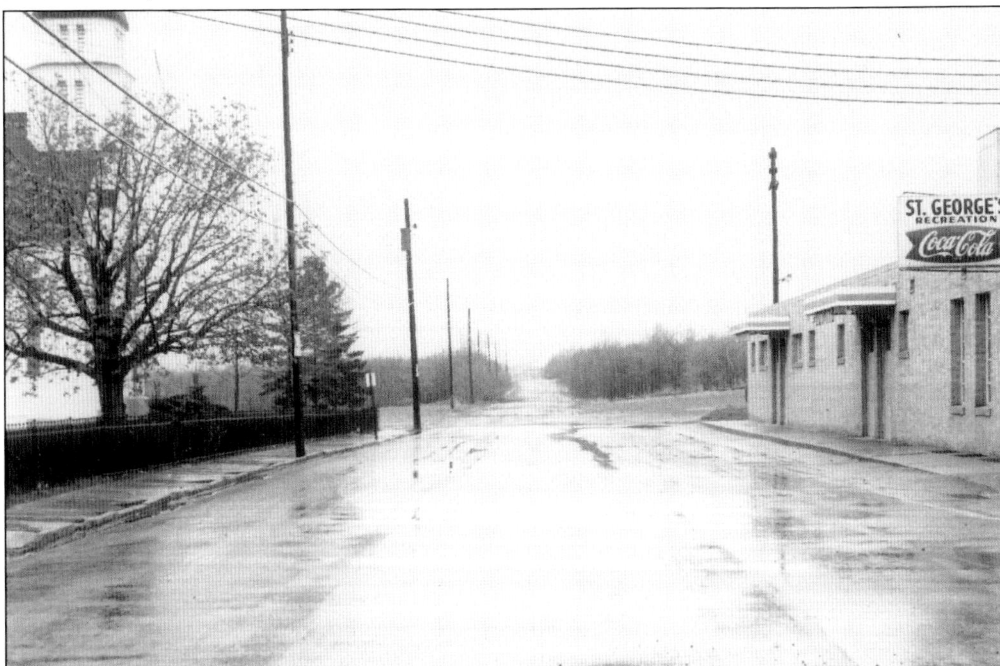

The New Road. This road connected the Patch with Taylor Proper. It also served as the location for St. George's Recreation Center, a local place for people of the community to socialize. (Courtesy of Dale Malecki.)

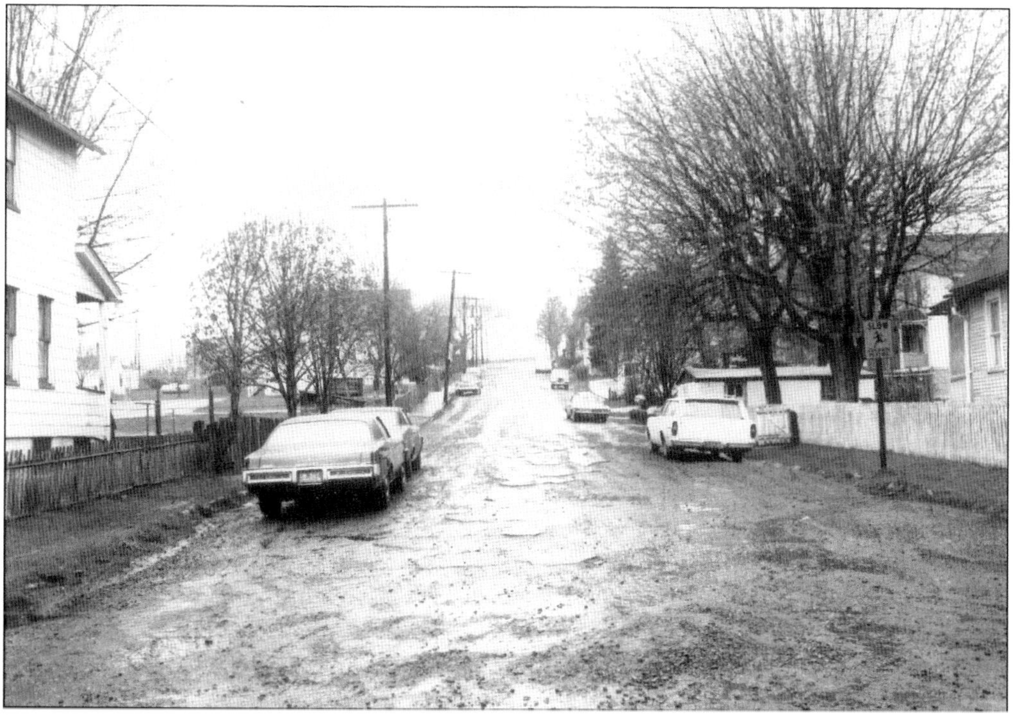

Fifth Street. Many homes adorn this block. The area next to the house on the left was the former site of Garfield Elementary School. (Courtesy of Dale Malecki.)

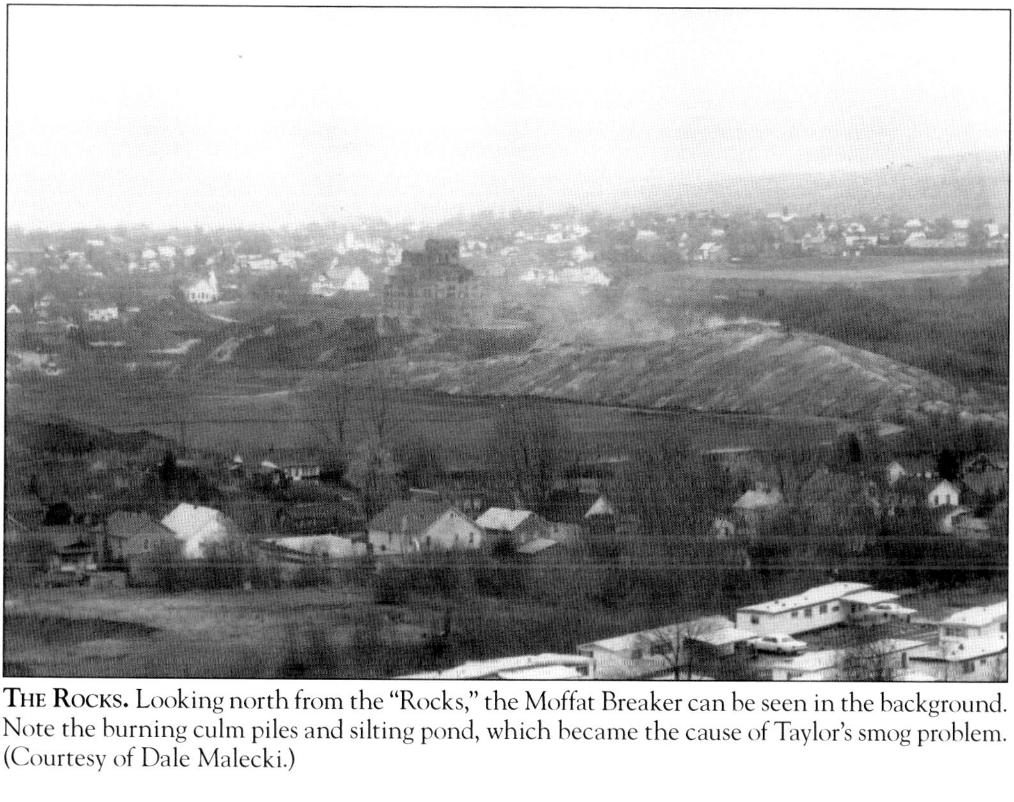

The Rocks. Looking north from the "Rocks," the Moffat Breaker can be seen in the background. Note the burning culm piles and silting pond, which became the cause of Taylor's smog problem. (Courtesy of Dale Malecki.)

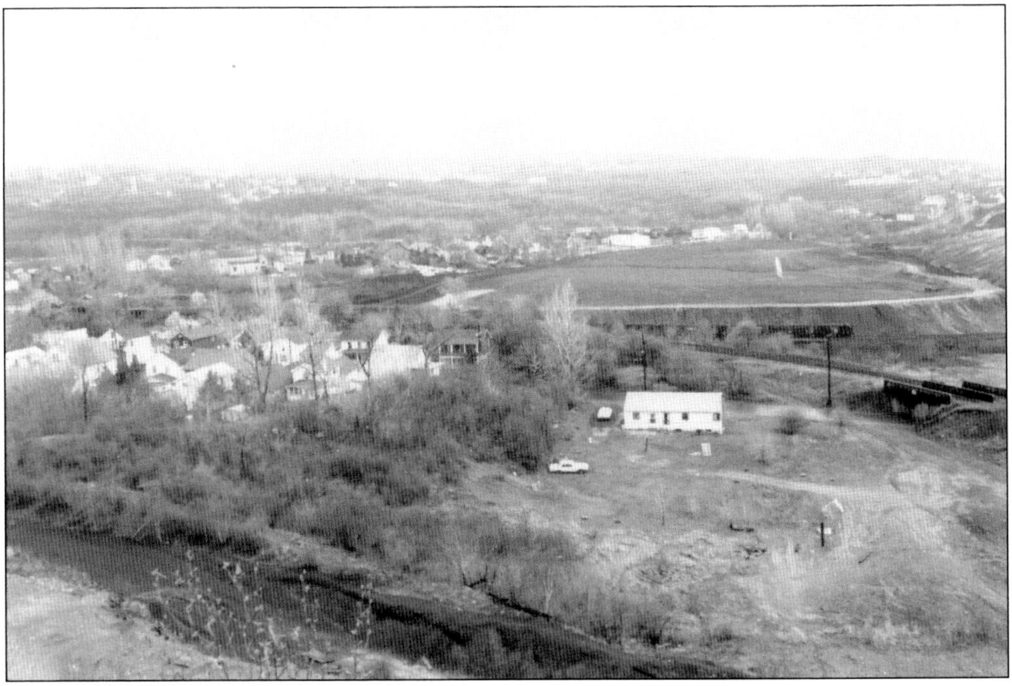

SILTING POND. Here is an aerial view of the silting pond, pictured in the background. Heavy wind would blow dust from the pond over the homes and businesses in the nearby vicinity. (Courtesy of Dale Malecki.)

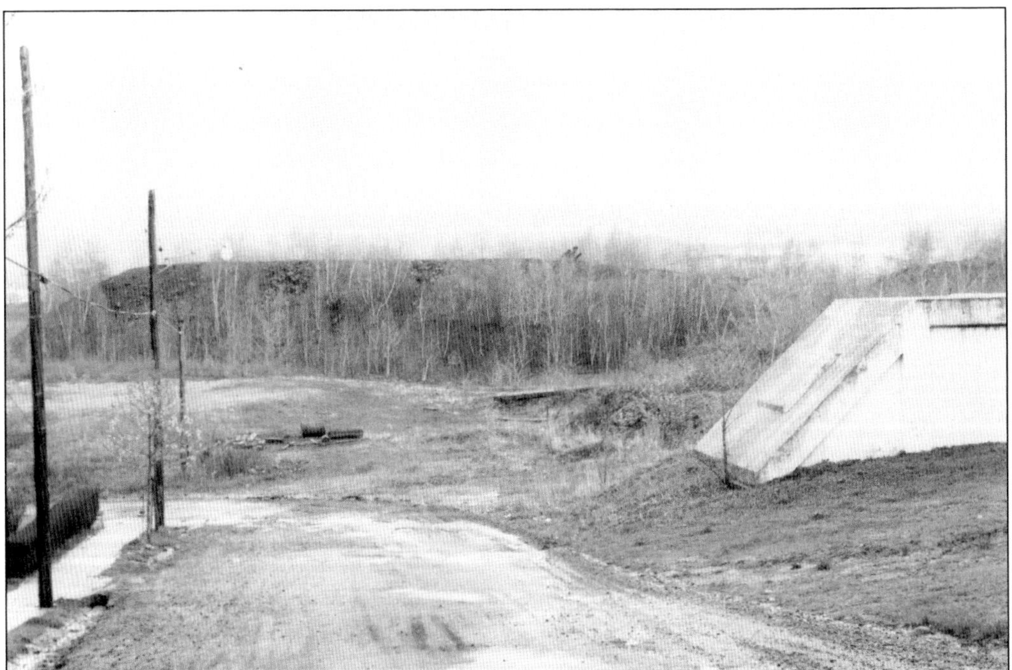

THE FAN. A piece of equipment owned by the Moffat Coal Company, the fan, was used as a ventilation system, pushing air in a deliberate flow pattern throughout the entire mine so that no dust or poisonous, explosive gases could build up. (Courtesy of Dale Malecki.)

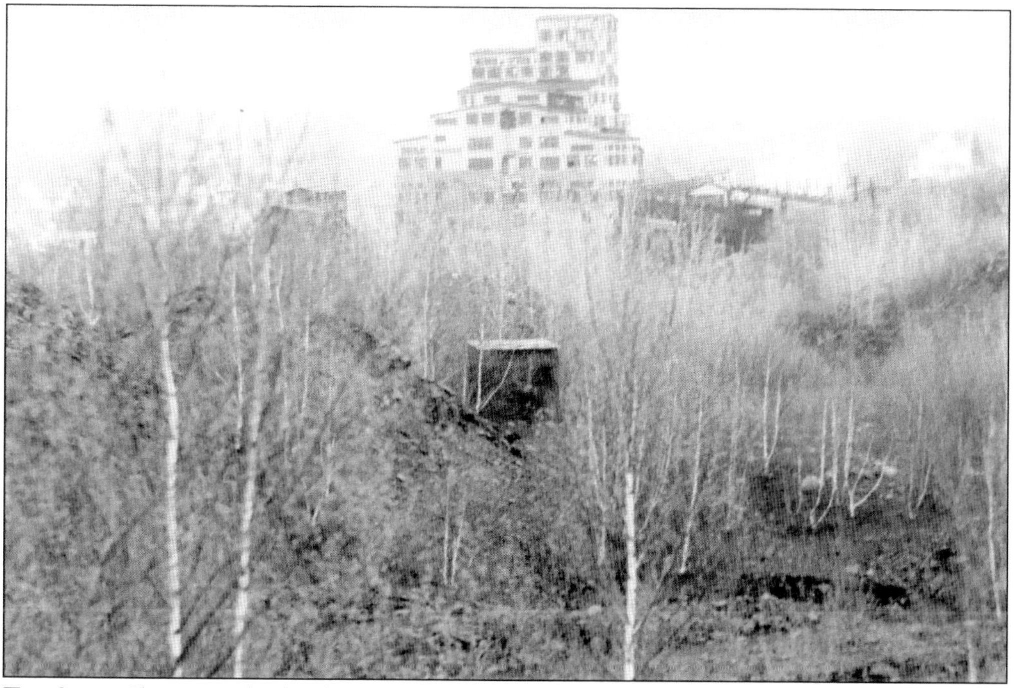

THE SHED. Shown in the forefront is the shed used by the breaker workers to store their tools. Looming in the distance is the familiar site of the Moffat Breaker. Today the boiler house is the only thing that remains of the breaker. (Courtesy of Dale Malecki.)

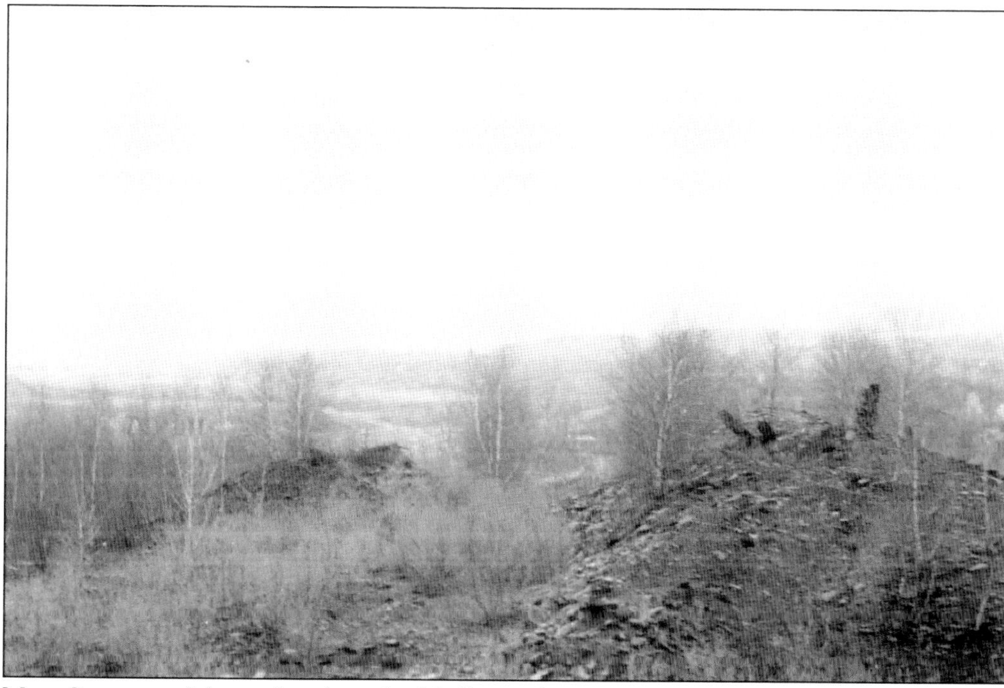

MINE STRIPPING. Mine refuse from the Moffat Coal Company is seen in this picture taken from Pine and Third Streets. Strip mining is the process through which a seam of coal is exposed by removal of the overlaying earth and rock. (Courtesy of Dale Malecki.)

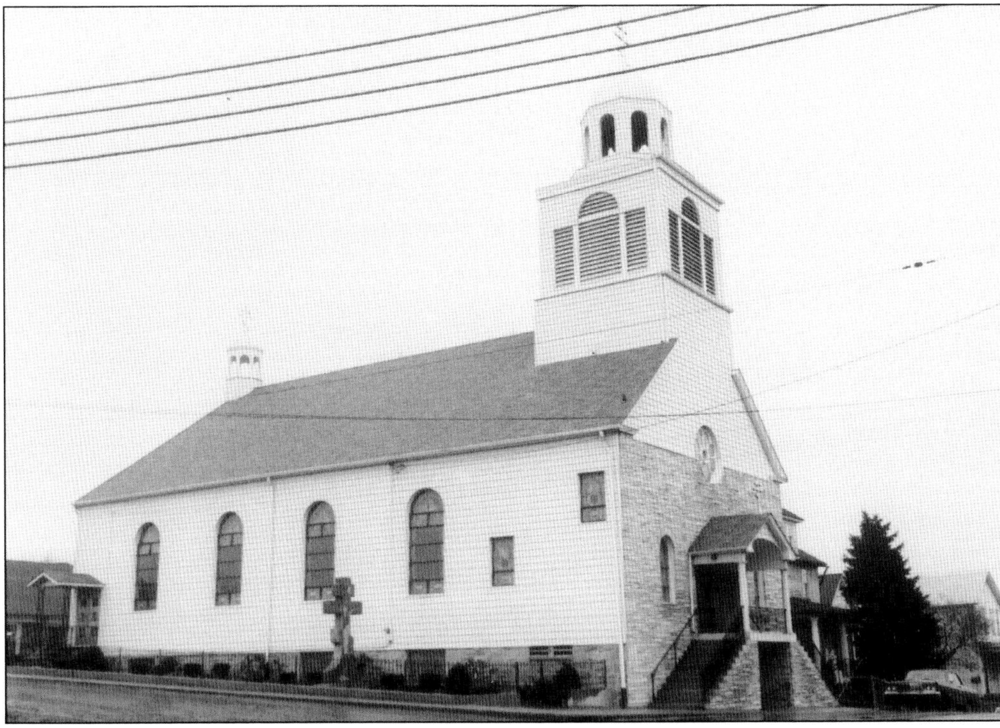

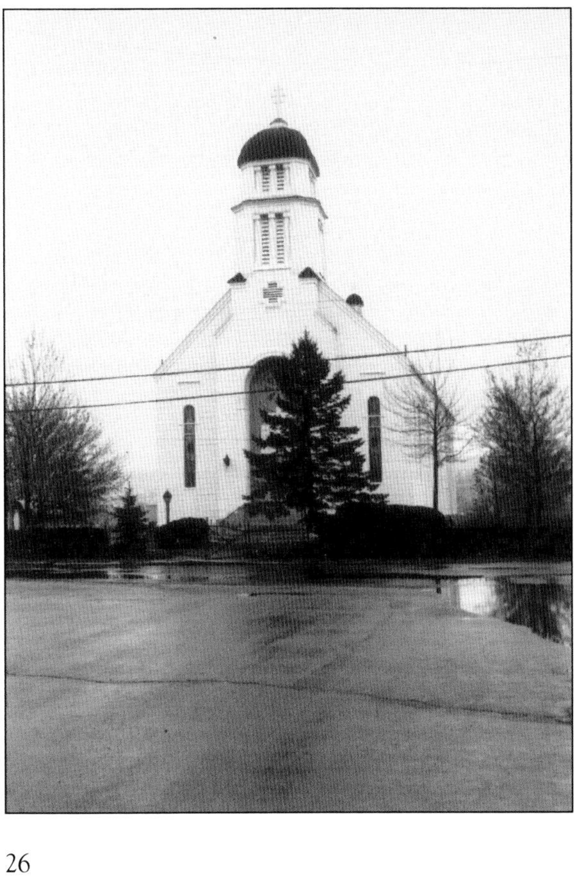

ST. GEORGE'S GREEK ORTHODOX CHURCH. The church was founded in 1907 by a group of Greek Orthodox Catholics. Due to the church's lack of wealth, the building took some time; finally on October 3, 1937, the cornerstone was laid and dedicated. Its original location was Fourth and Pine Streets, but because of many mine subsidences in the Patch, Lackawanna County Redevelopment condemned 200 homes, many businesses, and two churches, so St. George had to relocate in the 1970s. They purchased land on South Keyser Avenue, and the new church was dedicated in 1978. (Courtesy of Dale Malecki.)

ST. MARY'S GREEK CATHOLIC CHURCH. The church shared the same block with St. George's on opposite sides of the street. The building burned in the 1940s and is currently located at the top of Oak Street. (Courtesy of Dale Malecki.)

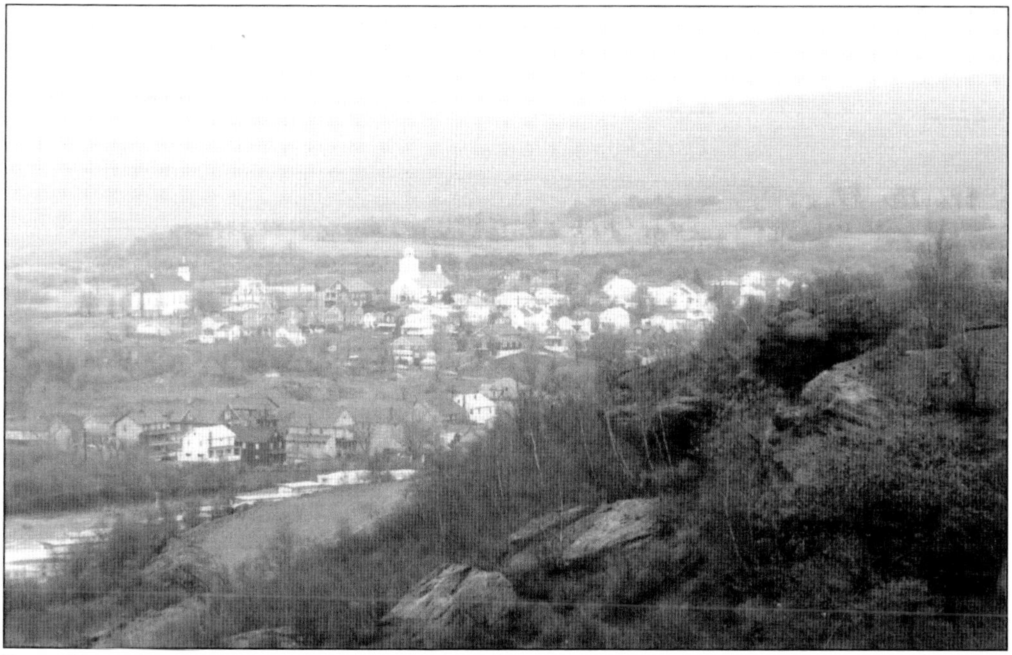

Pine Hills Golf Course. This would be the future site of the golf course. Seen in the picture is St. Mary's Church (left) and St. George's. The Alliance Landfill was not yet a part of Taylor at the time the photograph was taken. (Courtesy of Dale Malecki.)

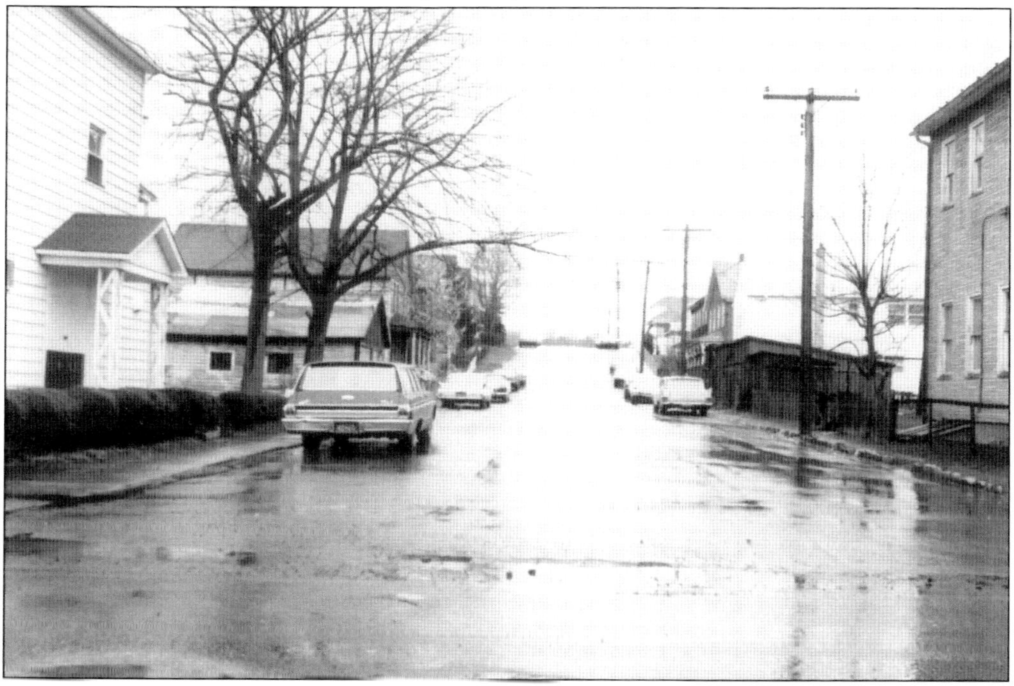

Semian's Funeral Home. Looking up Second Street from Oak Street, the building located on the left is Semian's Funeral Home. Presently it is located on Union Street. The funeral home, when on Oak, was operated by Andrew Semian, the father of Tammy Semian Souter, who now operates it at the present address. (Courtesy of Dale Malecki.)

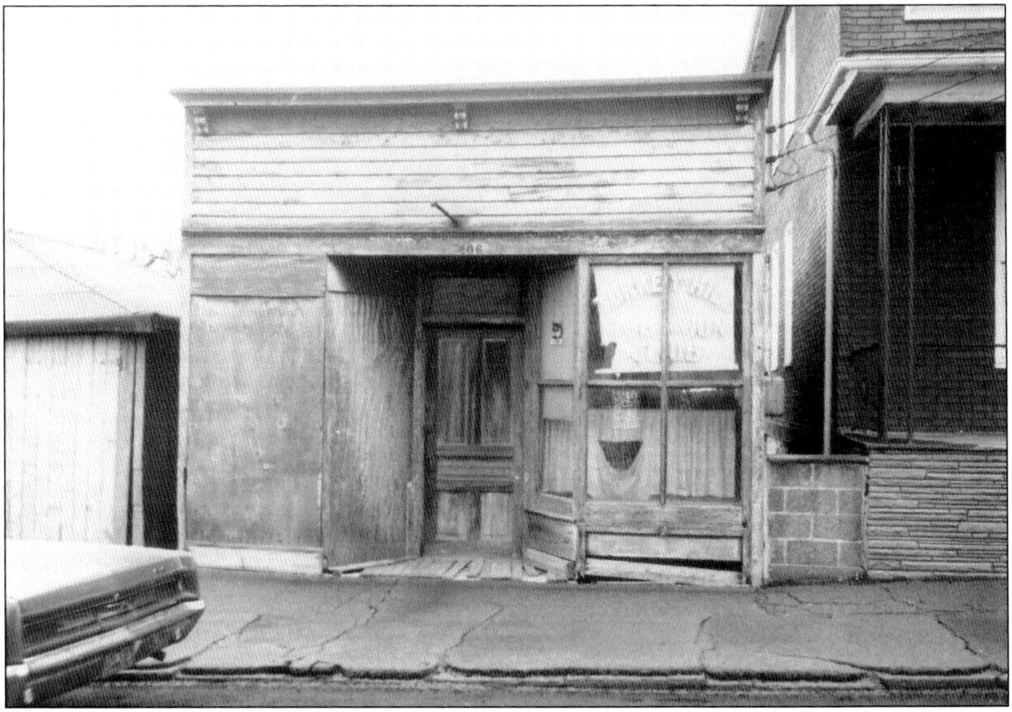

Hudzina Dry Goods. This is the original site of Paul and Anna Hudzina's store, located on Fourth Street. In later years, it became the home of the Turkey Hill Rod and Gun Club, which is still in existence today. (Courtesy of Dale Malecki.)

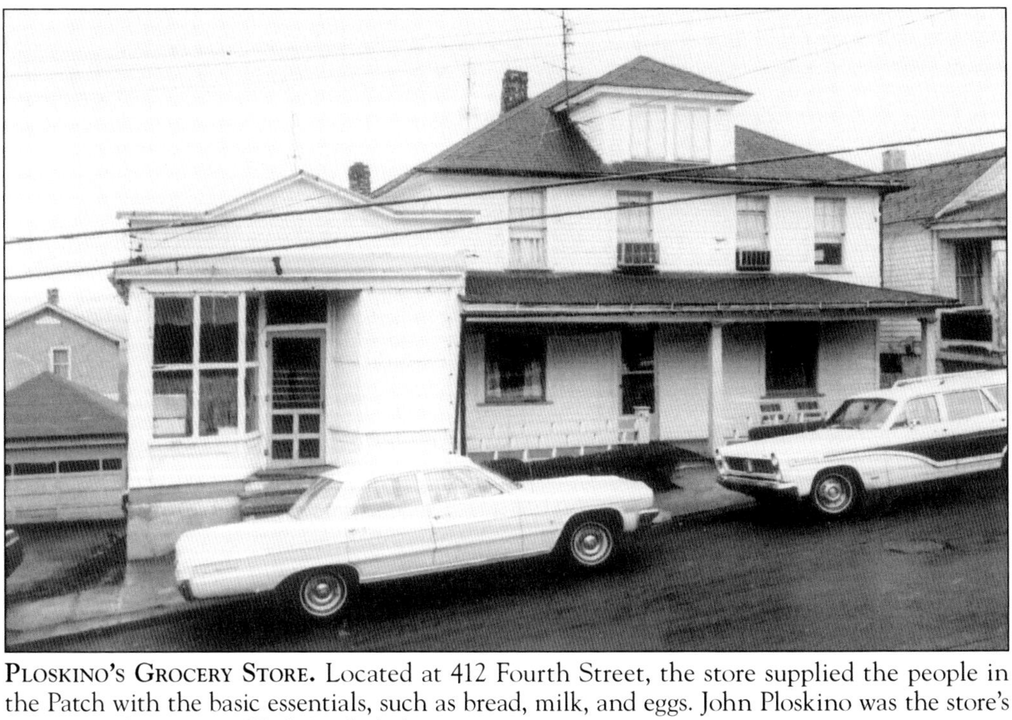

Ploskino's Grocery Store. Located at 412 Fourth Street, the store supplied the people in the Patch with the basic essentials, such as bread, milk, and eggs. John Ploskino was the store's proprietor. (Courtesy of Dale Malecki.)

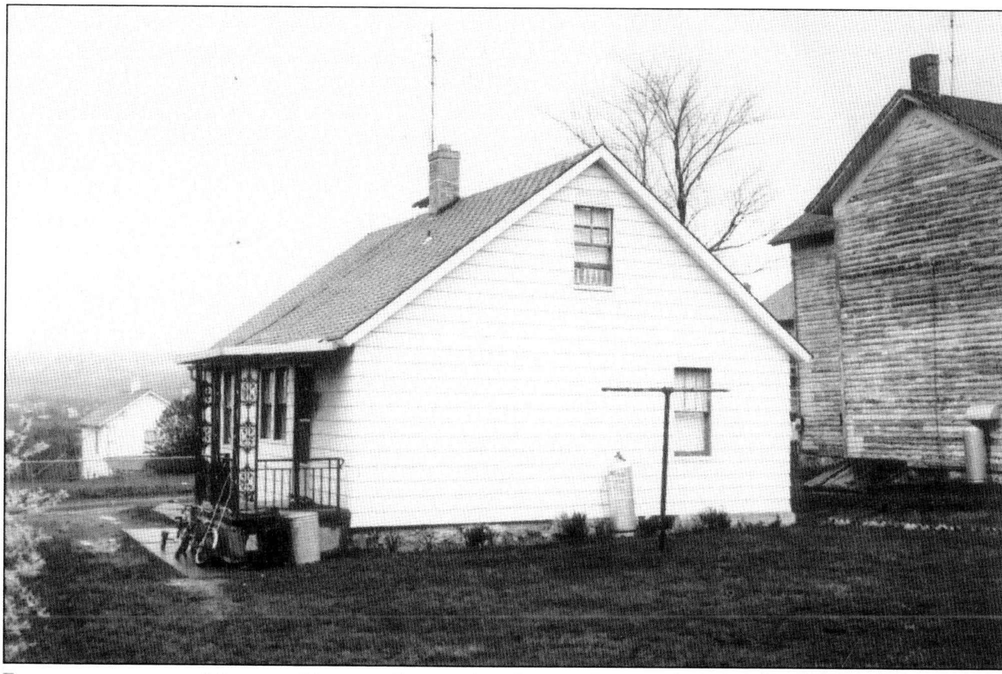

Residence of the Malecki Family. Pictured is the residence of Michael and Mary Malecki. At one time it was the site of the original grain and storage building for Ploskino's Grocery Store. (Courtesy of Dale Malecki.)

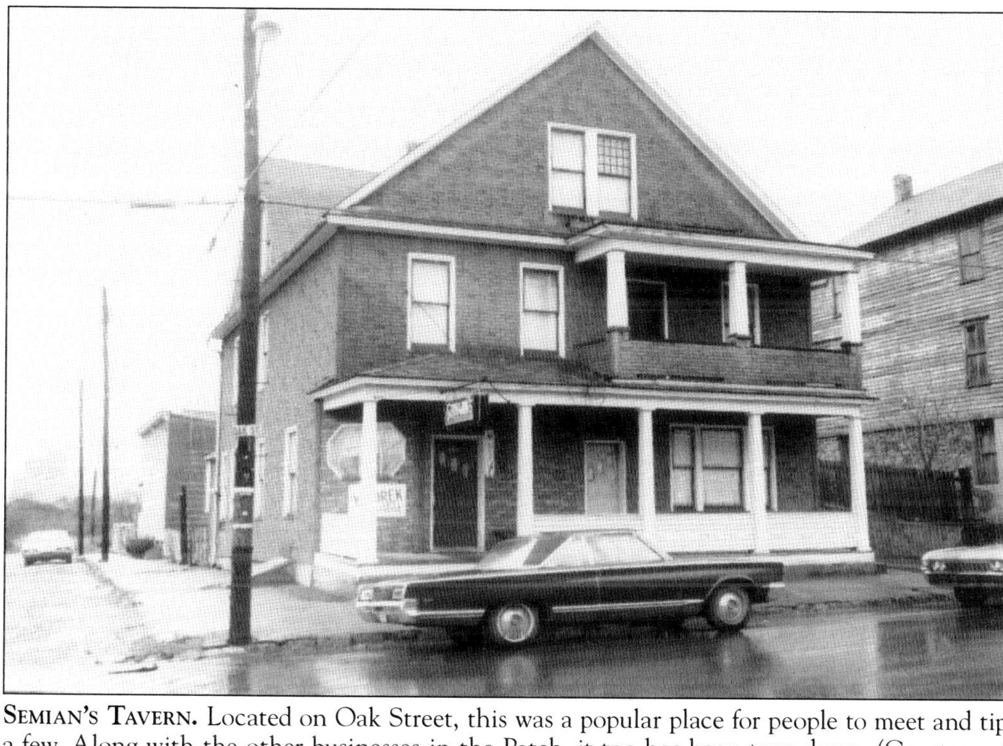

Semian's Tavern. Located on Oak Street, this was a popular place for people to meet and tip a few. Along with the other businesses in the Patch, it too has been torn down. (Courtesy of Dale Malecki.)

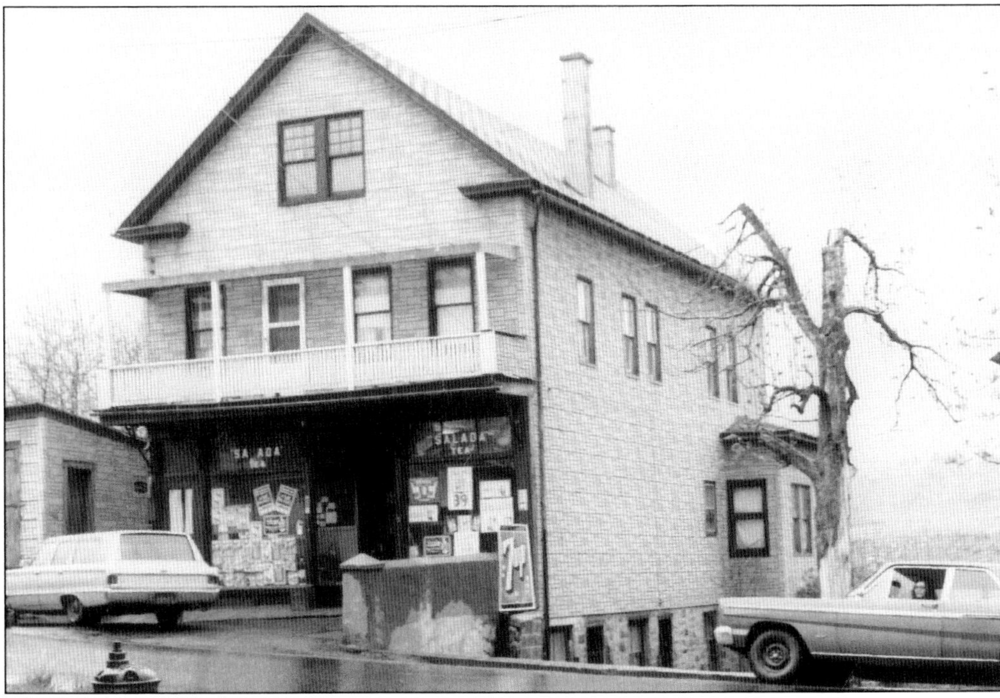

ECKER'S MARKET. This market located on Oak Street was a favorite place to shop among the Jewish community and others in the Patch. Many may remember the potbelly stove in the store. Joe Ecker was the proprietor. (Courtesy of Dale Malecki.)

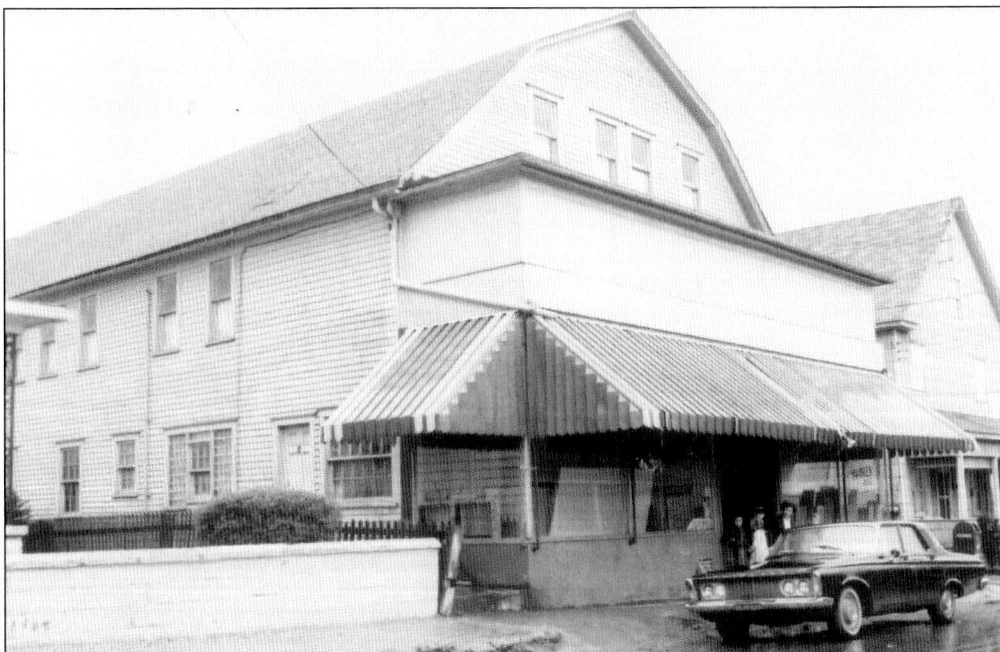

HARRY MARCK'S. Harry Marck's Appliances and Toys sold a little bit of everything from toasters to refrigerators. He was another of Taylor's prominent Jewish merchants. (Courtesy of Dale Malecki.)

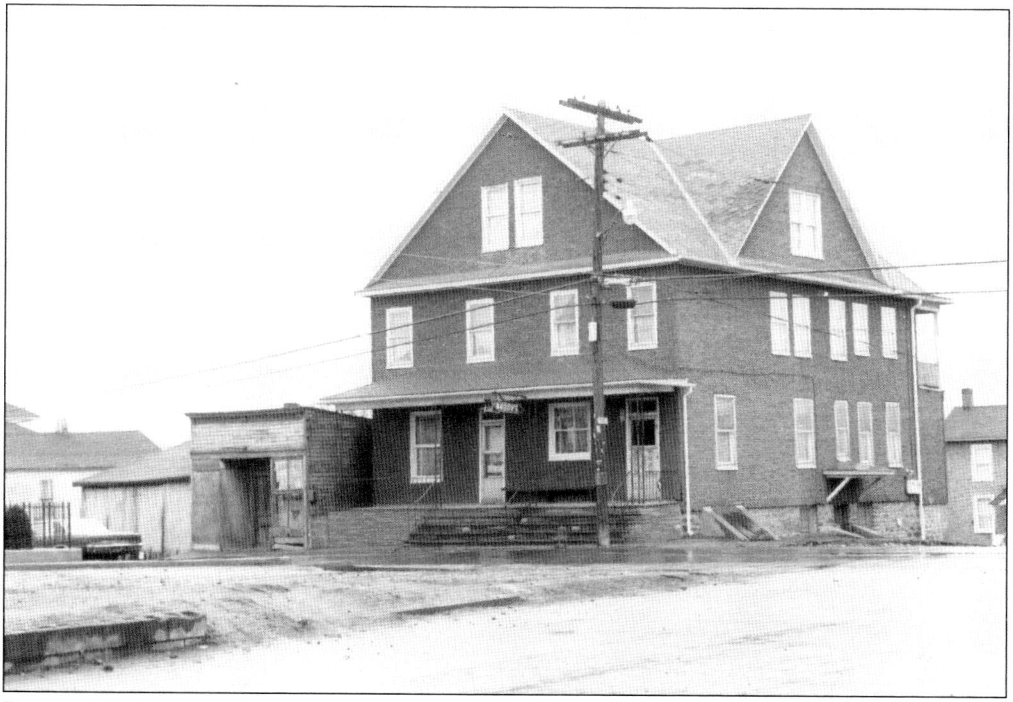

Ruddy's Café. Located at the corner of Fourth and Pine Streets, this was another of the Patch's favorite places where people would socialize after a hard day at work. Elizabeth Ruddy was the proprietor. (Courtesy of Dale Malecki.)

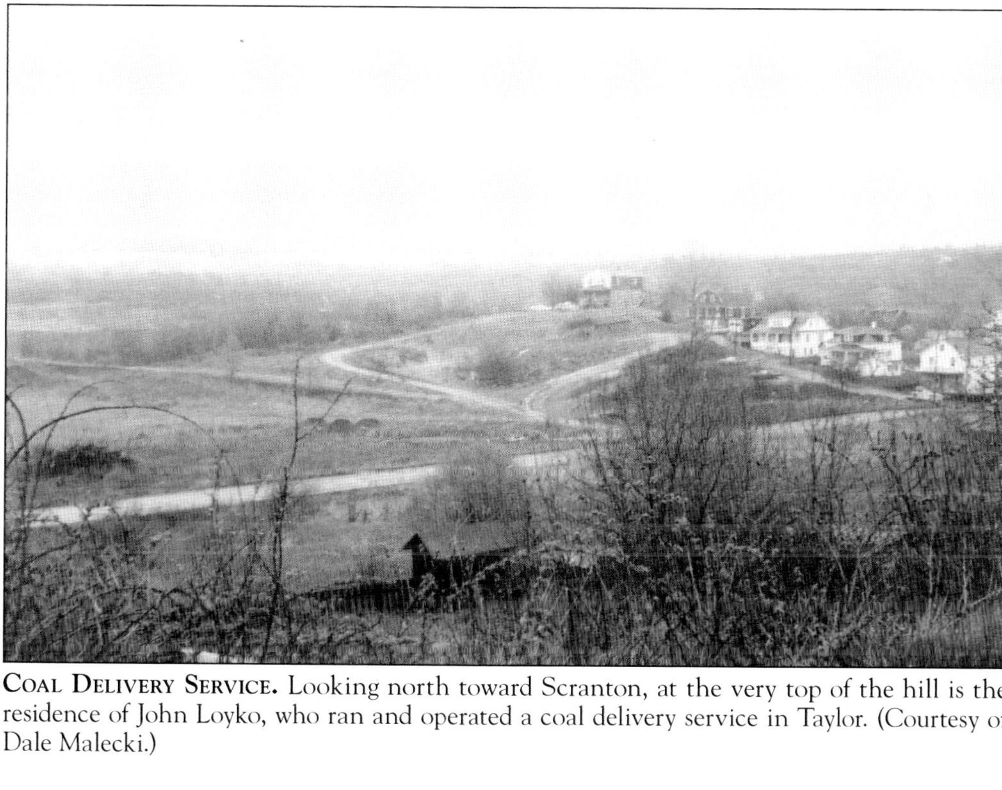

Coal Delivery Service. Looking north toward Scranton, at the very top of the hill is the residence of John Loyko, who ran and operated a coal delivery service in Taylor. (Courtesy of Dale Malecki.)

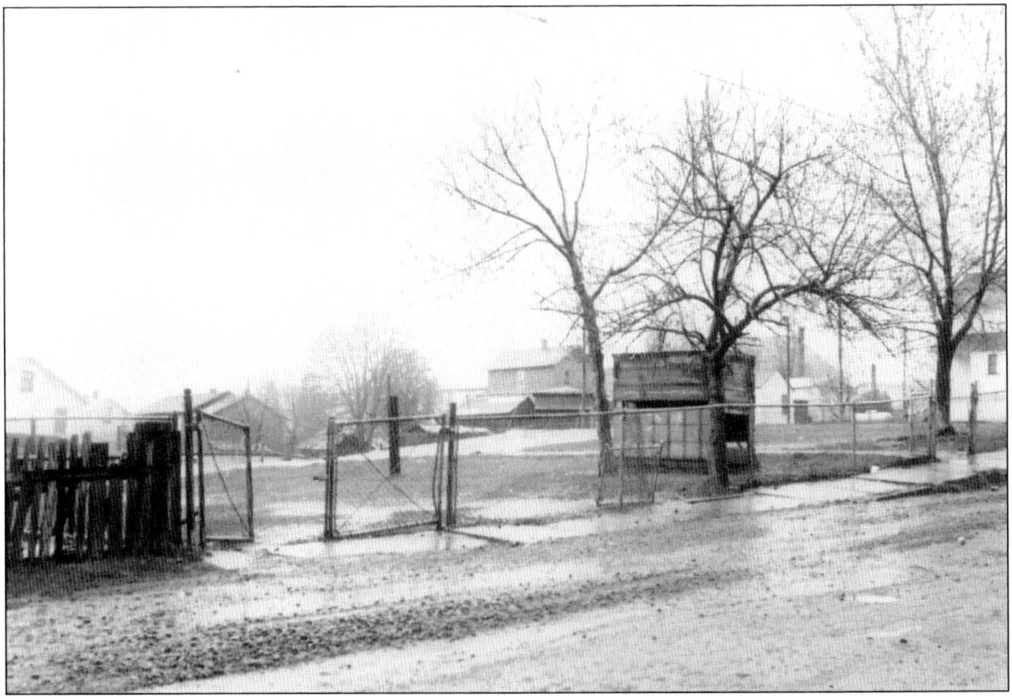

GARFIELD ELEMENTARY SCHOOL. This is the lot of the elementary school, located on Fifth Street. Many of the children in the Patch section were educated here. The school was closed down after being deemed no longer safe due to mine subsidences. The fence still remains. (Courtesy of Dale Malecki.)

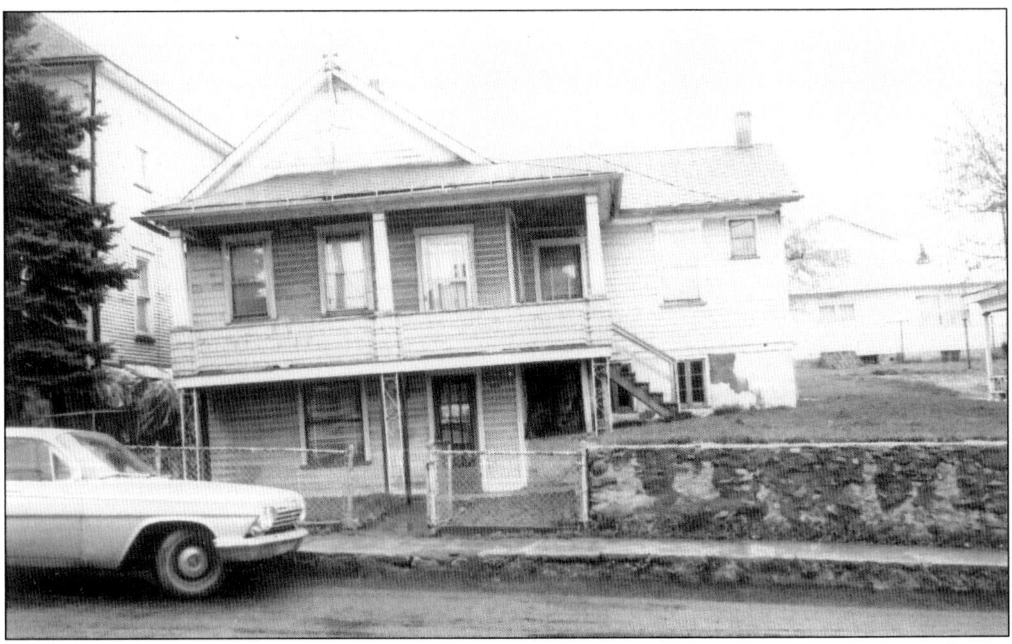

PETRO FAMILY RESIDENCE. Note the significant tilt to the Petro family home; this was due to a mine cave-in, a very common occurrence in this section of Taylor that eventually led to its demise. (Courtesy of Dale Malecki.)

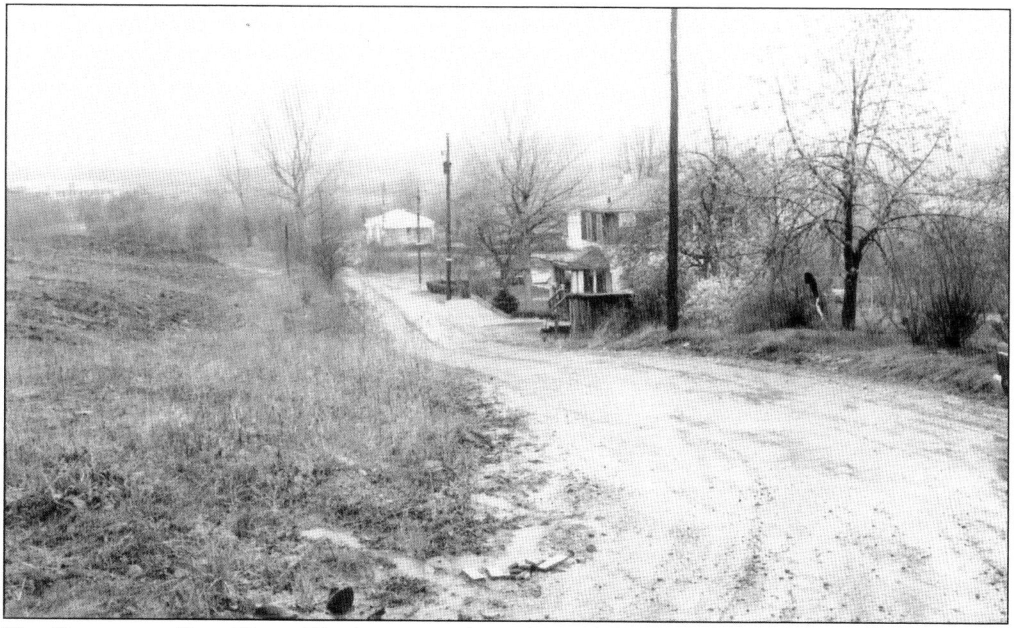

The Barber of Dog Hole. The house on the right in the photograph served as both residence and barbershop of Michael Semo. At that time, you could still get a shave and a haircut for two bits. (Courtesy of Dale Malecki.)

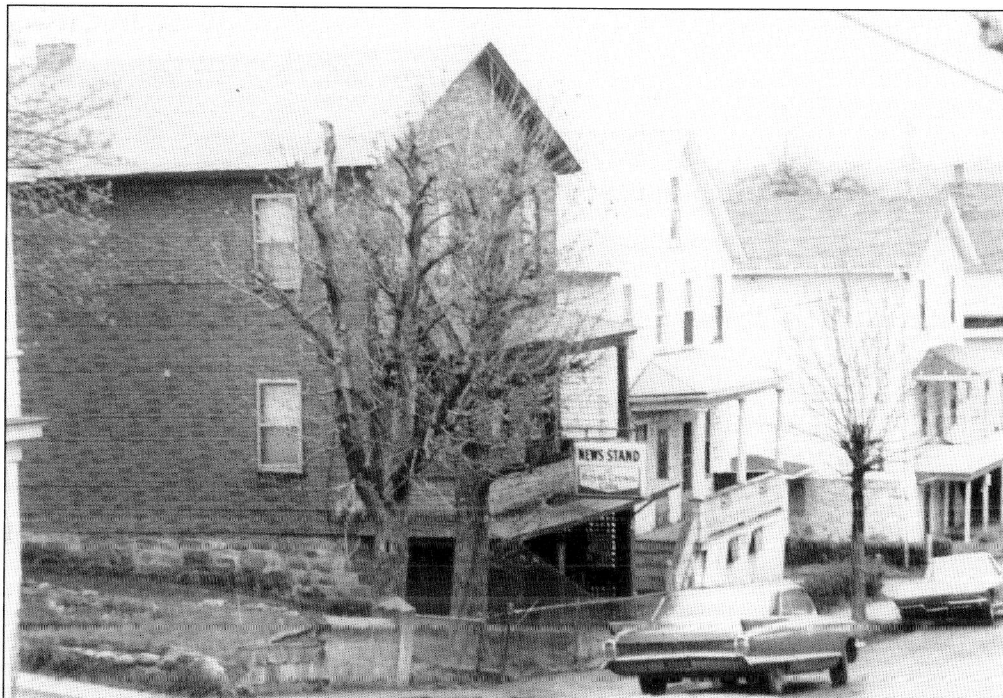

Sepa's Newsstand. Also known in the neighborhood as Penny's Newsstand, Sepa's was a small grocery store on Fourth Street that sold books, cigarettes, and other products. Peter Sepa was the proprietor; he also served on the board of directors of Taylor High School. (Courtesy of Dale Malecki.)

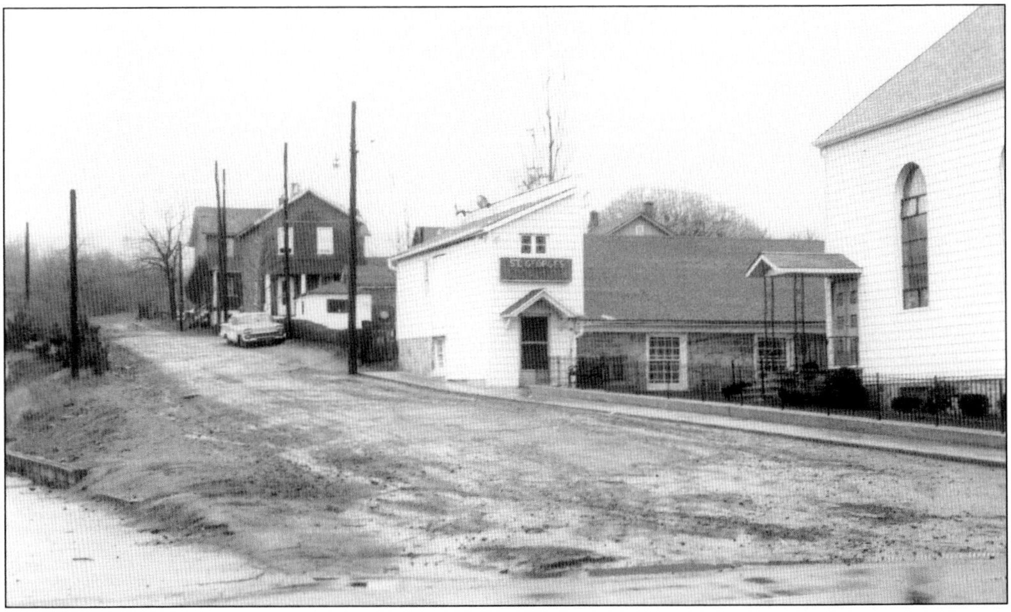

St. George's Social Club. In August 1954, St George's Hall was destroyed by an explosion. Plans were made to quickly reconstruct the social club rooms. It was completely rebuilt and reopened in November 1954. (Courtesy of Dale Malecki.)

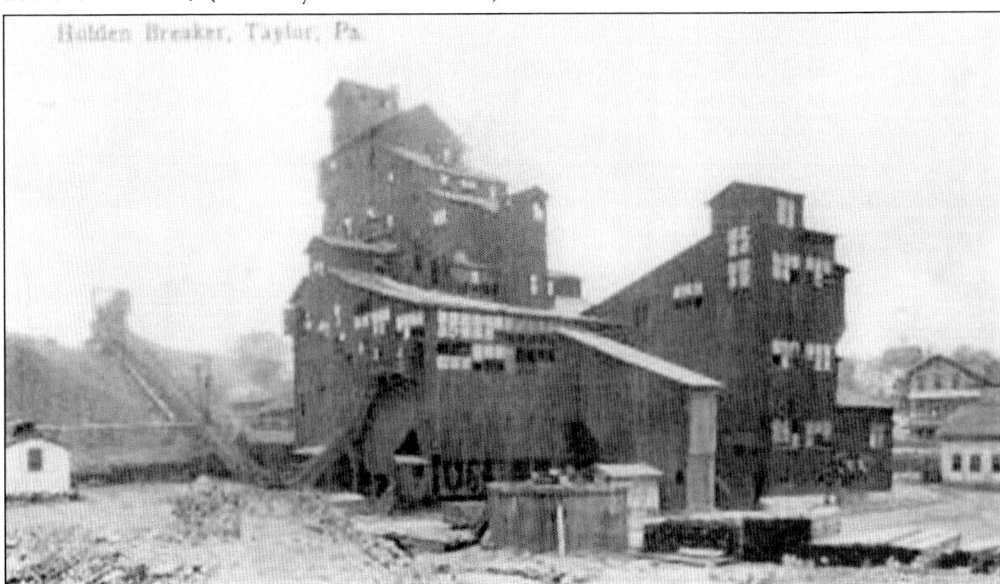

Holden Breaker. One of the worst mining disasters in Taylor occurred here on March 2, 1907. A gas explosion erupted in what was known as the barn road in the Clark vein, about a mile from the shaft. There are conflicting stories due to the cause of the explosion, but it was later surmised an accumulation of gas was ignited by a miner or laborer's naked lamp. The explosion came with such force it was felt by men working in the Pyne Colliery a mile away. According to the 1907 Department of Mines report, the following are the names of the men who perished in the Holden Mine Disaster: William Z. Williams, Thomas Williams (father and son), Frank Cososki, John Washnock, Chesmes Cosfoski, and John Zerzava. (Courtesy of Daniel Zeliniak.)

Three

CHURCH LIFE

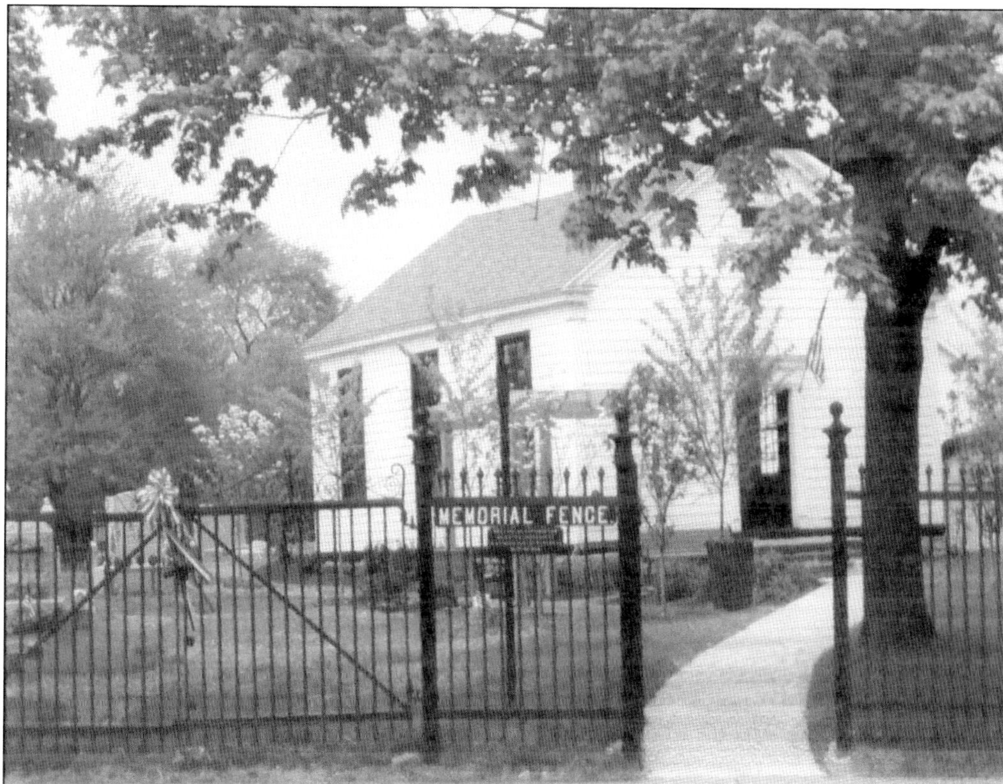

CORNELIUS ATHERTON. A man of much piety, Atherton was instrumental in organizing the weekly prayer meeting in Taylor. Historical papers read before the Daughters of the American Revolution describe how he stood in an old puritanical style with his arms outstretched and his hands and face upturned to heaven, invoking blessings for his family and friends. Cornelius referred to the land surrounding the First Presbyterian Church (pictured) as "God's Acre." (Courtesy of Shawn Murphy and Taylor Community Library.)

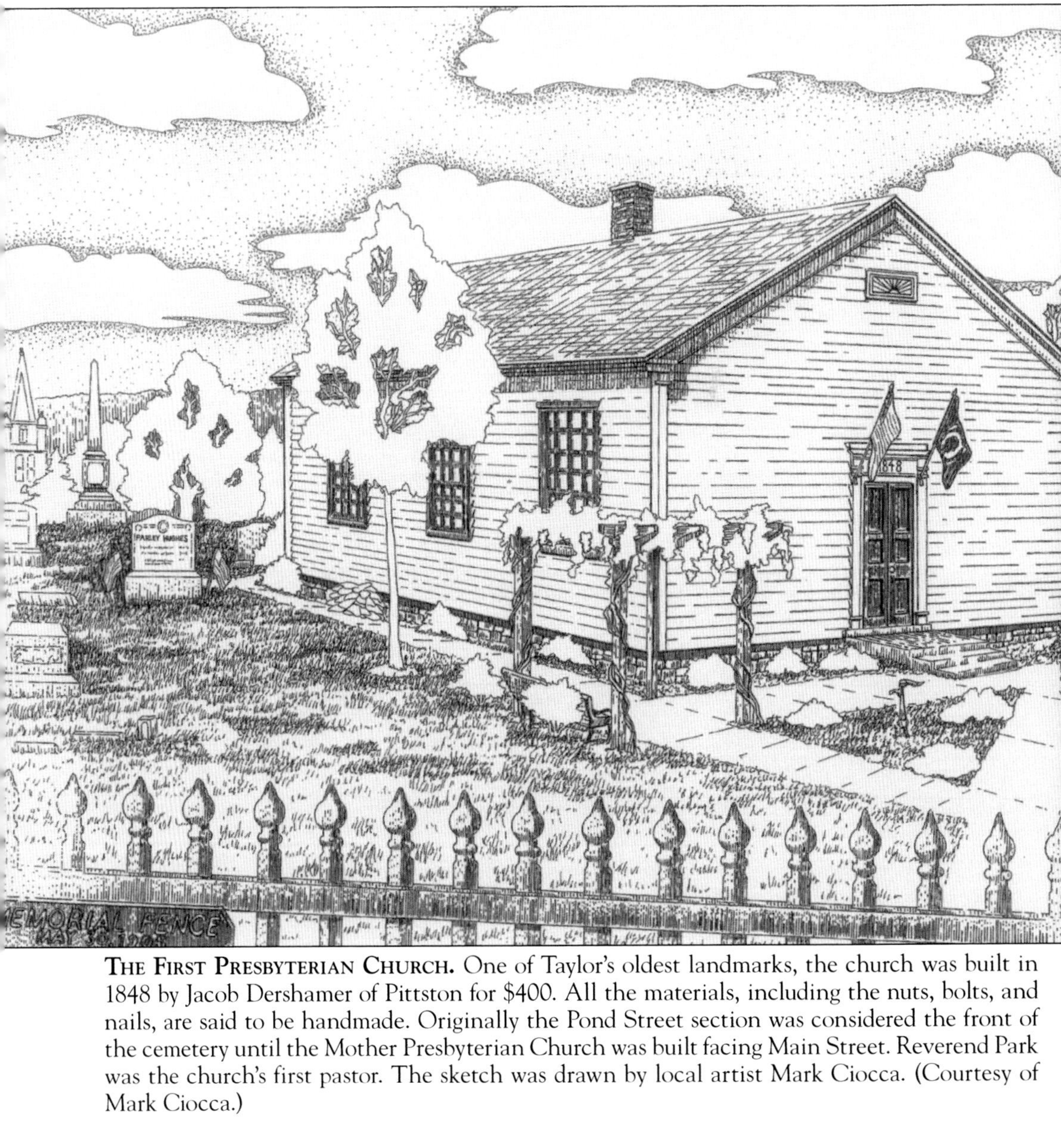

The First Presbyterian Church. One of Taylor's oldest landmarks, the church was built in 1848 by Jacob Dershamer of Pittston for $400. All the materials, including the nuts, bolts, and nails, are said to be handmade. Originally the Pond Street section was considered the front of the cemetery until the Mother Presbyterian Church was built facing Main Street. Reverend Park was the church's first pastor. The sketch was drawn by local artist Mark Ciocca. (Courtesy of Mark Ciocca.)

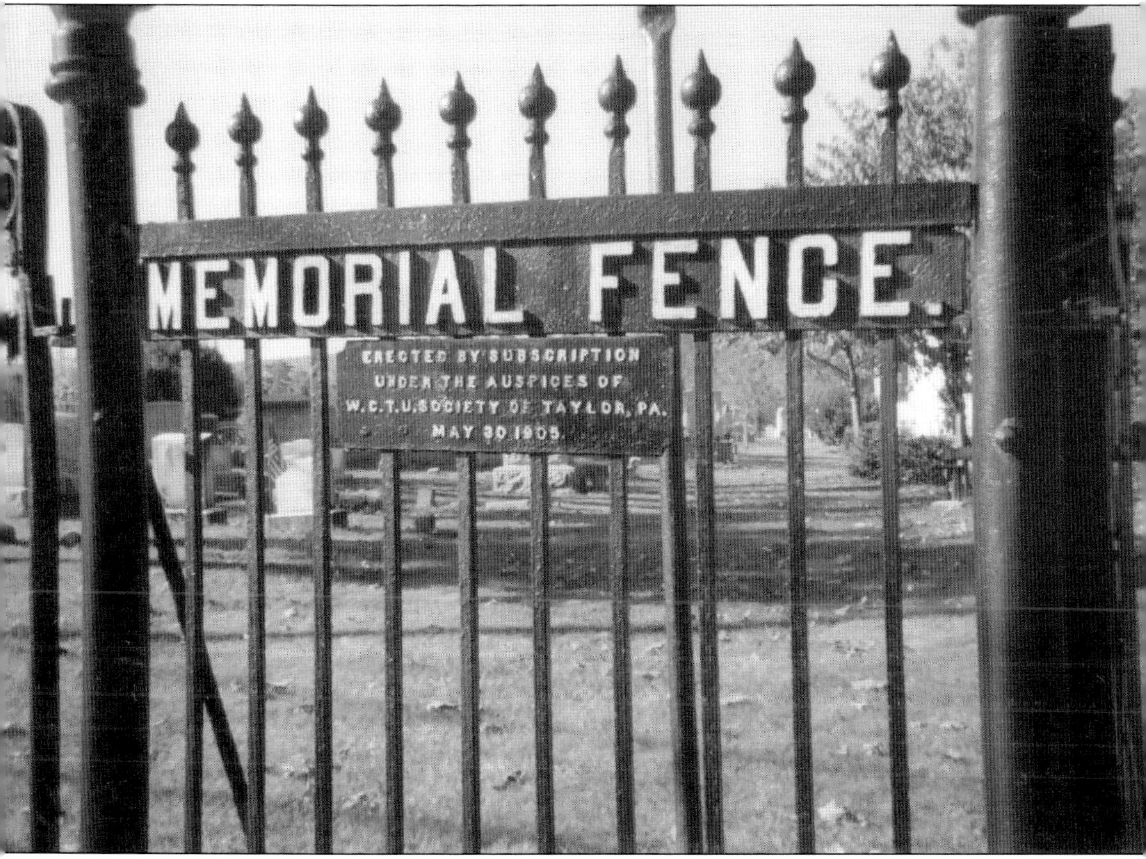

TAYLOR MEMORIAL CEMETERY. The second of Taylor's oldest landmarks, the cemetery, dates back to the late 1700s, at which time a local farmer used the land to bury family members. The entire area of the cemetery was purchased in 1855 for $100. Twenty-four veterans of war are buried here. John Price, a cavalryman in the Civil War, was captured by Confederate troops at Darbytown Road and was held at a prisoner of war camp in Richmond. The conditions in the camp were deplorable. He and four other prisoners were forced to live in knee-deep water for five years. When he was finally released, he had mold growing on his hair and body. He died shortly after returning to his home in Taylor. The cemetery holds a lot of history both above and below ground. In 1905, the Women's Christian Temperance Union Society of Taylor raised money to replace the original wooden fence with the current iron fence. Renovations were also made to the church. A dedication ceremony took place on Memorial Day 1905. (Author's collection.)

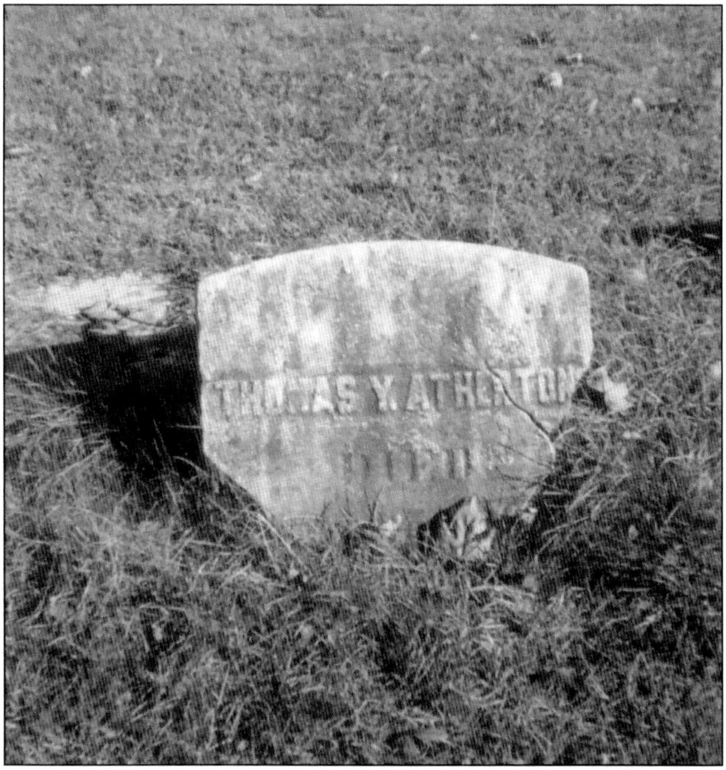

Oldest Tombstone. This tombstone belongs to Thomas Y. Atherton, who was born in 1834 and died the same year at the age of three months. He was the infant son of Joseph and Phoebe Atherton. (Author's collection.)

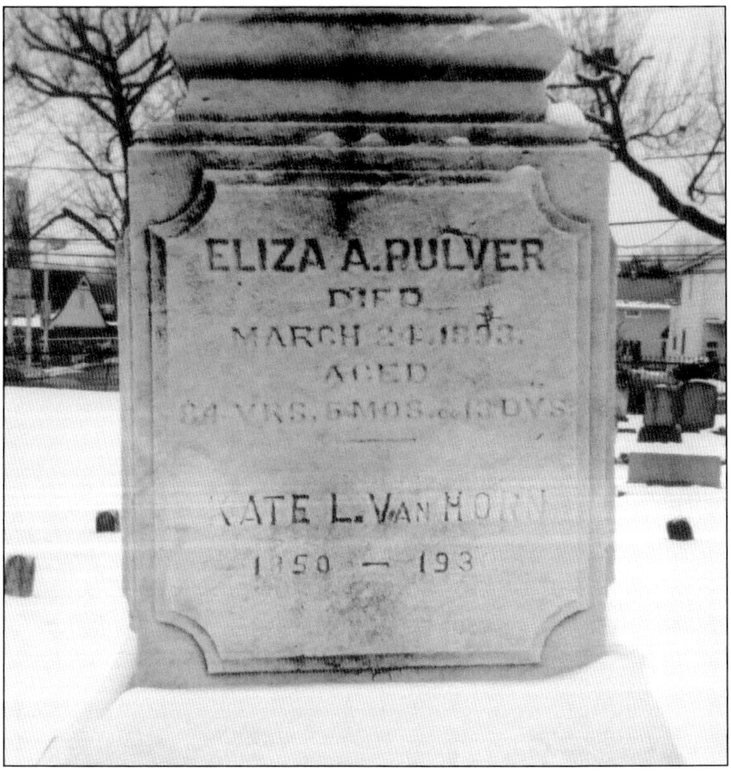

Eliza Pulver. Pulver was a teacher who stands out in Taylor's history for having taught Pres. Grover Cleveland during his boyhood in New York State. She died on March 24, 1893, at the age of 84. Though not noticeable in the picture, her tombstone is the tallest in the Taylor Memorial Cemetery. (Author's collection.)

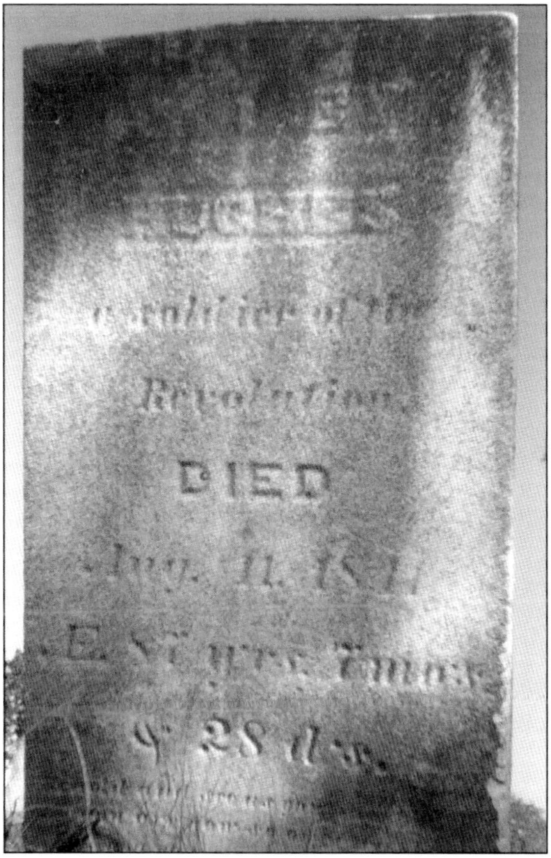

Parley Hughes. Born in Killingly, Connecticut, on December 14, 1753, Hughes came to Taylor where he died on August 11, 1841. He served as a soldier in the Revolutionary War: He enlisted in January 1776 for one year, was discharged in January 1777, and re-enlisted for a three-year term. Legend tells that Parley served as a personal bodyguard, or "lifeguard" as they were referred to then, to Gen. George Washington; however, no affidavits were ever discovered to back up this claim. His epitaph reads, "Behold and see as you pass by / As you are now so once was I / As I am now soon you must be / Prepare for death and follow me." In 1929, the Historical Society of the Taylor High School (shown below) erected a new stone in his honor. (Author's collection.)

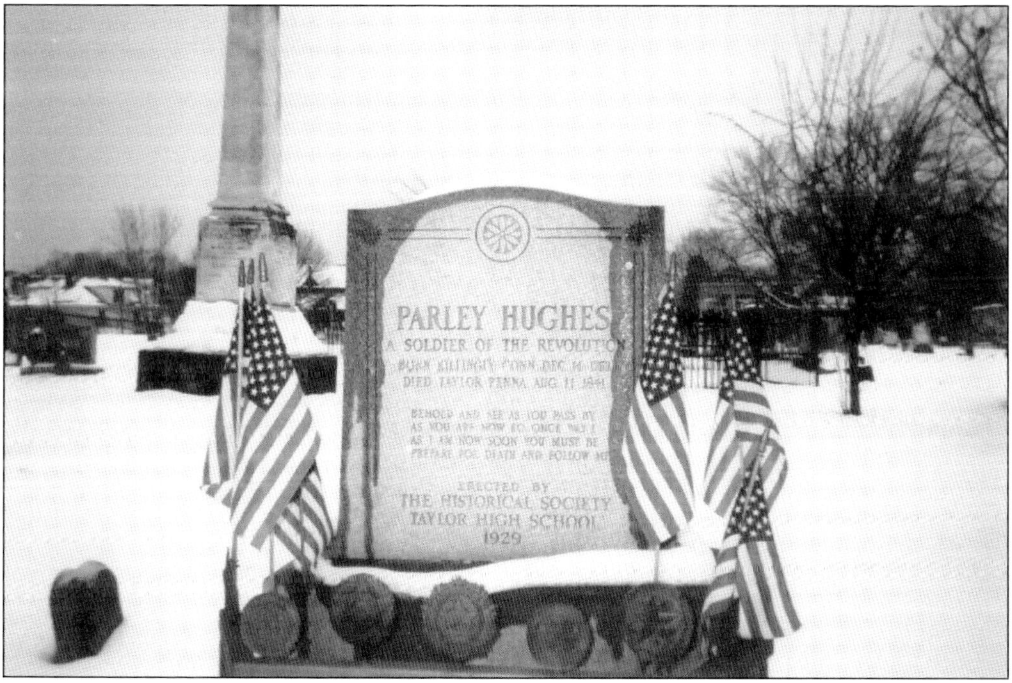

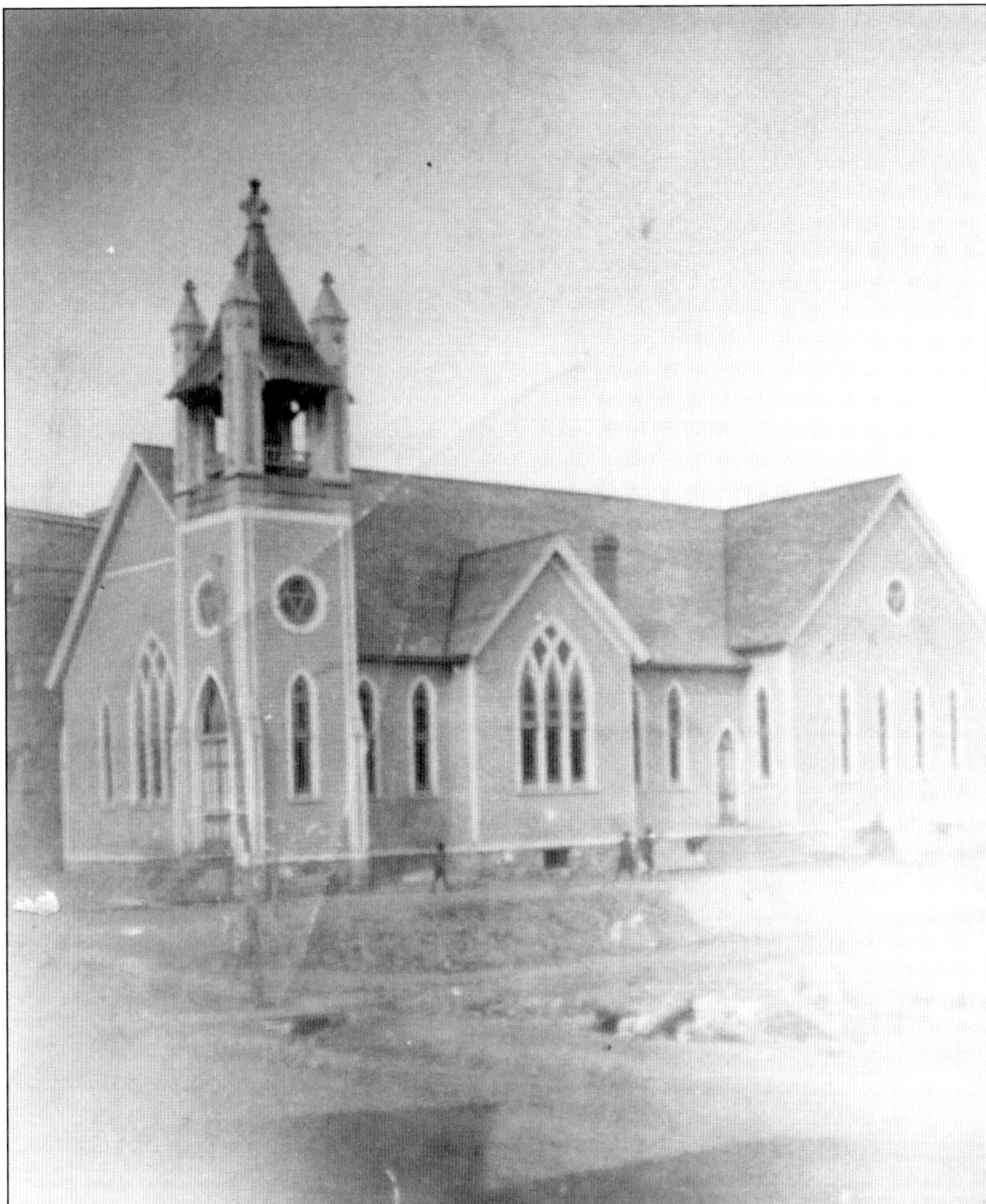

CALVARY BAPTIST CHURCH. Between 1888 and 1890, a dissention arose in the Welsh Baptist Church over the constant use of the Welsh language, and many members of the congregation left and formed an English Baptist Church, also known as the Calvary Baptist Church. In 1942, a fire swept through the church causing much damage: A $3,200 pipe organ donated by philanthropist Andrew Carnegie was destroyed, and the interior of the building was left in ruins. Presently it is the site of the United Baptist Church. (Courtesy of Marie Eskra.)

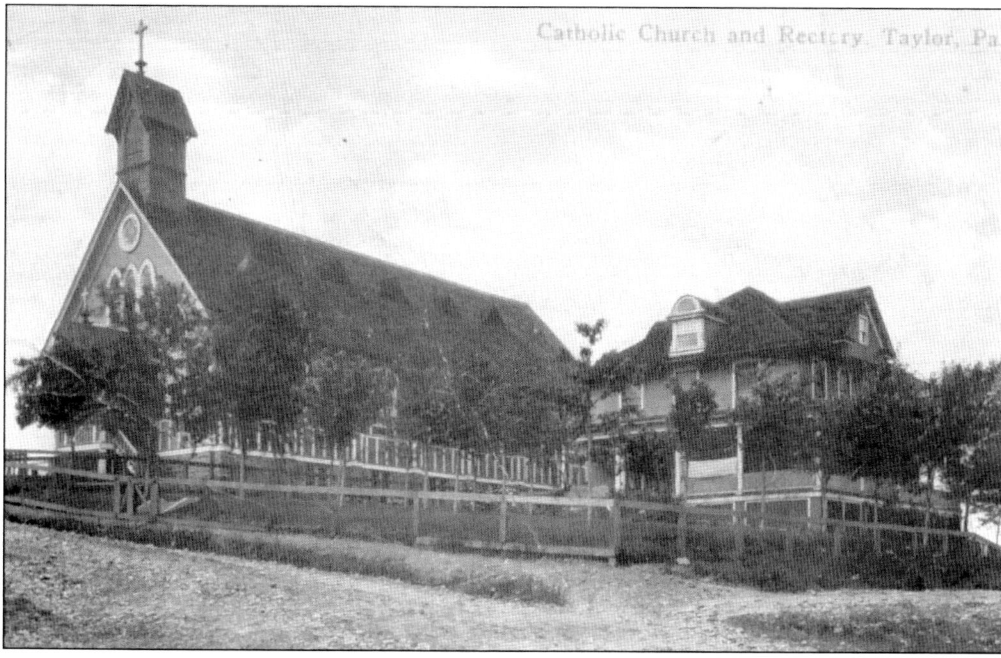

IMMACULATE CONCEPTION CHURCH. Also known as the "Irish Church," it was built in 1889. The first pastor was Rev. James A. Moffit. The church and rectory were located at 202 Church Street. The building remains standing today, but no services are held there. (Courtesy of Shawn Murphy and Taylor Community Library.)

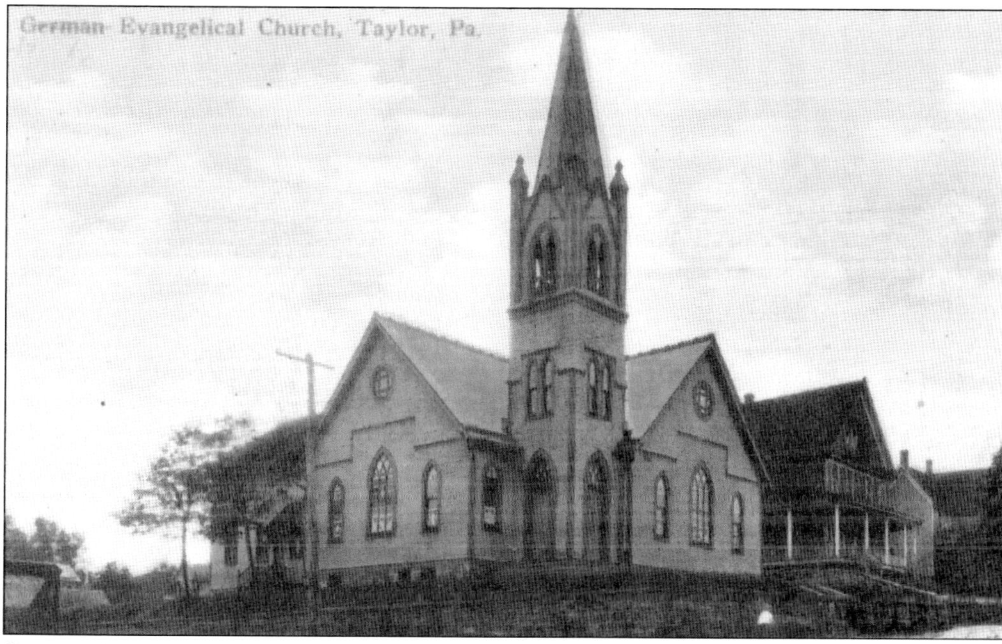

GERMAN EVANGELICAL CHURCH. Also known as St. Paul's Evangelical Church, the many Swiss and German settlers assembled and organized their congregation in the little old schoolhouse located on the site of Weber's Rink on August 15, 1874. In 1887, the church edifice was erected. Reverend Summers, of Pittston, was its first pastor. (Courtesy of Nancy and Bob Thomas.)

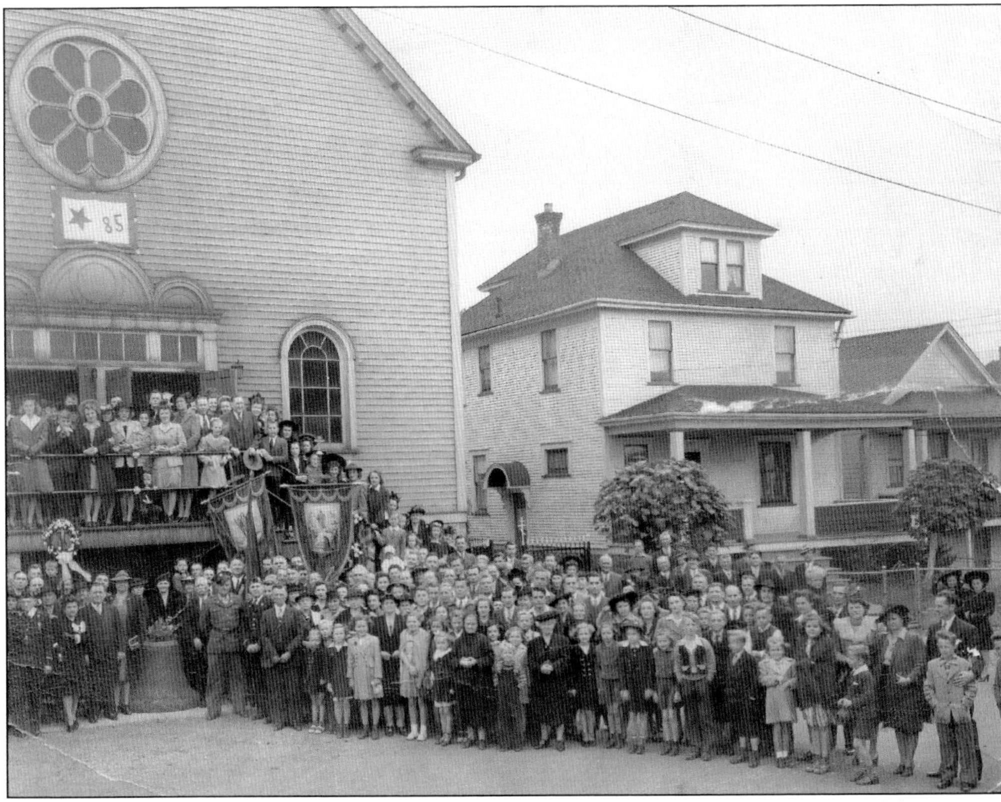

DEDICATION OF THE BELL, C. 1940. During wartime, nearly the entire congregation of the original St. George's Orthodox Church in the Patch section of Taylor gathered for the dedication of the bell (shown in center). (Courtesy of Kathleen Olekszulin.)

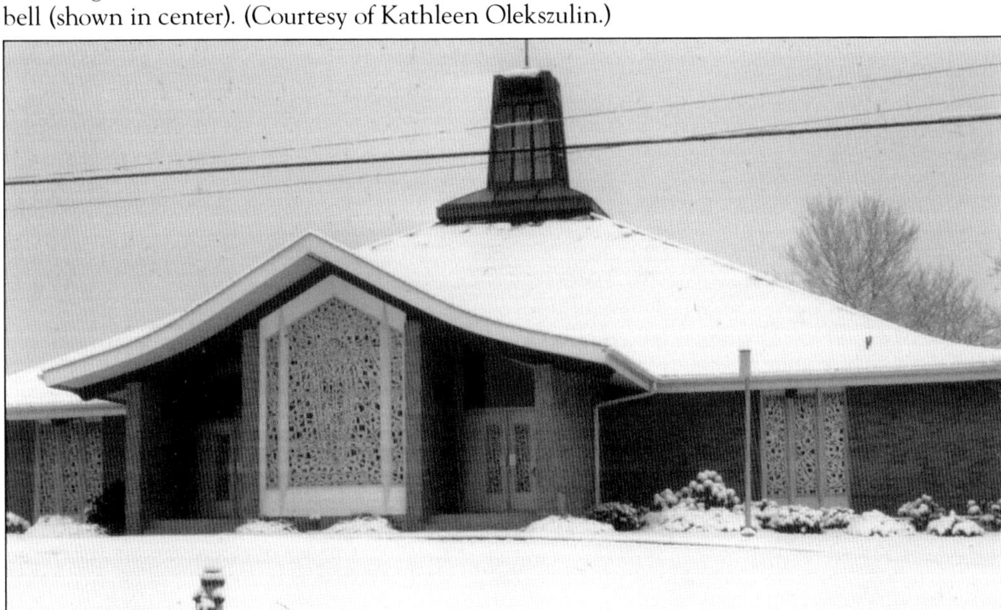

ST. JOHN THE BAPTIST CATHOLIC CHURCH. Situated in the "Frogtown" section of Taylor, this church just recently closed in 2009. (Courtesy of Shawn Murphy.)

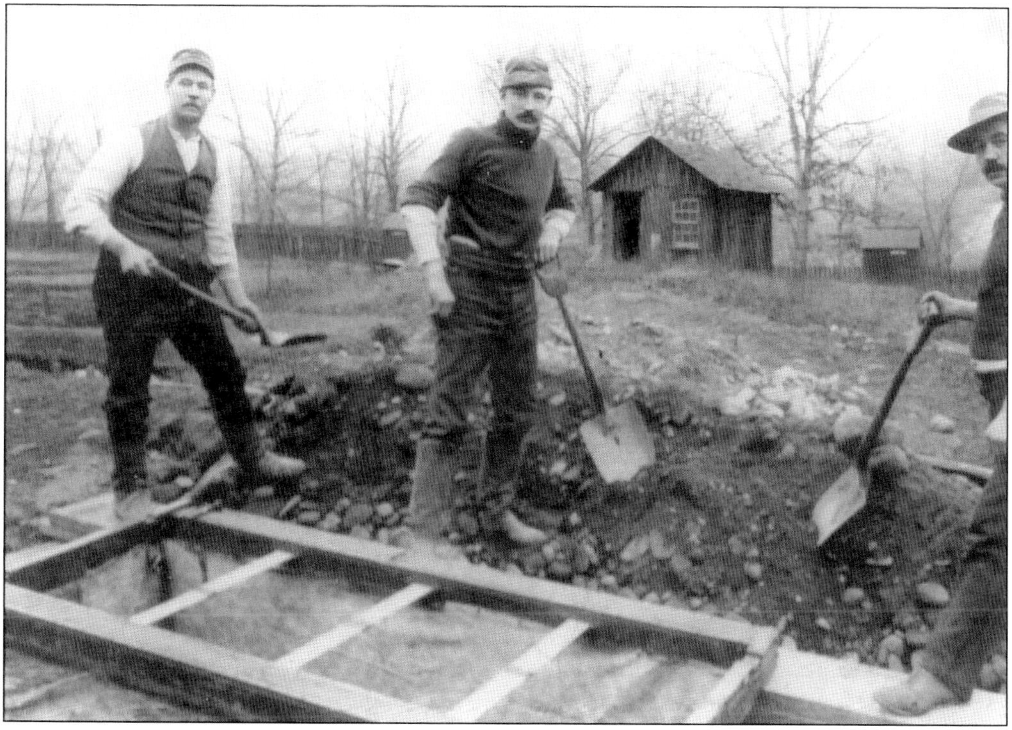

Gravediggers. Three men are seen around 1900 digging a grave at the Forest Home Cemetery. Morgan B. Morgan, a burgess and justice of the peace from Taylor's early days, is buried here. (Courtesy of Shawn Murphy.)

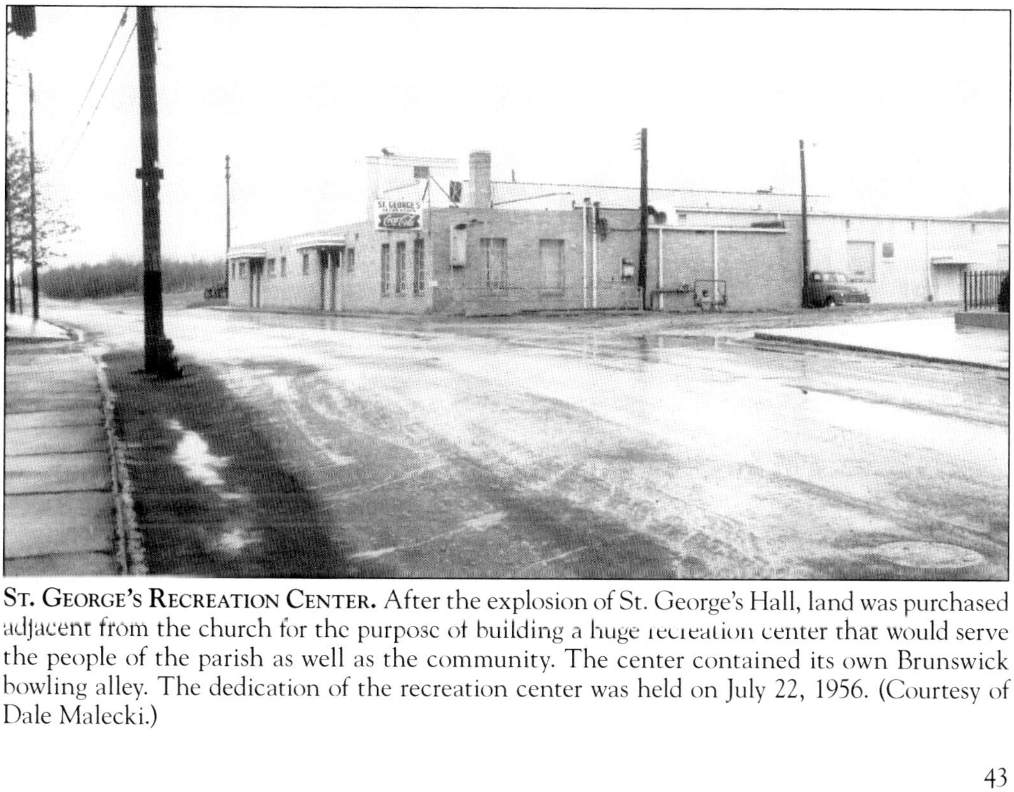

St. George's Recreation Center. After the explosion of St. George's Hall, land was purchased adjacent from the church for the purpose of building a huge recreation center that would serve the people of the parish as well as the community. The center contained its own Brunswick bowling alley. The dedication of the recreation center was held on July 22, 1956. (Courtesy of Dale Malecki.)

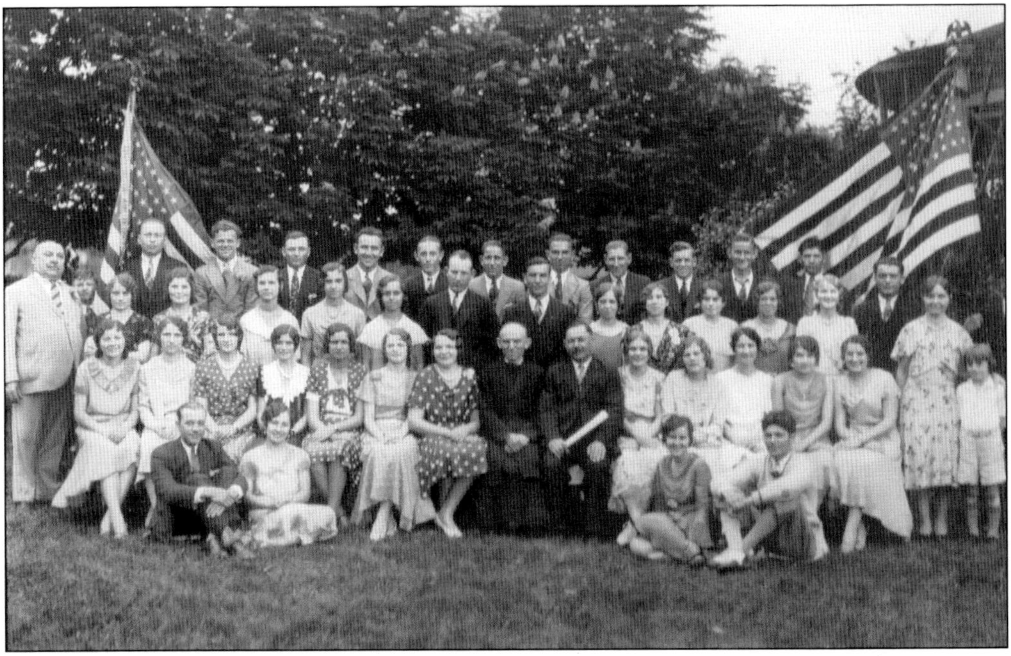

ST. MARY'S CHOIR. This is a photograph of members of St. Mary's Choir taken in the late 1920s or possibly early 1930s. (Courtesy of Kathleen Oleckszulin.)

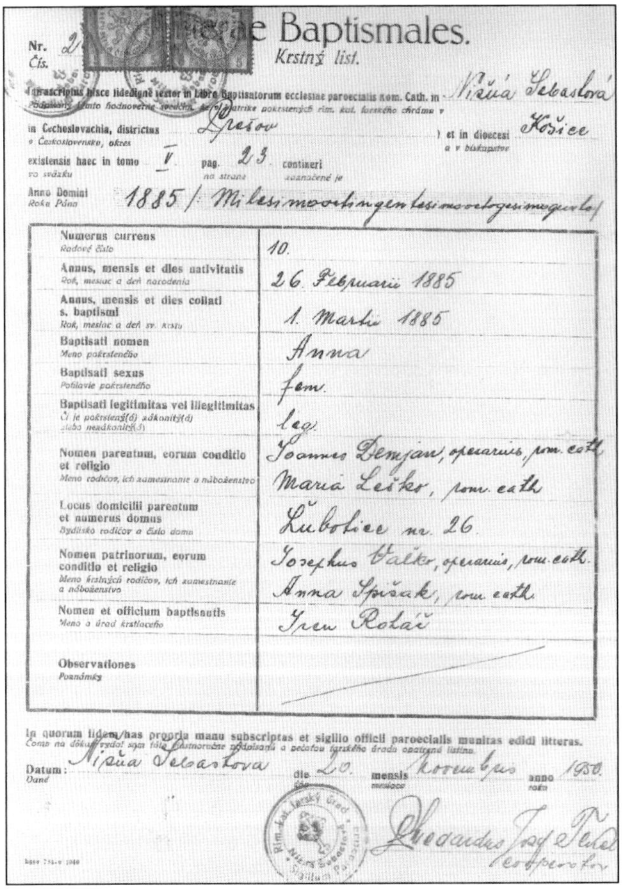

Litterae Baptismales.
Krstný list.

Nr. 2
Čís.

Infrascriptus hisce fidedigne testor in Libro Baptisatorum ecclesiae parocialis Rom. Cath. in Nižňa Šebastová
Podpísaný týmto hodnoverne svedčím, že v matrike pokrstených rím. kat. farského chrámu v

in Čechoslovachia, districtus Prešov) et in dioecesi Košice
v Československu, okres a v biskupstve

existensis haec in tomo V. pag. 23. contineri
vo zväzku na strane zaznačené je

Anno Domini 1885 / Millesimooctingentesimooctogesimoquinto /
Roku Pána

Numerus currens Radové číslo	10.
Annus, mensis et dies nativitatis Rok, mesiac a deň narodenia	26. Februarii 1885
Annus, mensis et dies collati s. baptismi Rok, mesiac a deň sv. krstu	1. Martii 1885
Baptisati nomen Meno pokrsteného	Anna
Baptisati sexus Pohlavie pokrsteného	fem.
Baptisati legitimitas vel illegitimitas Či je pokrstený(á) zákonitý(á) alebo nezákonitý(á)	leg.
Nomen parentum, eorum conditio et religio Meno rodičov, ich zamestnanie a náboženstvo	Joannes Demjan, operarius, rom. cath. Maria Leško, rom. cath.
Locus domicilii parentum et numerus domus Bydlisko rodičov a číslo domu	Ľubotice nr. 26.
Nomen patrinorum, eorum conditio et religio Meno krstných rodičov, ich zamestnanie a náboženstvo	Josephus Valko, operarius, rom. cath. Anna Spišak, rom. cath.
Nomen et officium baptisantis Meno a úrad krstiteľa	Joan. Rohái
Observationes Poznámky	

In quorum fidem has propria manu subscriptas et sigillo officii parocialis munitas edidi litteras.
Čo na dôkaz vydal som toto vlastnoručne podpísané a pečaťou farského úradu opatrené listina.

Datum: Nižňa Šebastova die 20. mensis Novembris anno 1950.
Dané dňa mesiaca roku

Rím. kat. farský úrad Nižná Šebastová Sigillum Parochiale

Alexander Jozef Tekel cooperator

BAPTISMAL CERTIFICATE. This is the baptismal record of Anna Demjan. Born in Eastern Europe, she immigrated to the United States and settled in Taylor, where she and husband, Alexander Matician (also spelled Metisin), raised a family. Alexander worked for the Delaware, Lackawanna and Western Railroad. The couple belonged to the St. Mary's Greek Catholic Church. (Courtesy of Mary Ann Matsko.)

FIRST HOLY COMMUNION. This c. 1915 photograph shows Anna Matician (later Matsko) dressed to receive her First Holy Communion at St. Mary's Greek Catholic Church. Next to her is Sister Mary and seated is Sister Agnes. Anna's parents emigrated from Eastern Europe. She was their eldest child and the first to celebrate this important religious rite. (Courtesy of Geraldine Matsko Kashuba.)

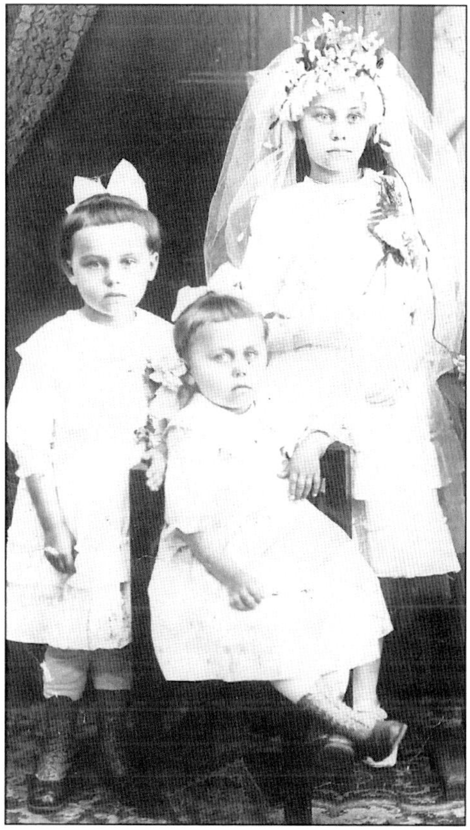

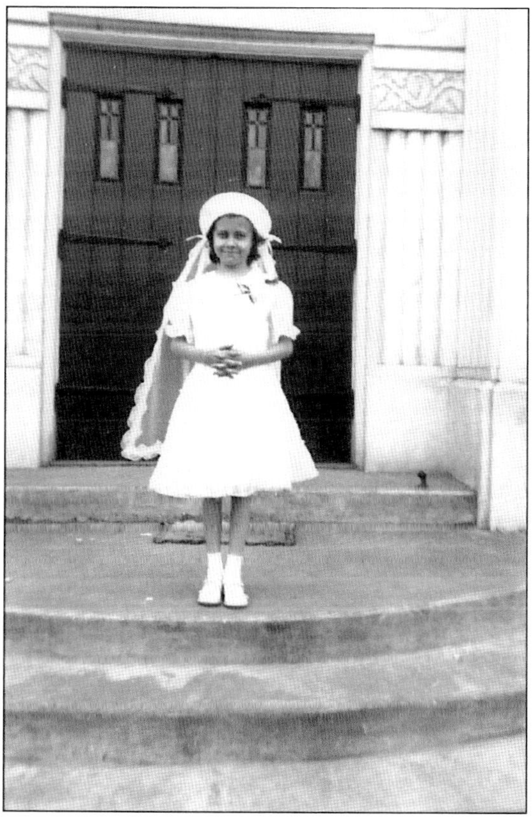

GERALDINE MATSKO FIRST HOLY COMMUNION. This c. 1950 photograph shows Geraldine Matsko on the steps of St. Mary's Greek Catholic Church on the day of her First Holy Communion, an important day in the life of a Catholic child. The parish was founded by immigrant families who wished to practice their faith as they had in Eastern Europe. A Byzantine Rite Catholic parish, it followed the Julian calendar for religious holidays at this time. (Courtesy of Geraldine Matsko Kashuba.)

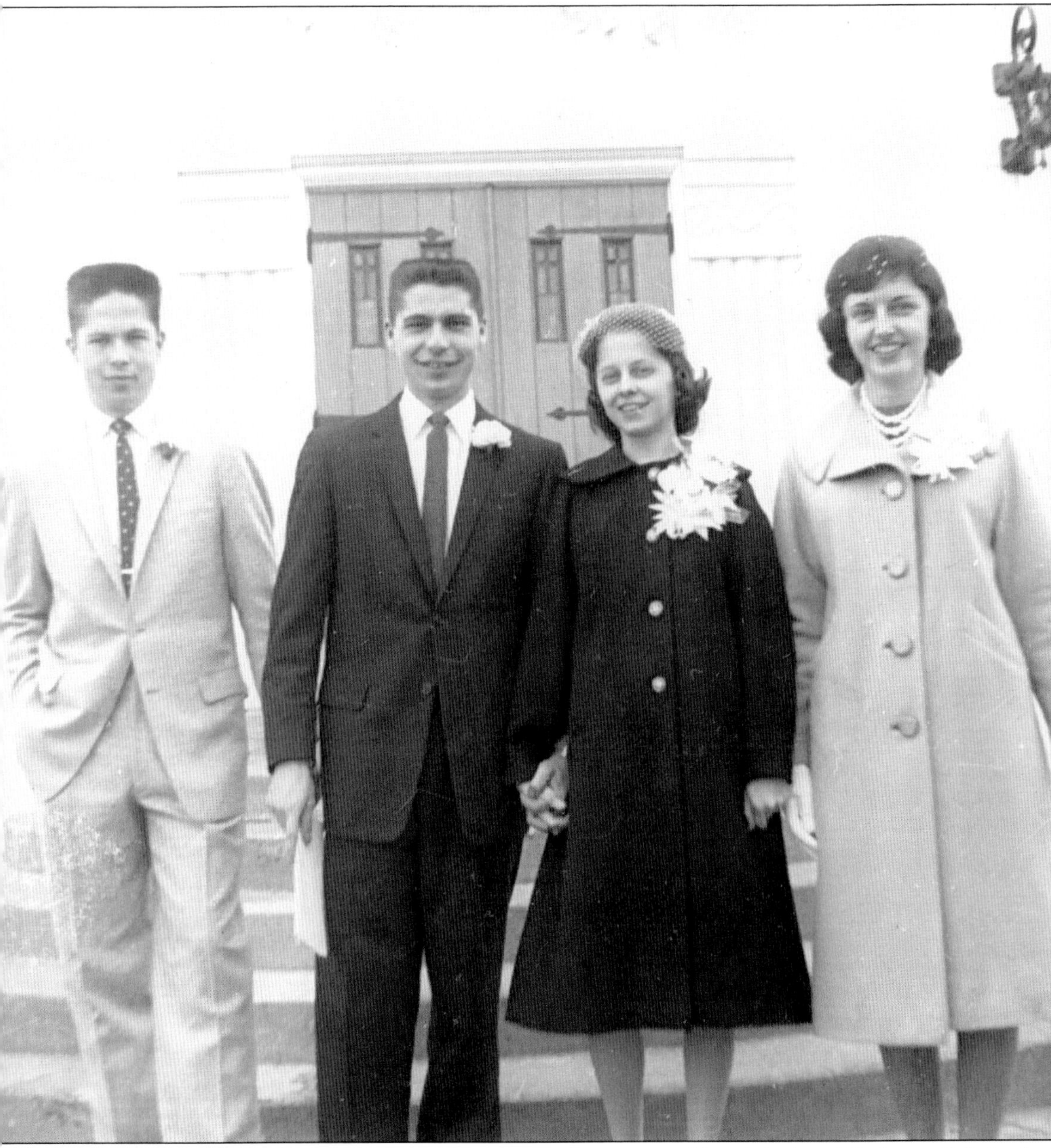

GERALDINE MATSKO AND MICHAEL KASHUBA WEDDING. Geraldine Matsko of Taylor and Michael Kashuba of Scranton stand outside St. Mary's Greek Catholic Church on their wedding day, January 27, 1962. With them are best man William Kashuba, brother of the bridegroom, and bridesmaid Jeanne Petrunich, cousin of the bride. (Courtesy of Geraldine Matsko Kashuba.)

Four

Open for Business

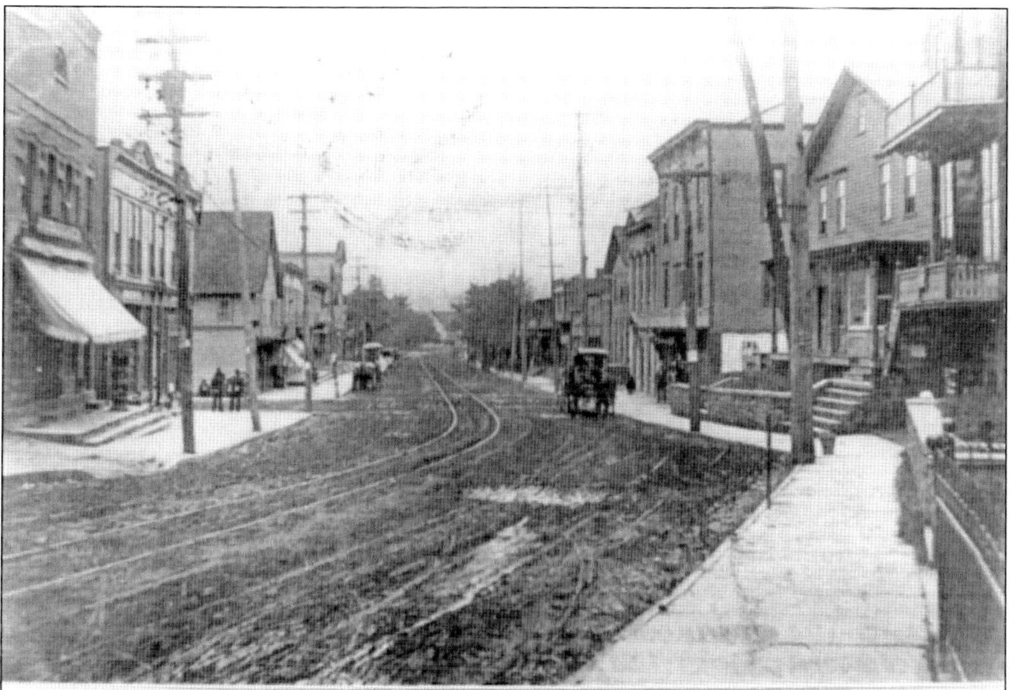

Main Street. In the heart of Taylor, businesses on Main Street have gone through many changes through the years. Shops have come and gone. The Taylor Discount and Deposit Bank once occupied the corner of Main and Union Streets. Where buildings once stood, the Veteran Bridge now connects Taylor to Scranton. This is what Main Street looked like in 1911. (Courtesy of Dan Zeleniak.)

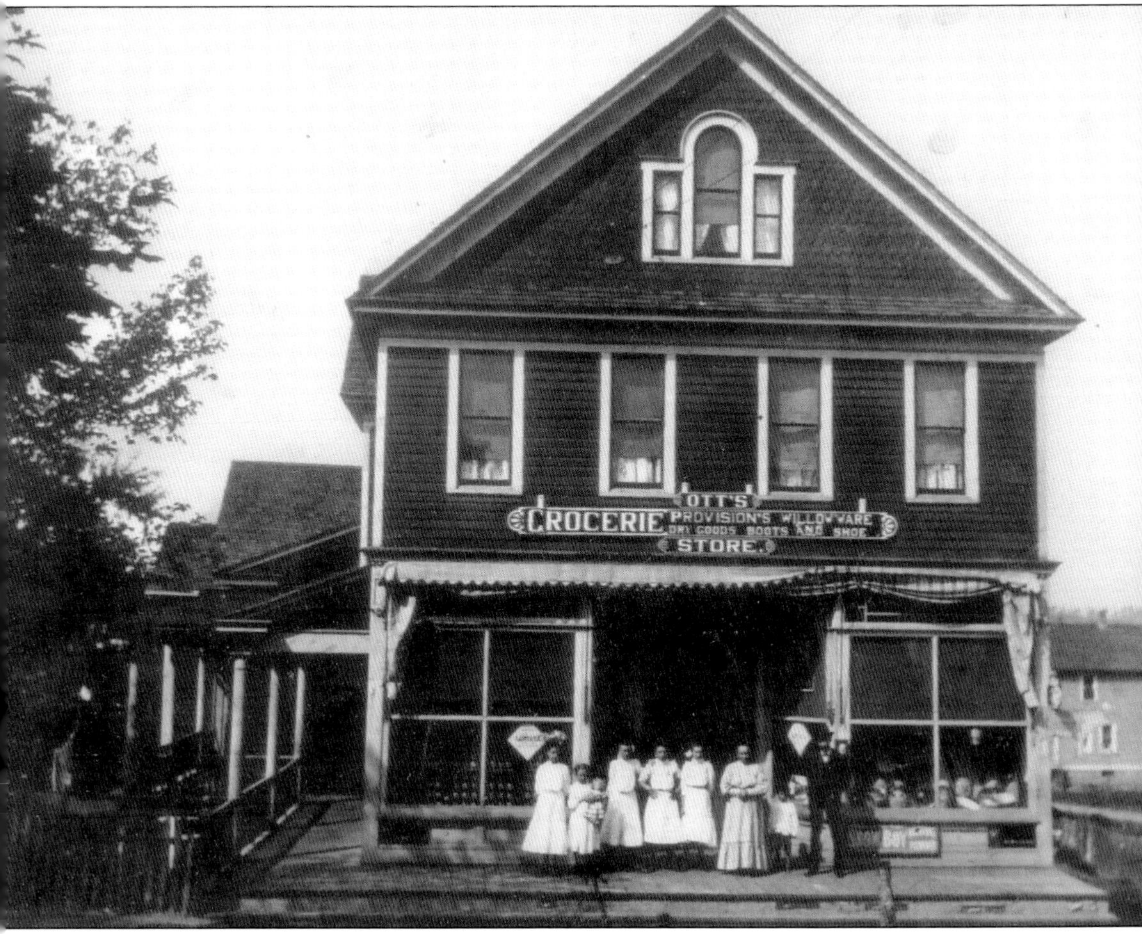

OTT'S GROCERIE STORE, C. 1880. At Ott's Grocerie Store customers could purchase dry goods, provisions, willowware (dishes), boots, and shoes. Casper Ott was the proprietor. In the early 1900s, the site became Englemeier's store, and in the 1980s, it once again changed hands and was Godino's Market. Years later, the building burned, and it is currently an empty lot. (Courtesy of Margaret M. Greco.)

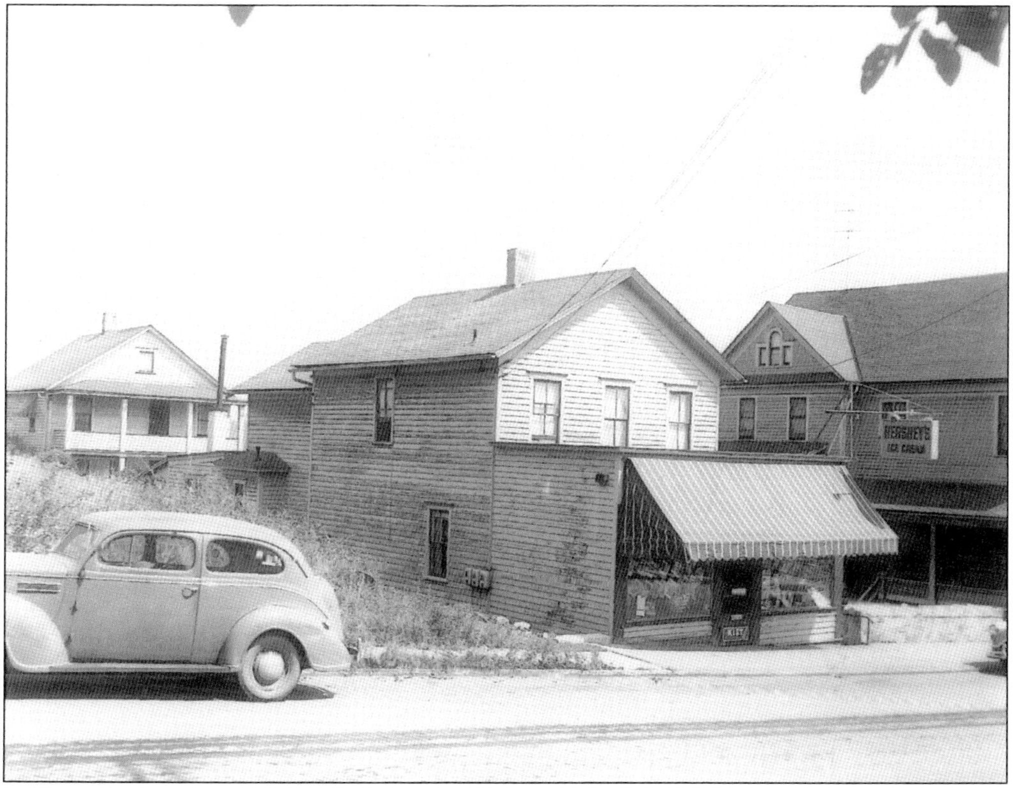

ENGLEMEIER'S STORE. In the early 1900s, Ott's Grocerie Store became Englemeier's store on Union Street. The store was run by two brothers. Residents in the Patch had to walk a great distance to shop at Englemeier's. (Courtesy of Nancy and Bob Thomas.)

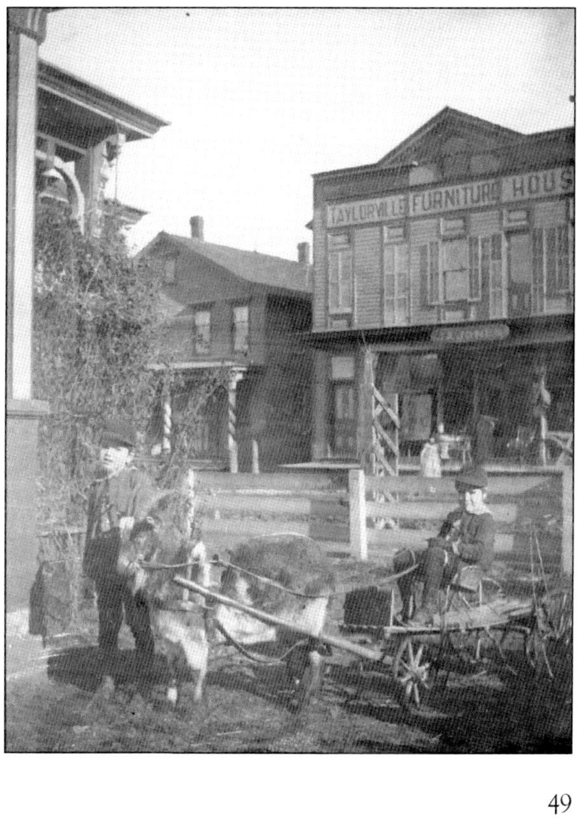

TAYLORVILLE FURNITURE HOUSE. This business dates back to the 1880s. Located on Main Street, today the site is home to the Diane Haduck School of Dance. (Courtesy of Nancy and Bob Thomas.)

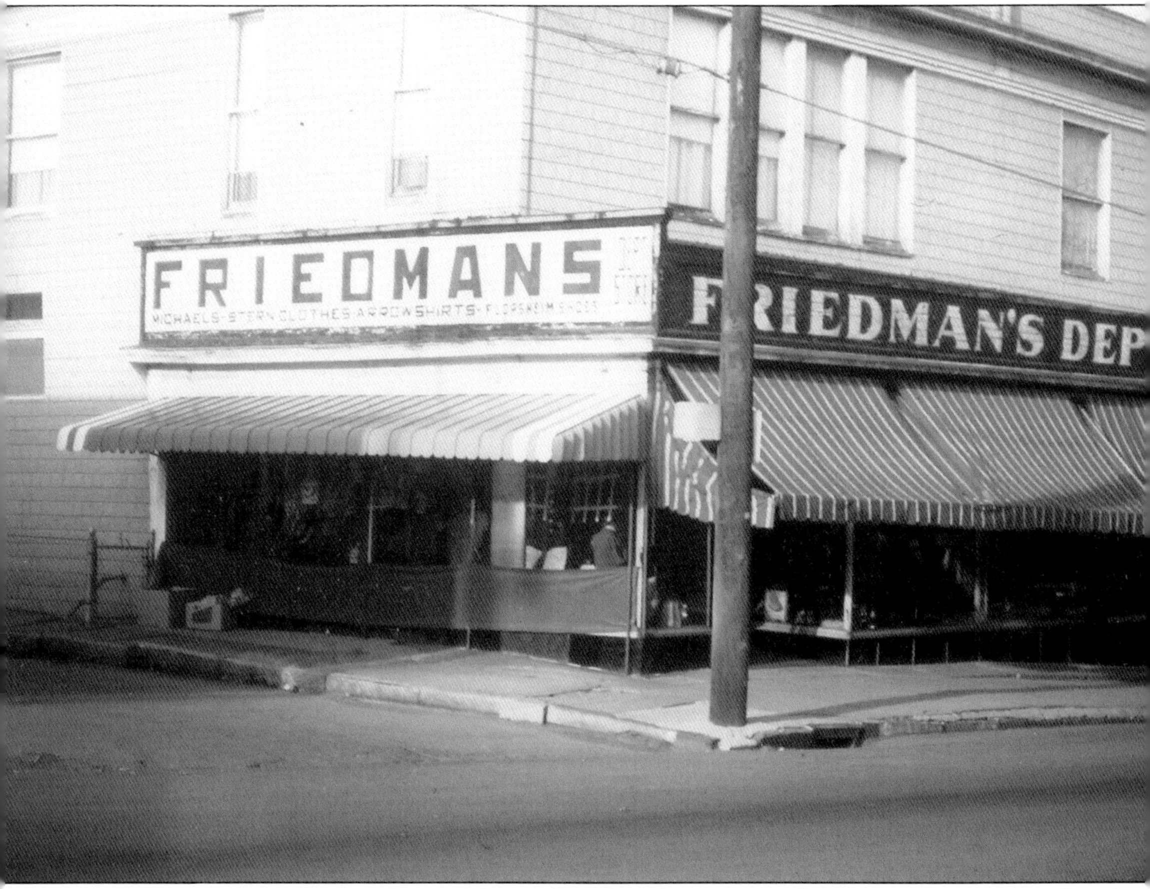

FRIEDMAN'S DEPARTMENT STORE. The worker's friend since 1897, the store on Main Street closed in the 1980s, and the building was razed to make room for Gaughan Auto Store. Proprietor Sam Friedman was among the prominent list of Taylor's Jewish merchants. (Courtesy of Shawn Murphy.)

PAUL HUDZINA SR. Owner and butcher of Hudzina's Market on Fourth Street in the Patch, Paul Hudzina Sr. is shown sharpening his knives in preparation of slicing the delectable meats he sold to his customers. (Courtesy of Dale Malecki.)

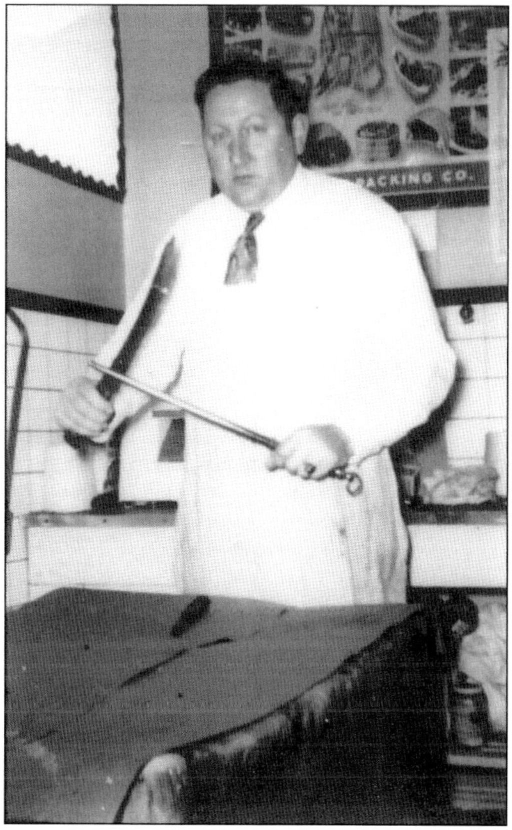

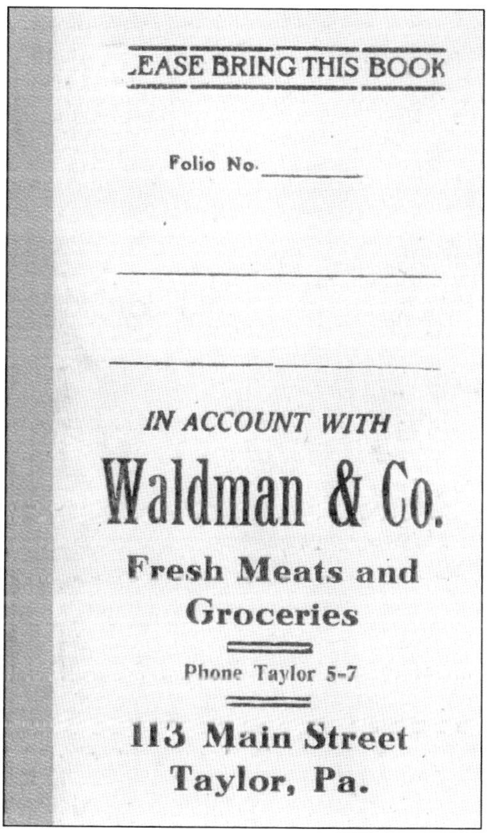

.EASE BRING THIS BOOK

Folio No.________

IN ACCOUNT WITH

Waldman & Co.

Fresh Meats and Groceries

Phone Taylor 5-7

113 Main Street
Taylor, Pa.

WALDMAN AND COMPANY. Situated at 113 Main Street, Waldman's sold fresh meats and groceries. Many people would pay "on the book" (as shown), meaning they would purchase items on credit and pay at the end of the week when they received their paycheck. (Courtesy of Shawn Murphy.)

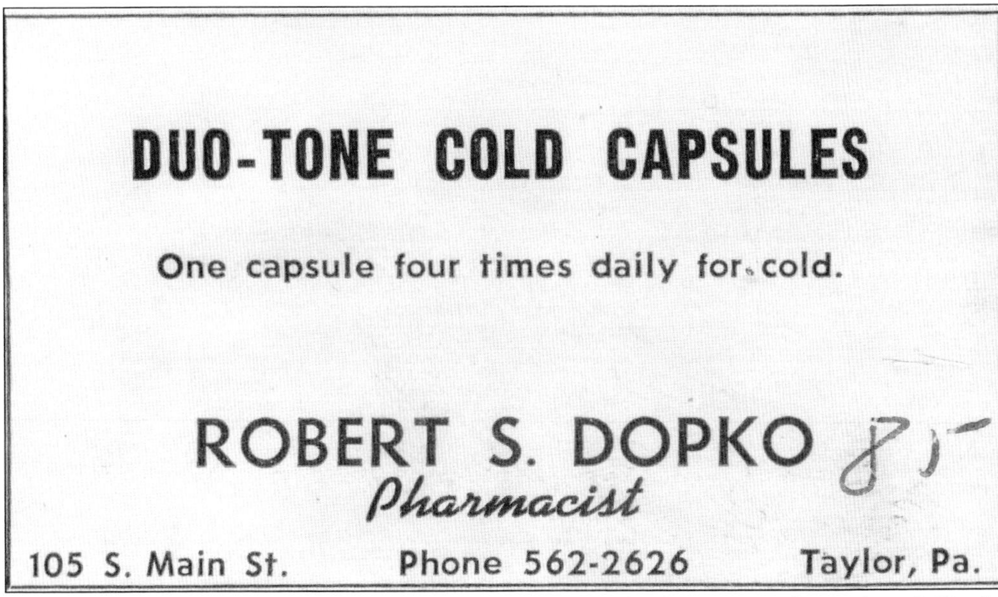

Dopko Pharmacy. Those with a cold take Duo-Tone capsules four times a day. Robert S. Dopko served as pharmacist at the Main Street store. (Courtesy of Jacob Davis Funeral Home.)

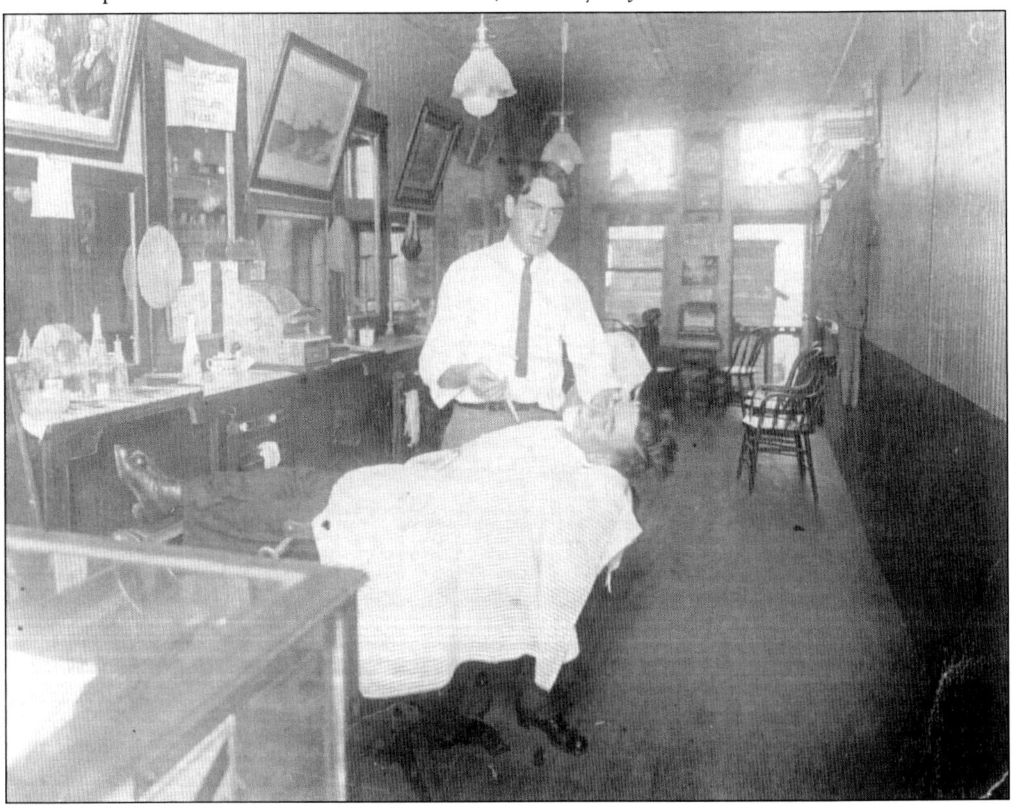

Griffith's Barbershop. Thomas Griffith is shown giving a customer a shave around 1930. The barbershop was located on Main Street. (Courtesy of Shawn Murphy and Taylor Community Library.)

Taylor Discount and Deposit Bank. Willard Atherton was vice president and director of the Taylor Discount and Deposit Bank established in 1905. The financial facility closed in 1932 due to the stock market crash. The Third National Bank opened on the site in the 1940s. (Courtesy of Shawn Murphy and Taylor Community Library.)

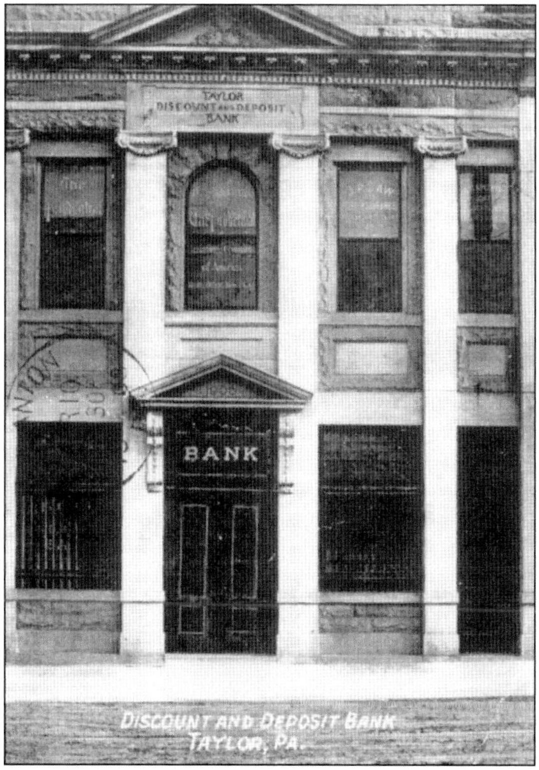

TAYLOR. 1907

146-3	C. R. R. OF N. J		
28-2	D., L. & W. R. R. CO	Station	
146-2	DAVIES, MRS. JOHN E. & SONS, Undertakers and Livery		
858-W2	DAVIS, C. E	Residence	Grove St

With a Long Distance Telephone on your desk, you have half the country at your elbow.

391-5	DAVIS, R. J	Undertaking	
391-2	DAVIS, THOMAS J	Undertaker and Livery	
378-3	ECONOMY SILK CO		
378-4	GRIFFITHS, DR. J. L	Physician	
372-4	HOUSER, DR. J. W	Physician	
858-W	JONES, D. E		Main St
337-2	JUDGE & CO	General Store	
858-Y	LAW, J. B	Residence	
391-4	LEUTHOLD, DR. H	Veterinary Surgeon	
337-4	MULHERIN, P	Residence	
378-2	NEIGER & POWELL	Furniture and Carpets	
378-5	OLMSTEAD, DR. W. H	Physician	
2115-2	REESE, J. W	Druggist	
28-3	RENARD, H. & CO		
520-5	TAYLOR WATER CO		
337-5	TAYLOR WORSTED MILL		
391-3	THOMAS, JOHN P	General Store	
372-2	TIMLIN, GEORGE	Undertaker and Livery	
41-3	VICTORIA SILK CO		High St
858Y-2	WATKINS, JAMES E	Residence	
372-3	WILLIAMS, D. M	Meat Market	Main St

Taylor Phone Directory. This directory is dated 1907. Listed are all the businesses and professional services available to the people of Taylor. Note the phone numbers: Residents could contact Dr. J. W. Houser if they were sick and in need of a house call by dialing 372-4. (Courtesy of Shawn Murphy and Taylor Community Library.)

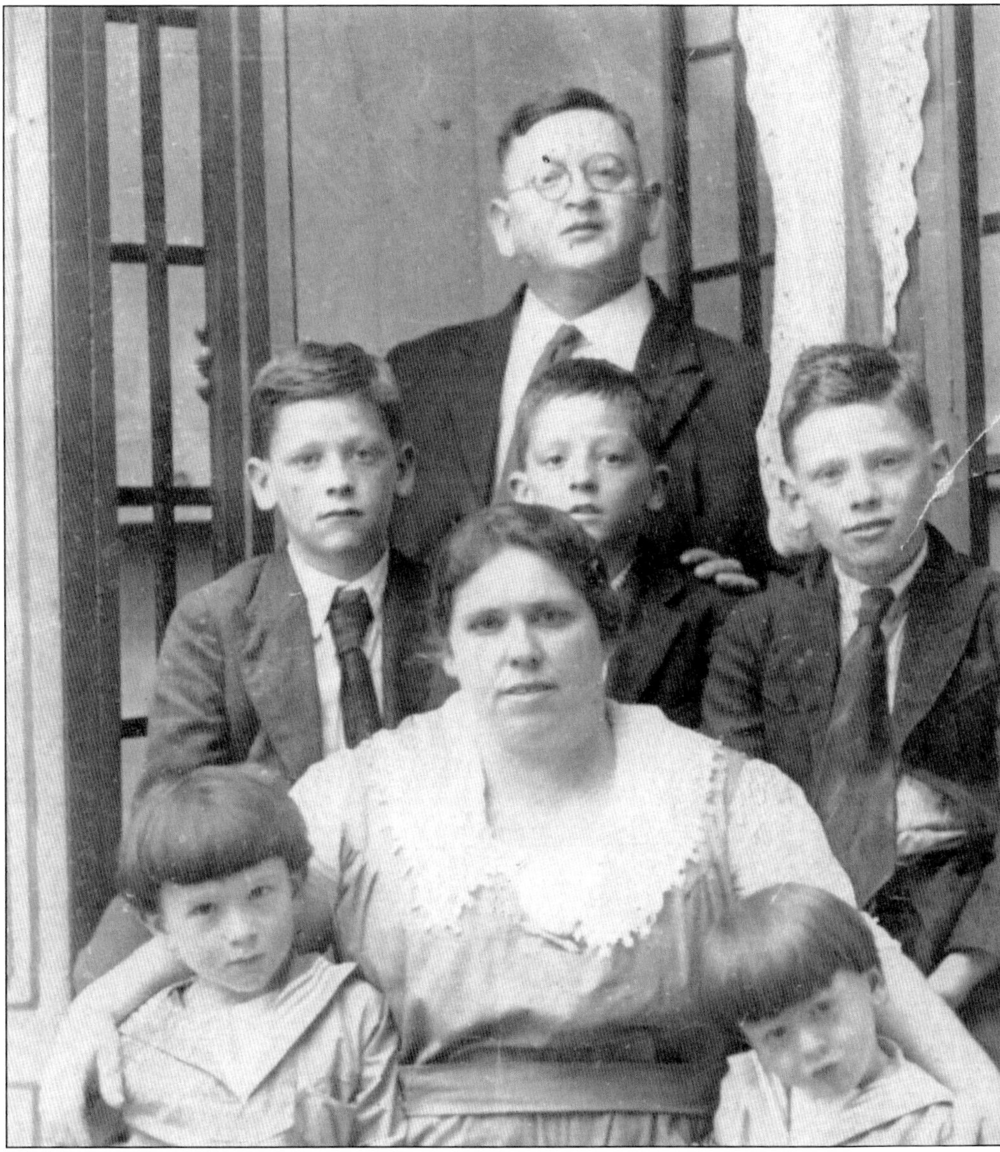

Powell's Grocery Store. The Powell family owned and operated the market at 230 Union Street. Pictured are, from left to right, (first row) Arthur Jr., Blanche, and William; (second row) John, David, and Howard (Red) Powell; (third row) Arthur. (Courtesy of Marie Eskra.)

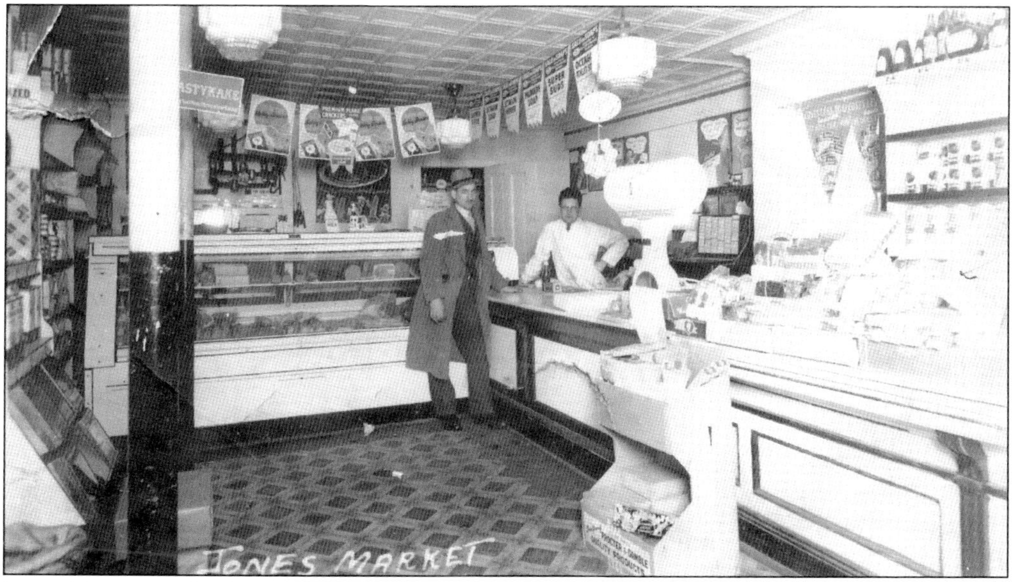

Jones Market. John Jones, owner, is shown behind the counter helping a customer. The business resided on Union Street. (Courtesy of Marie Eskra.)

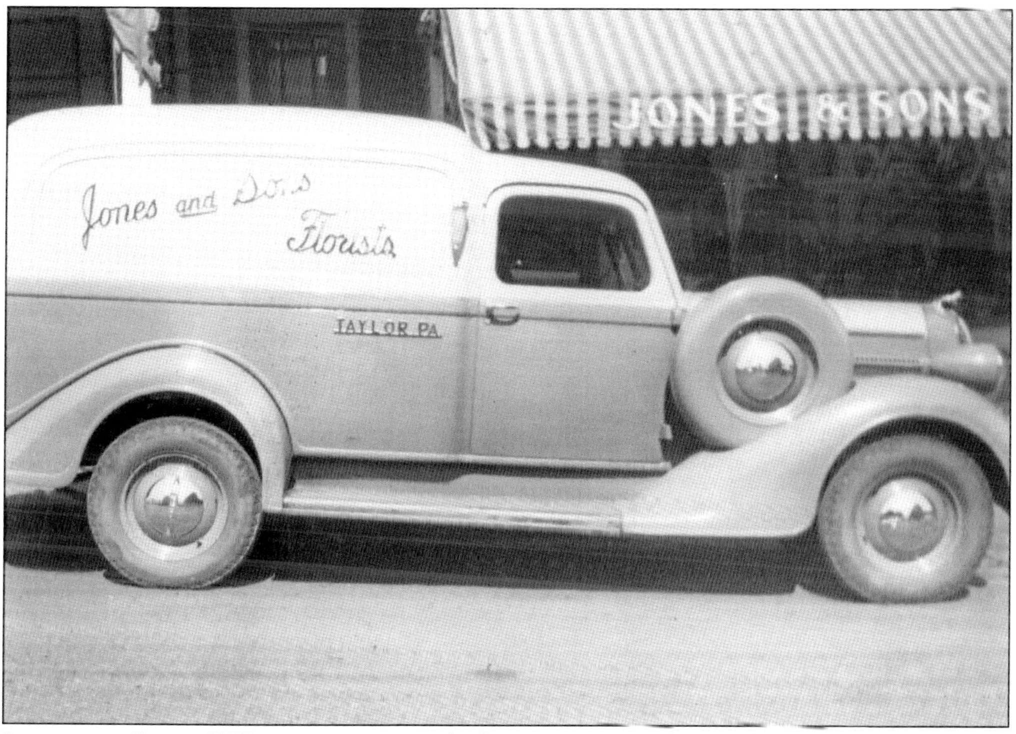

Jones and Sons. "When you say it with flowers, say it with our flowers." Jones and Sons florist shop was located at 224 Union Street from 1913 to 2003. The proprietors were Bob and Debbie Jones. Pictured is one of their delivery trucks. (Courtesy of Shawn Murphy and Taylor Community Library.)

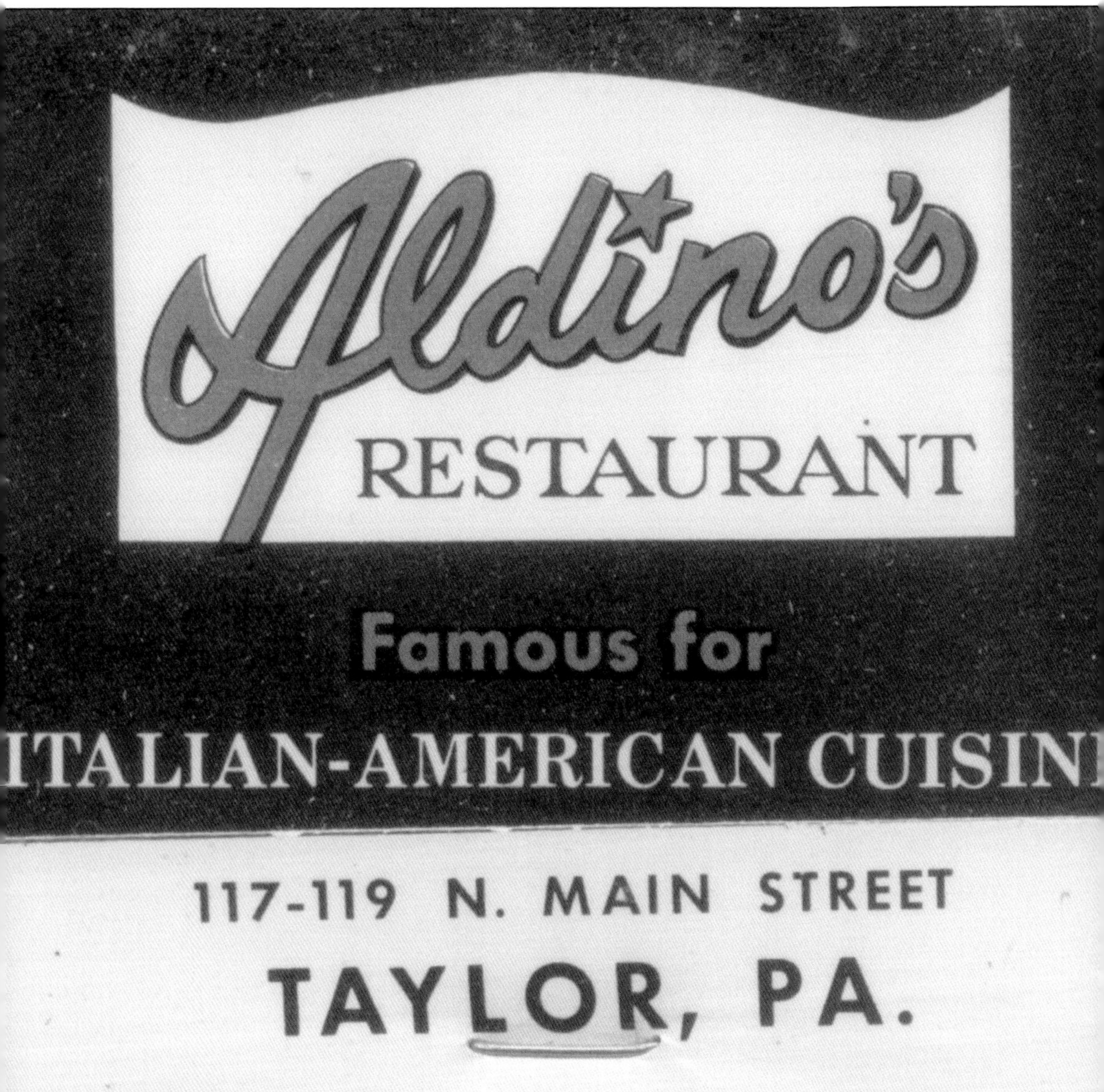

ALDINO'S RESTAURANT. A longtime favorite restaurant in Taylor, people would come from all over to sample its fine Italian cuisine. Owner Aldino Pierotti was a prominent figure in the community. (Courtesy of Shawn Murphy.)

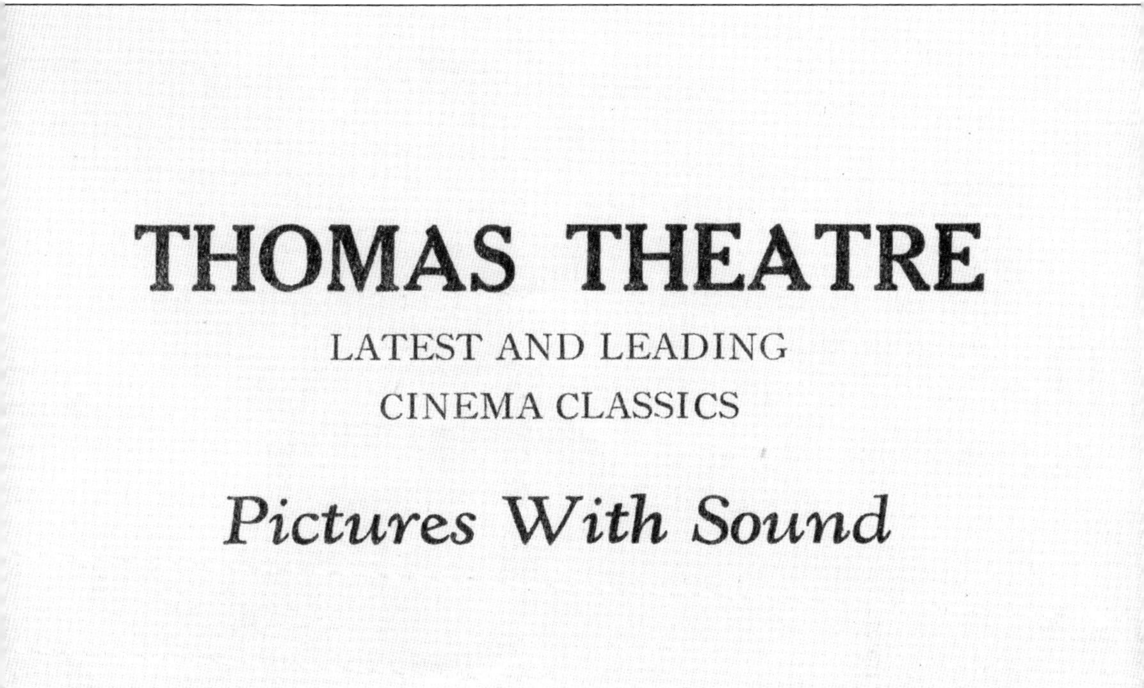

THOMAS THEATRE. Built in 1904 by John P. Thomas, the theater resided in the 100 block of Union Street. In the early days, it was a "nickelette," costing only 5¢ to take your date to the movies. Through the years, the theater was used for political rallies and school or social functions. Pres. Howard Taft made a speech there while running for office. It's a well-known fact that if a patron became unruly the owner would escort him or her out by the ear or by the seat of his pants. The theater remained open until 1968, at which time it was torn down and made into a parking lot. (Courtesy of Shawn Murphy and Taylor Community Library.)

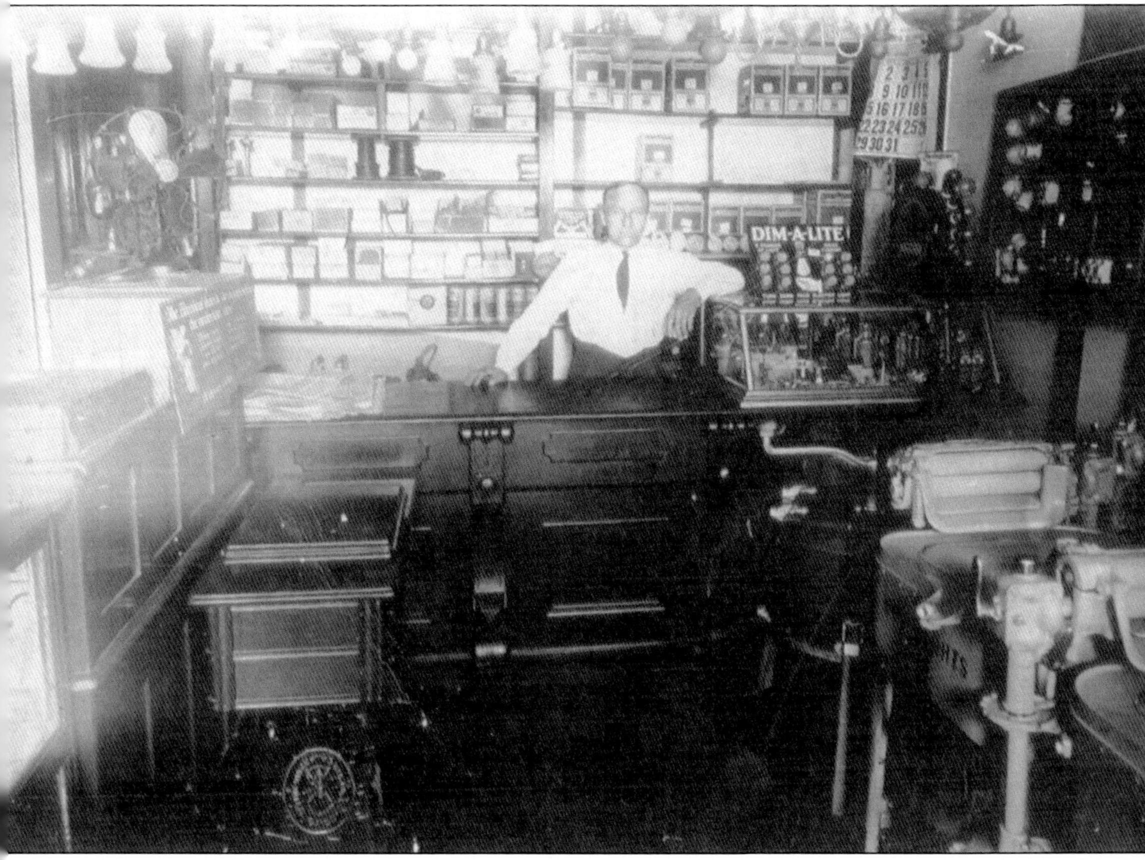

Strein's Hardware Store. The owner waits for a customer behind the counter. Strein's sold a variety of hardware to suit all the plumbing and electrical needs of area residents. Note the old crank washers in the photograph. The store was located on North Main Street. (Courtesy of Shawn Murphy.)

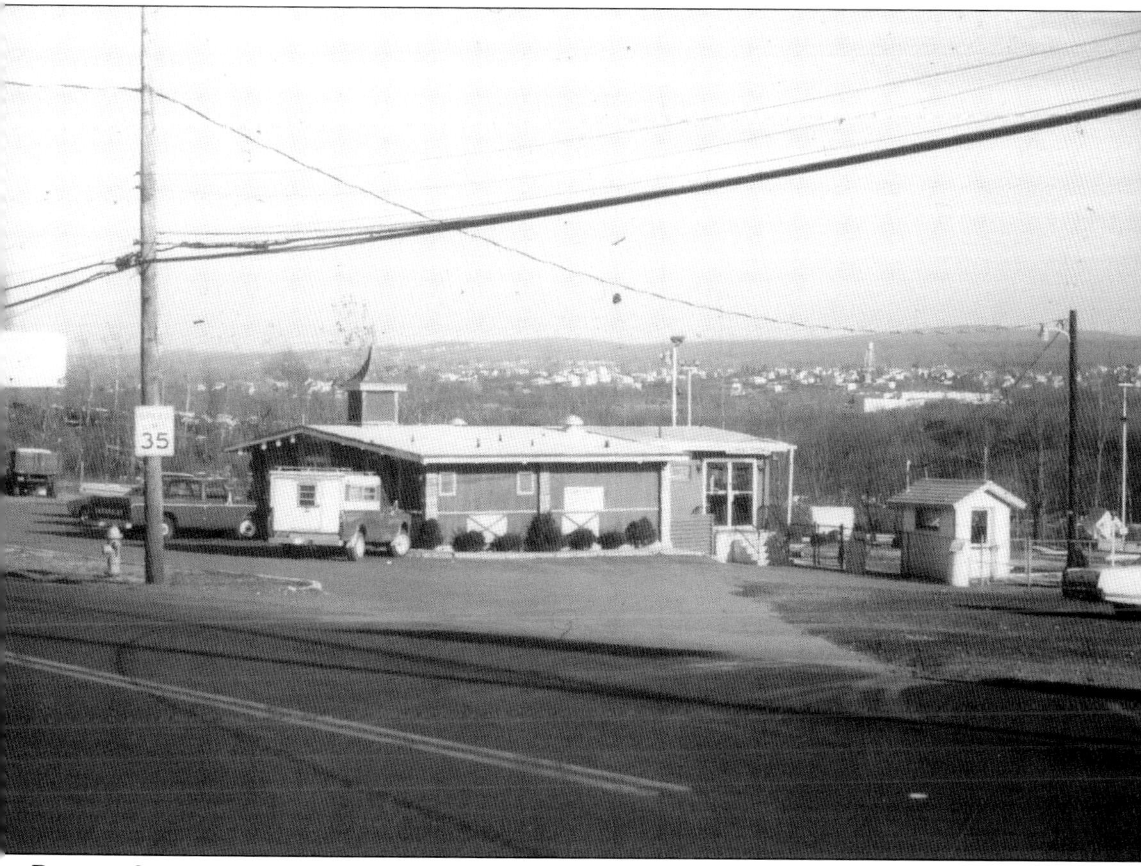

PUT AND SNACK DINER. A favorite Taylor spot for people to grab a bite to eat and play a few rounds of golf, it was equipped with an 18-hole miniature golf course and driving range. The business remained in Taylor for two decades and relocated to Lonesome Road in the 1980s. (Courtesy of Shawn Murphy.)

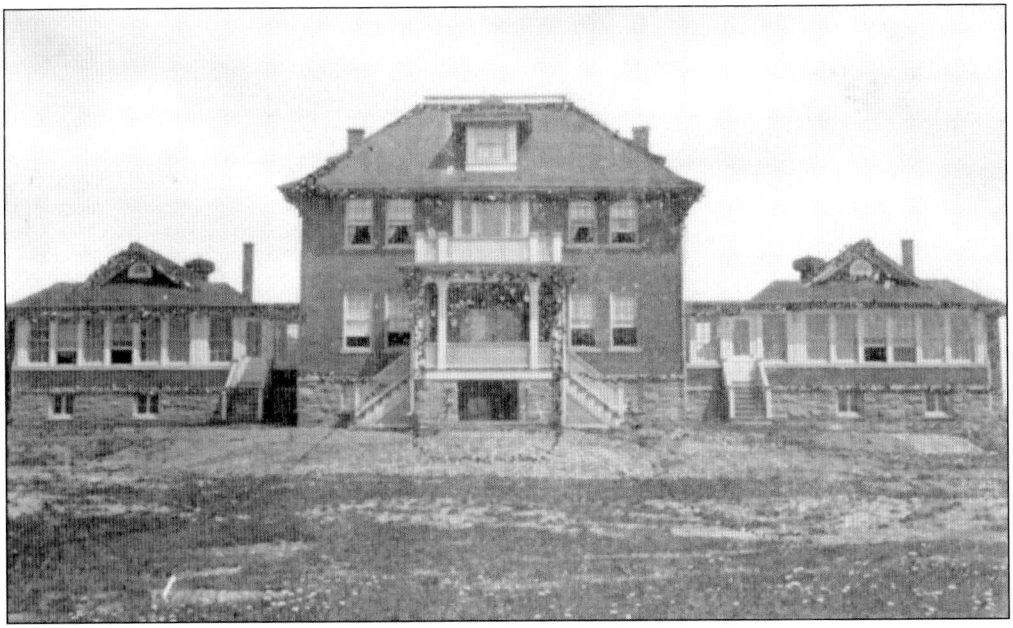

Taylor Hospital. Organized in 1903, thanks to the efforts of politicians Edward Jones and Scranton's mayor E. B. Jermyn, Taylor Hospital was used mainly as a miner's hospital. Originally it contained only 50 beds—not nearly enough to serve the health issues of the mining community. In later years, it was remodeled at the cost of $1.5 million. Today the building houses the Taylor Nursing Home on Hospital Street. (Courtesy of Shawn Murphy.)

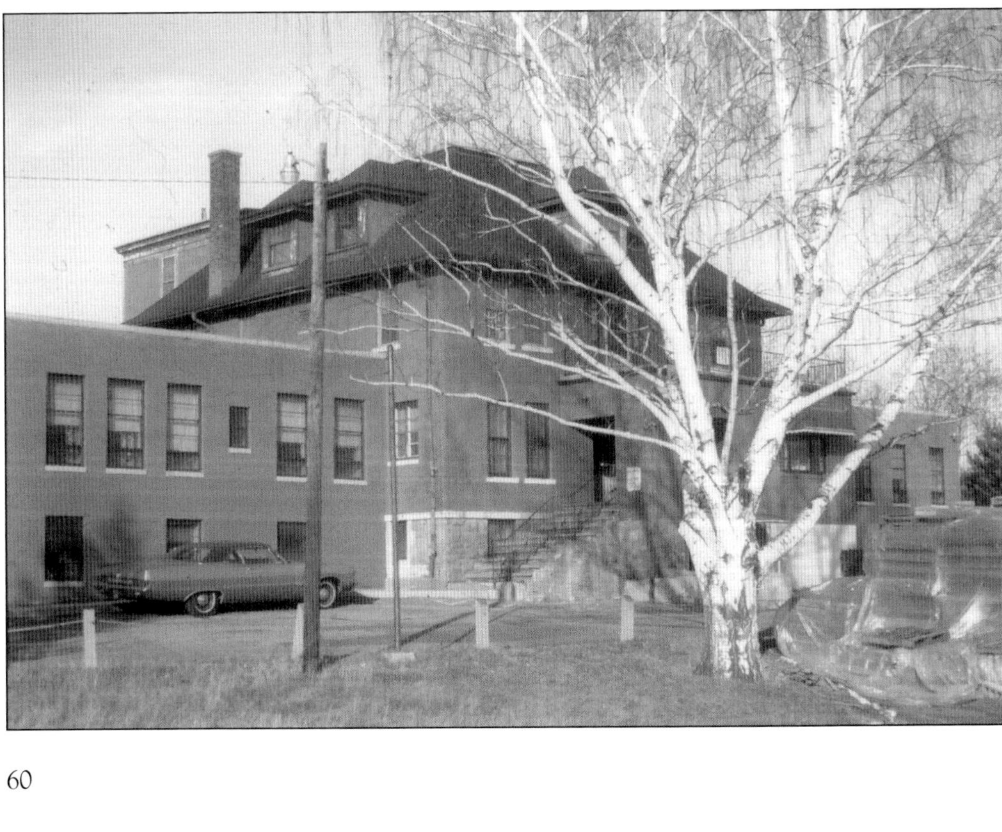

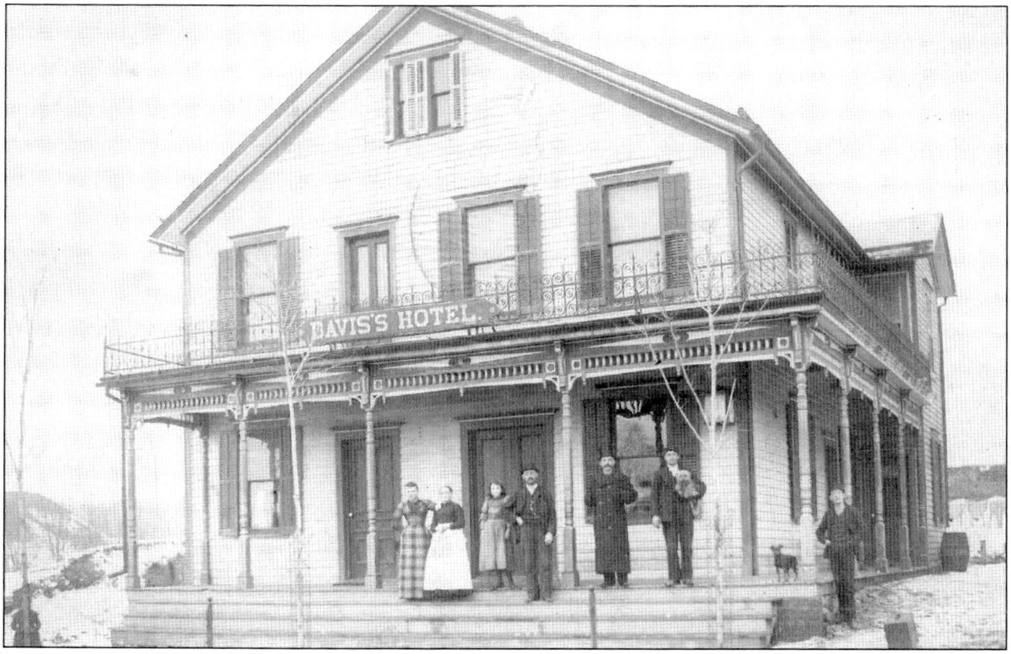

Davis's Hotel. The hotel opened its doors in 1889 on North Main Street, near the train depot in the Frogtown section. It would later become Davis Funeral Home. In the below photograph shown on the upper porch are, from left to right, Mary Jane, Great-Grandma Davis, Lizzie Uriverden, and Annie Price. In the carriage at right is Dick Davis holding the horses, and the driver is Will Davis. (Courtesy of the Jacob Davis Funeral Home.)

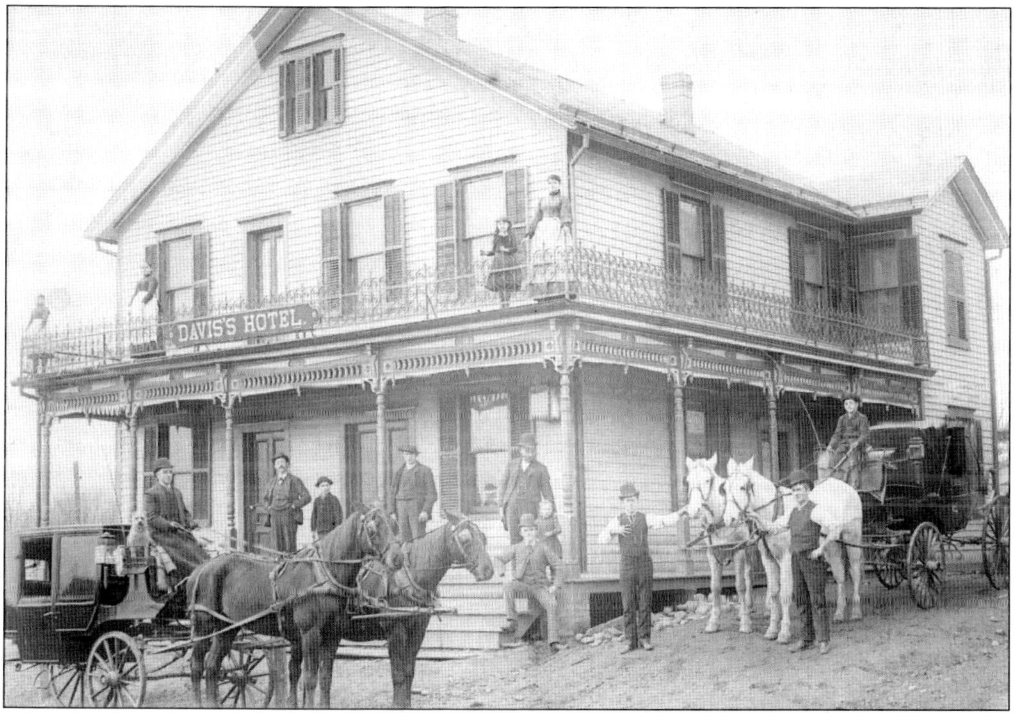

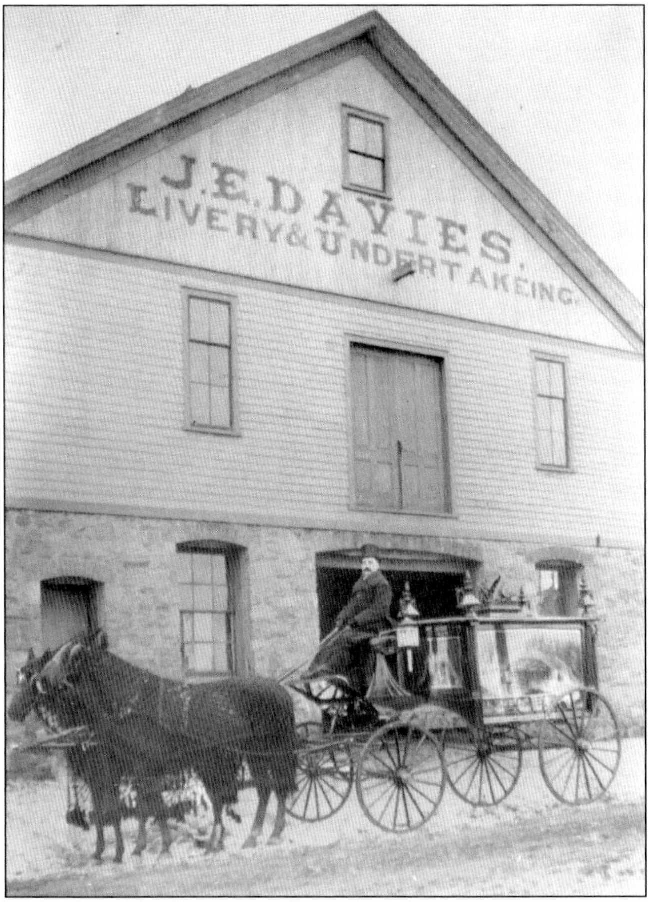

J. E. Davies Livery and Undertaking. In the late 1800s, it was a common practice for undertakers to own and operate a livery because of the horse-drawn hearses. Located on North Main Avenue, legend has it that the once-famous 12 Mule Detergent Horses rested there. (Courtesy of Shawn Murphy.)

Funeral Coach. An old horse-drawn hearse owned by the Jacob Davis Funeral Home when it was located on North Main Street and its driver are shown in the Frogtown section around the 1800s. (Courtesy of Jacob Davis Funeral Home.)

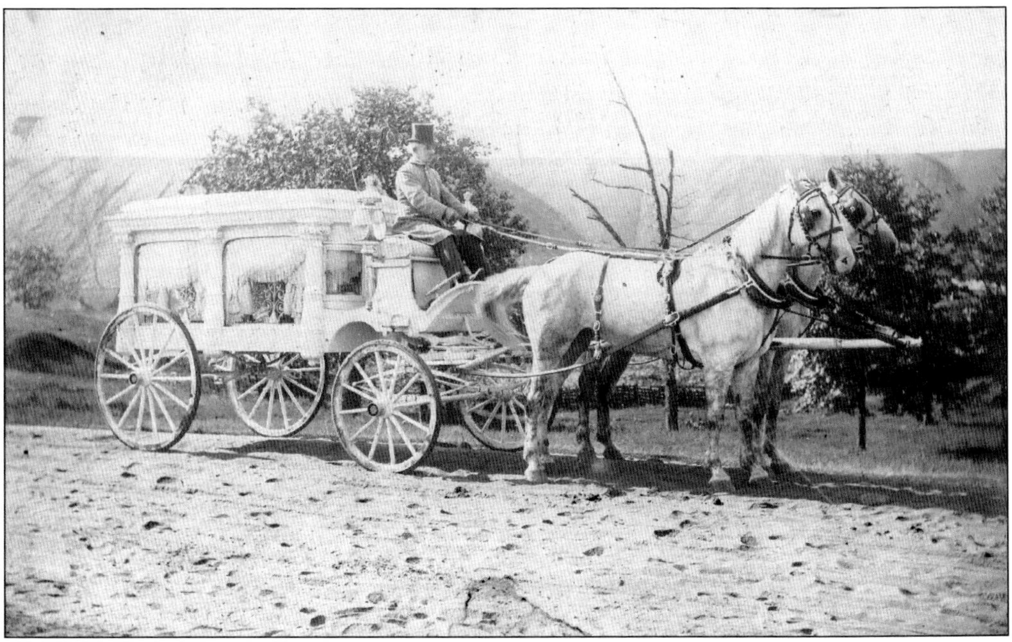

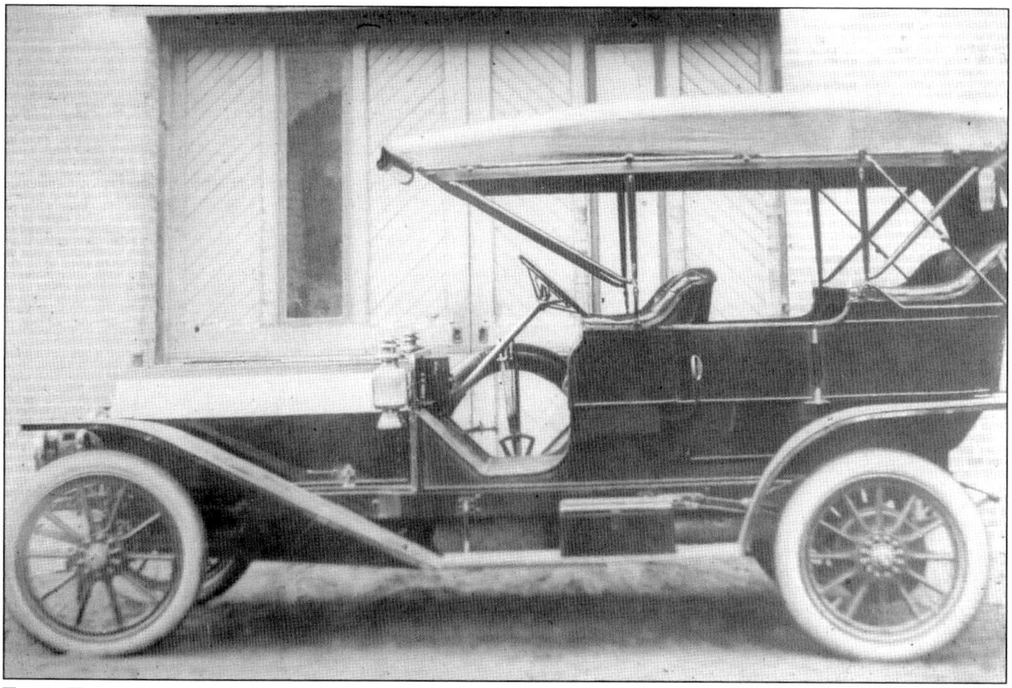

First Funeral Limousine. Also owned by the Jacob Davis Funeral Home, this was their first limousine after the horse-drawn hearse became a thing of the past. This photograph is from around the early 1900s. (Courtesy of Shawn Murphy.)

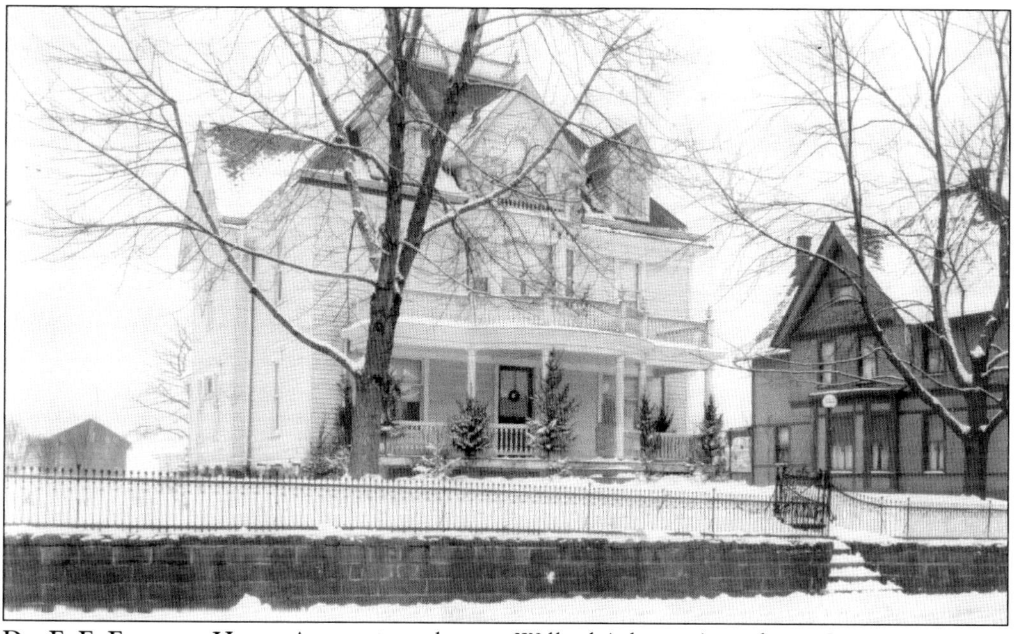

Dr. E. E. Edwards Home. At one time, this was Willard Atherton's residence. In 1923, Margaret Barron, Willard's first wife, sold the home to Dr. Edwards. The home was then purchased by the Davis family in the 1950s and is the current site of the Jacob Davis Funeral Home on South Main Street. The two trees in front are still standing and are the oldest in Taylor. (Courtesy of Nancy and Bob Thomas.)

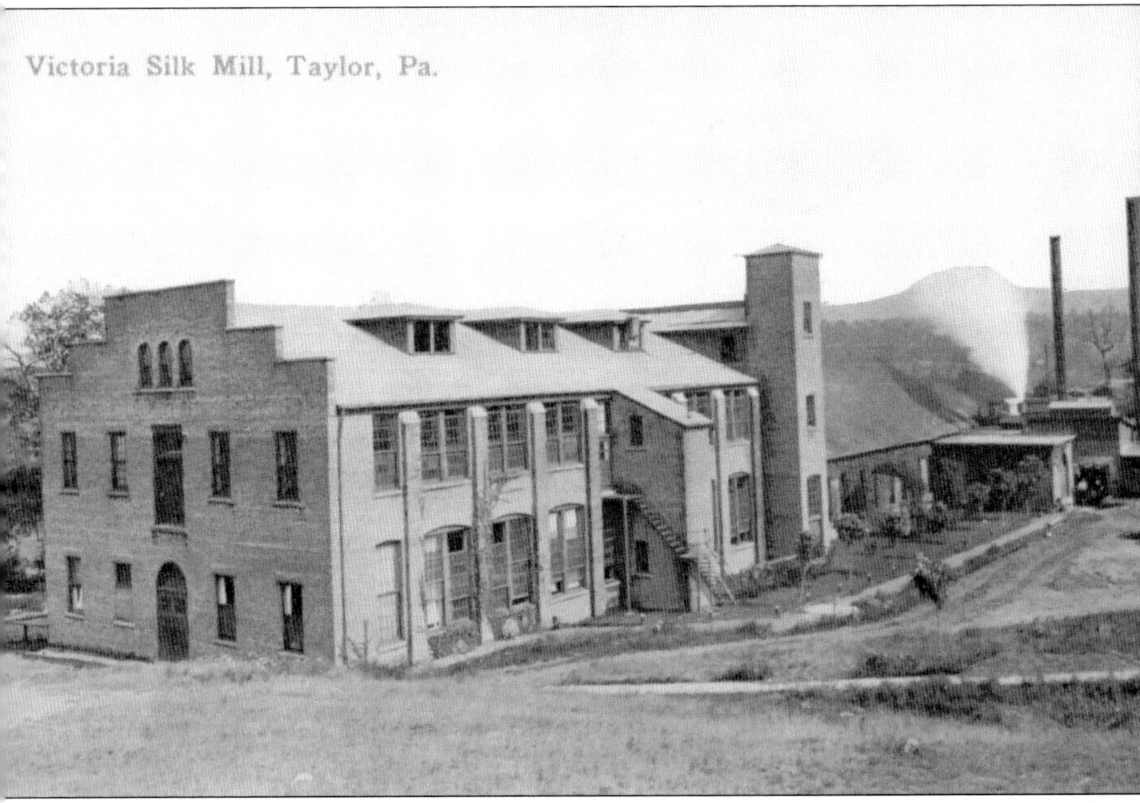

VICTORIA SILK MILL. Founded by William H. Davis, born in Paterson, New Jersey, known as the "Silk City," the Silk Mill, located at Cooper and High Streets, was incorporated on August 22, 1902. Charles E. Davis was the president and general manager. The silk was sent from Patterson, New Jersey, to Taylor to be woven into cloth and dyed. The original building was demolished around 1947–1948, but additional buildings were built. Taylor was the home to three silk mills in total: Victoria, Fromberg, and Laurel. Each mill employed an estimated 200 people, most of whom were women. (Courtesy of Cecile B. Champagne.)

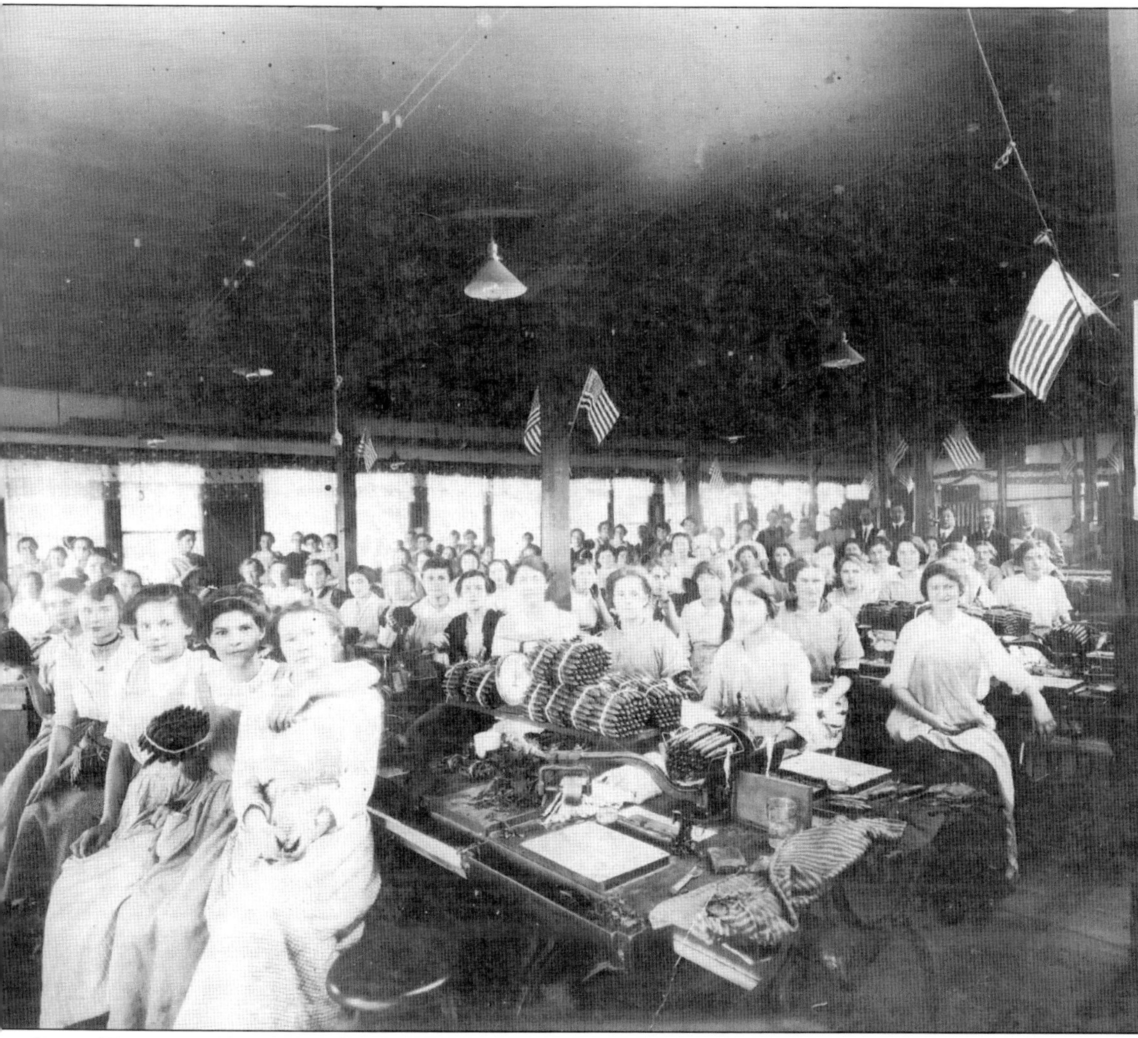

Cigar Factory. The General Cigar Factory was located in the upper section of Taylor. Girls as young as 14 years old would leave school and find employment in the factory to help their families, much like the breaker boys in the mines. (Courtesy of Dan Zeleniak.)

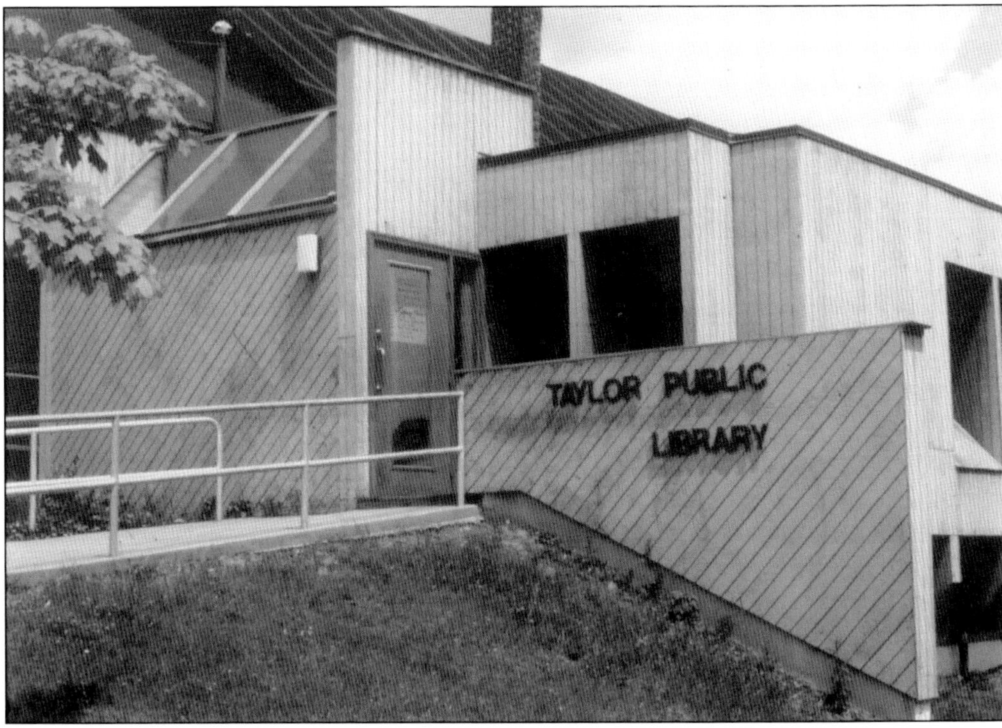

Taylor Public Library. In 1953, a group of Taylor residents launched a campaign to raise $4,000 in order to open a public library in the borough. A year later, a program to dedicate the Taylor's new public library was held in the borough building. Reba Griffiths was president of the library association. After the borough building burned in the 1970s, the library relocated to another building on Union and North Pond Streets and remained there until the spring of 2005, when its new facility, the Taylor Community Library (pictured below), opened its doors and the pages of its many books to the public. Jeanie Sluck is the library's director. (Both, courtesy of Shawn Murphy.)

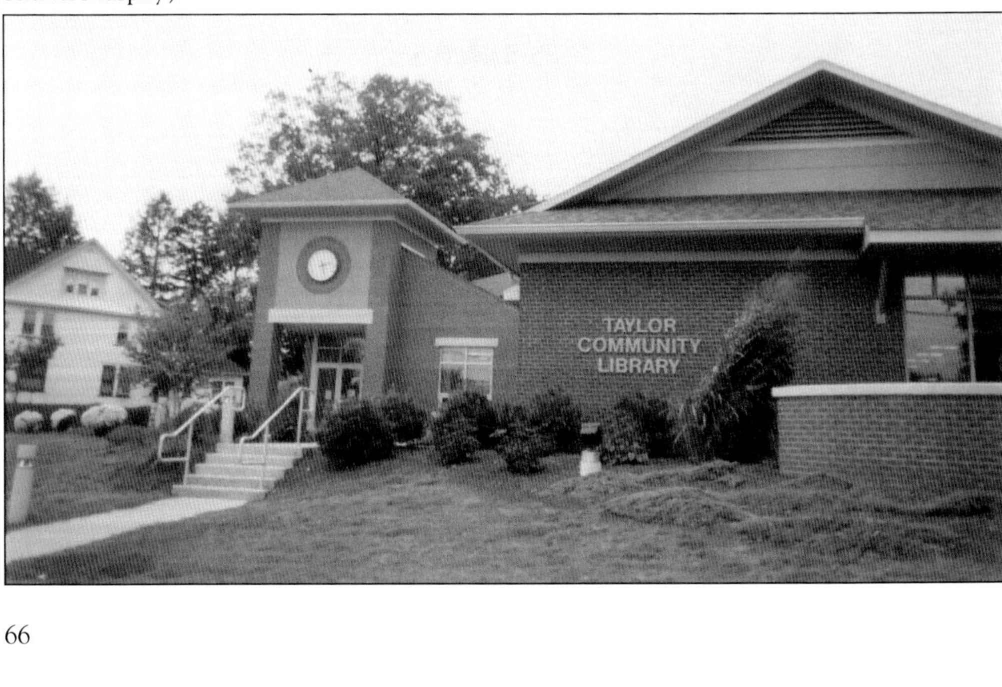

Five

TAYLOR AND ITS PEOPLE

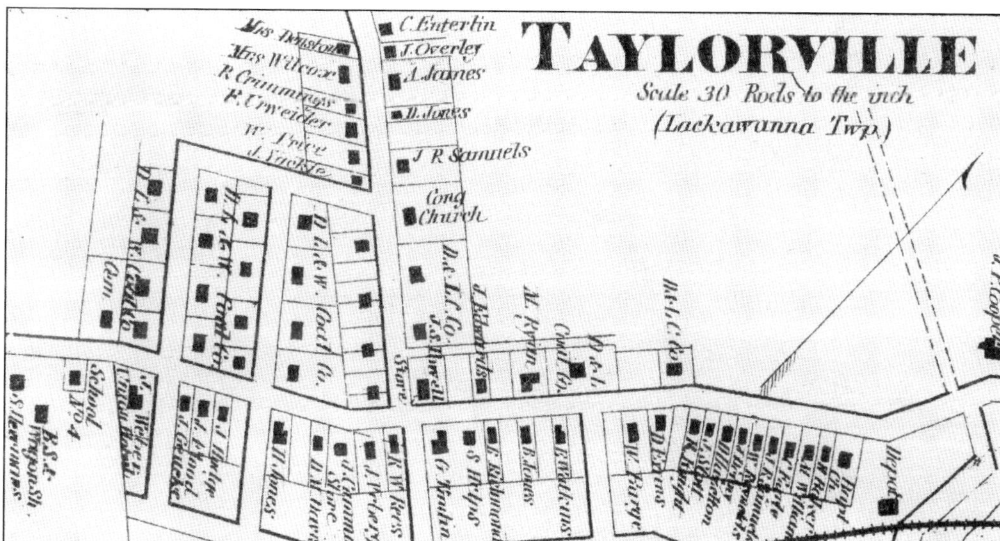

LACKAWANNA TOWNSHIP/TAYLORVILLE MAP. The latitude of Taylor is 41.394N and the longitude is -75.706W, with an elevation of 722 feet. In 2008, the estimated population was 6,151. Back when mining was its main industry the estimated population in 1927 was nearly 12,000. Lackawanna Township was created in 1838; Old Forge Township was formed in 1871, which divided Lackawanna Township in half at Union Street. Taylor was granted a temporary incorporation as a borough in November 1893. It was officially made a borough in May 1894. This map is from the Atlas of Luzerne County, Pennsylvania, from actual surveys by and under the direction of D. G. Beers. (Courtesy of Lackawanna Historical Society.)

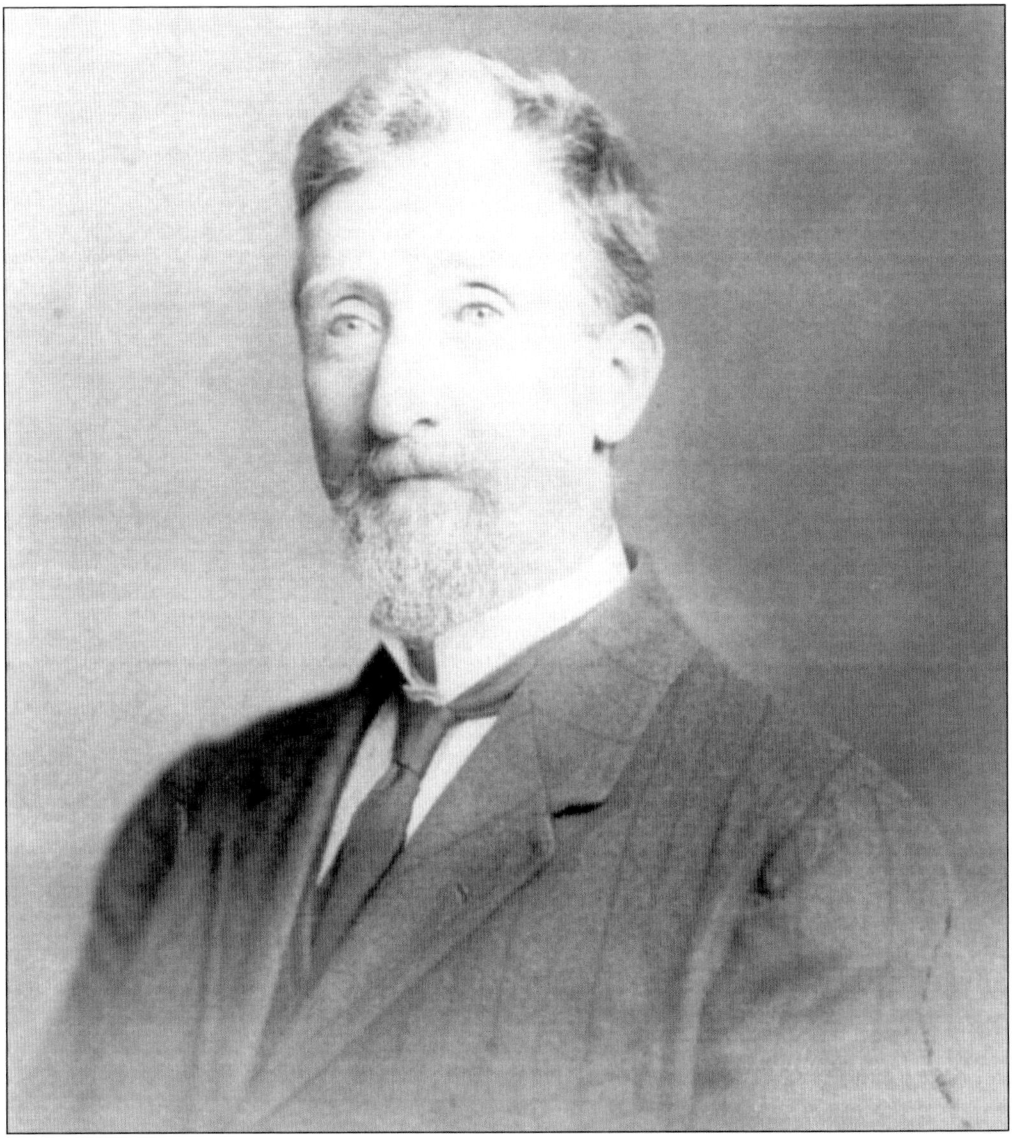

Morgan B. Morgan. One of Taylor's early burgesses, Judge Morgan was an institution in Taylor, having served as burgess for two terms and four terms as justice of the peace. He came to the United States from Wales and resided in Taylor for 33 years. He was known for his lovely tenor voice and the musical performances he treated the community to. For the Fourth of July parade each year, he would dress up as Uncle Sam; he was well-loved by the citizens of Taylor. (Courtesy of Joyce Morgan.)

EARLY EUROPEAN IMMIGRANT FAMILY. Thomas and Anastasia Lisowski and their children are Polish immigrants who settled in Taylor in the late 1800s; the actual year is not known for certain. Lisowski's Café on Union Street was owned and operated by members of their family for many generations. (Courtesy of Shawn Murphy.)

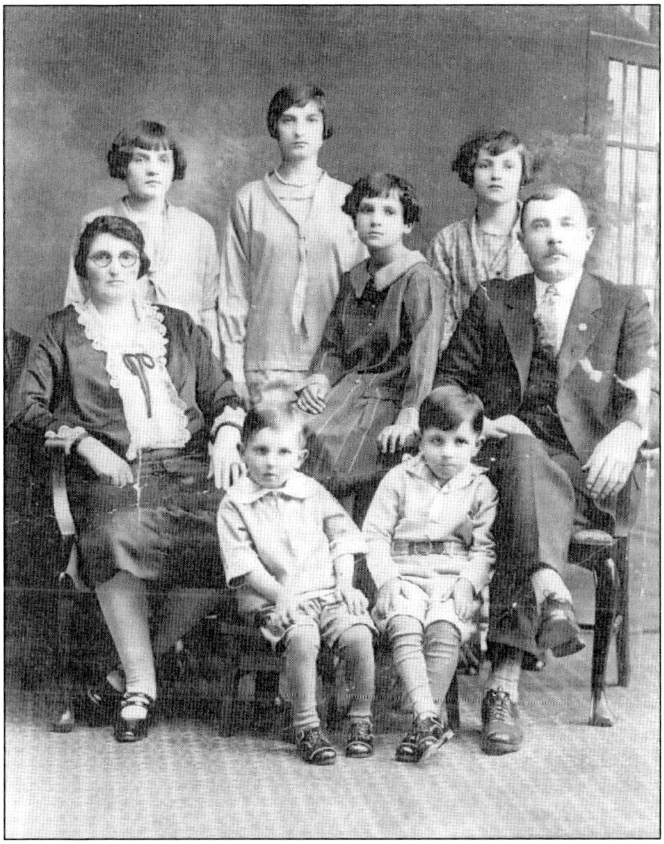

THE DORIN WEDDING. This photograph shows the Dorin family who lived in Feltsville on Fourth Street, directly behind Potkul's Tavern. Descendents of the family recently visited Taylor and were saddened to see nothing left of the Patch but their childhood memories. The people in this early-1900s photograph cannot be identified. (Courtesy of the Gawel family.)

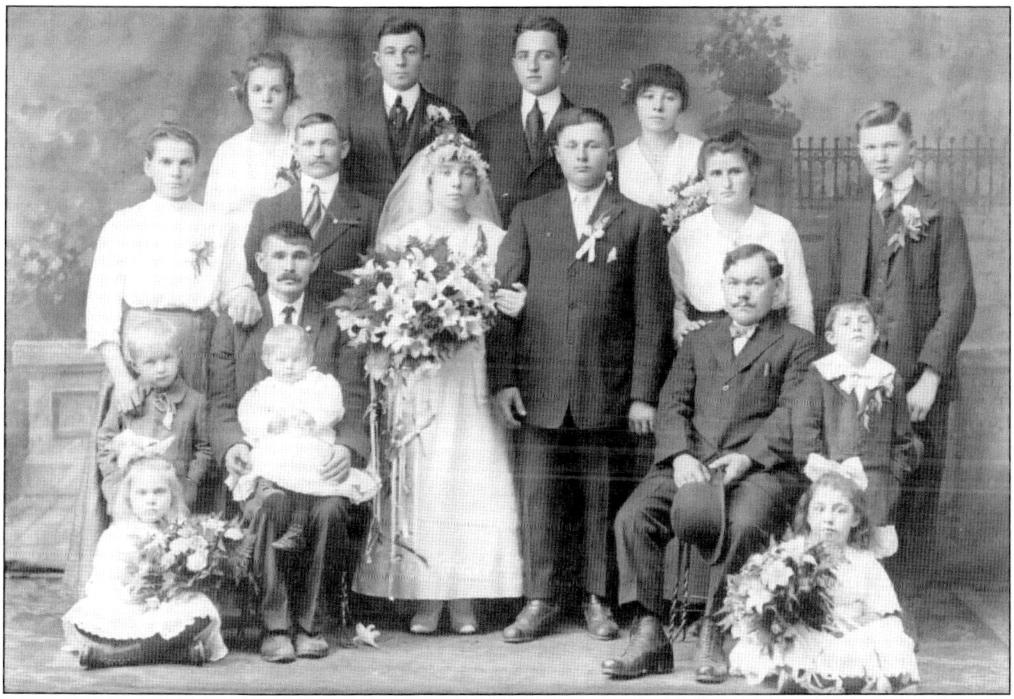

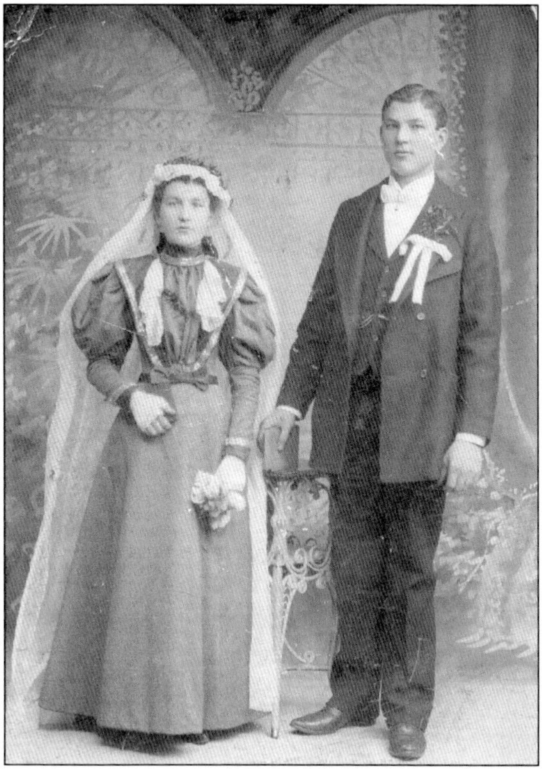

Victorian Bride and Groom. John Galka and Victoria Bonionr were married in February 1897. As with so many immigrants who came through Ellis Island, their names were often misspelled. Their marriage license has their name spelled "Gouka." (Courtesy of Mildred G. Zvonchenko.)

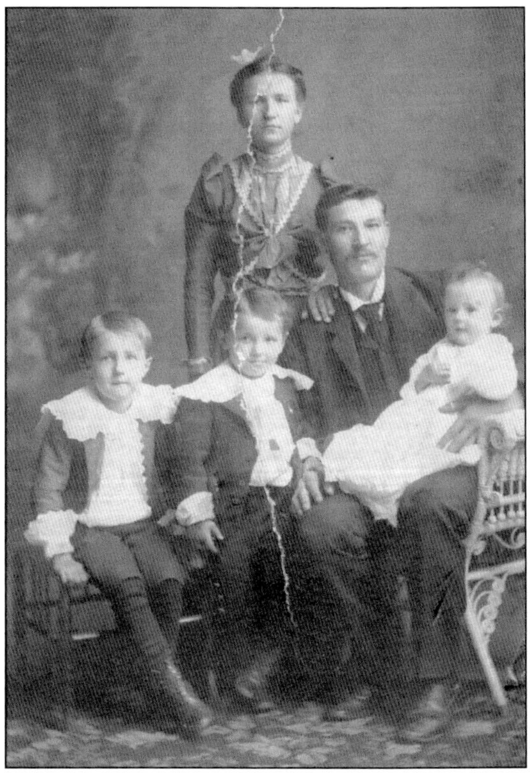

The Galka Family. In this 1900s portrait, John and Victoria pose with their children, from left to right, Anthony, Frank, and Amelia (infant). The family moved to the area in 1909 from Seattle. John was a huckster; he sold fruits and vegetables out of his horse and buggy. (Courtesy of Mildred G. Zvonchenko.)

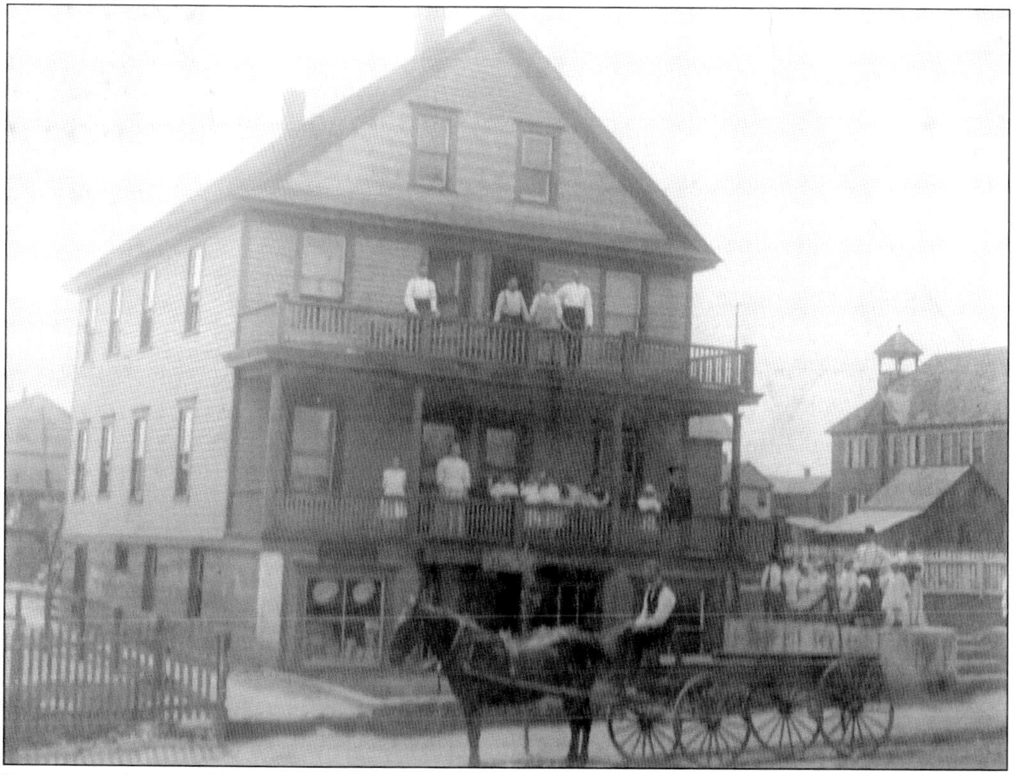

Reynolds Avenue Neighborhood. Standing in front of the Galka family home, all the residents living on Reynolds Avenue came out to have their picture taken around 1914. In the background is the Lincoln School. (Courtesy of Mildred G. Zvonchenko.)

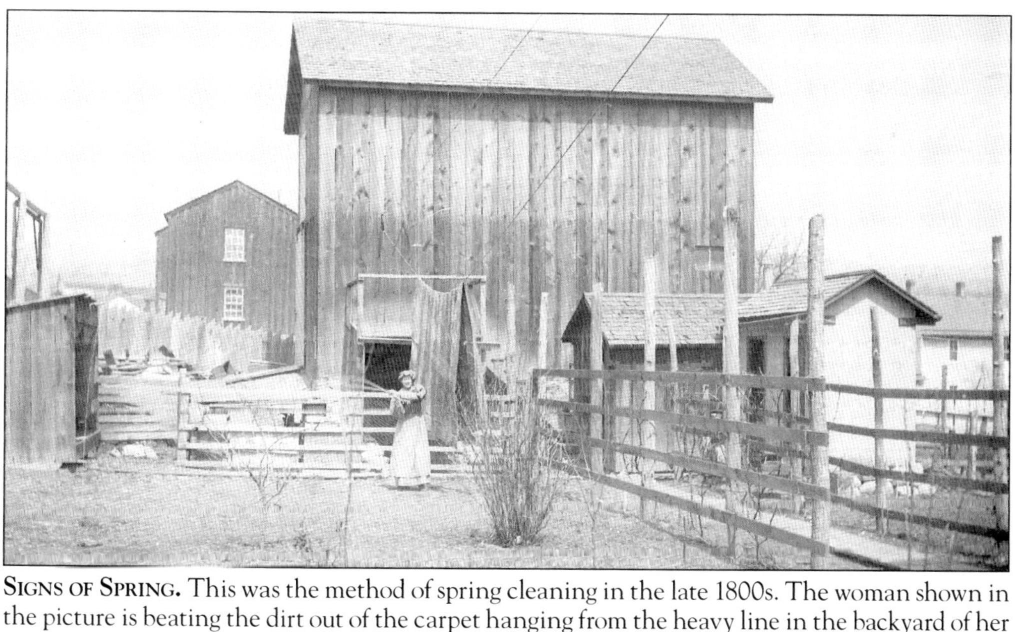

Signs of Spring. This was the method of spring cleaning in the late 1800s. The woman shown in the picture is beating the dirt out of the carpet hanging from the heavy line in the backyard of her home. This is the future site of Friedman's Department Store. (Courtesy of Shawn Murphy.)

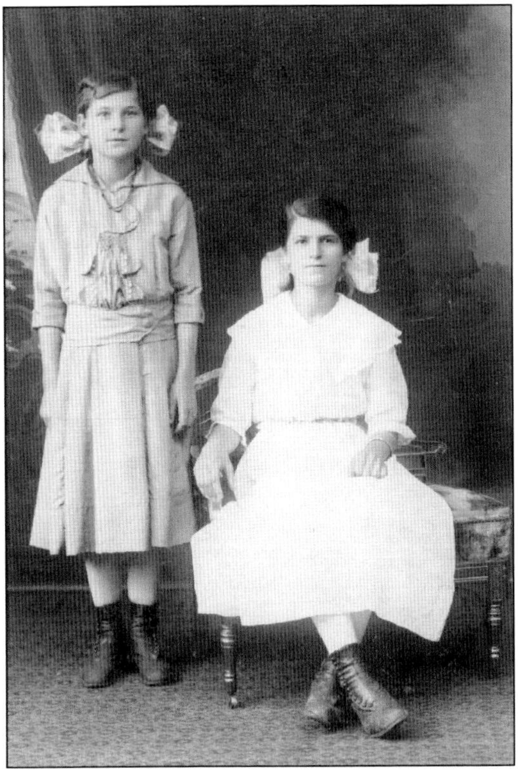

Victorian Couture. These young ladies are modeling the stylish clothing worn around the turn of the 20th century. The button-up ankle boots and large hair bows were all the rage of that time period. Shown are Amelia Wacendak (seated) and Julia ? (standing). (Courtesy of Barbara Hordich Togher.)

Neighborhood Shoemaker. Jason Powell, seen here at age 86, was one of Taylor's prominent shoemakers for many years. His shop was located on Main Street. (Courtesy of Barbara Hordich Togher.)

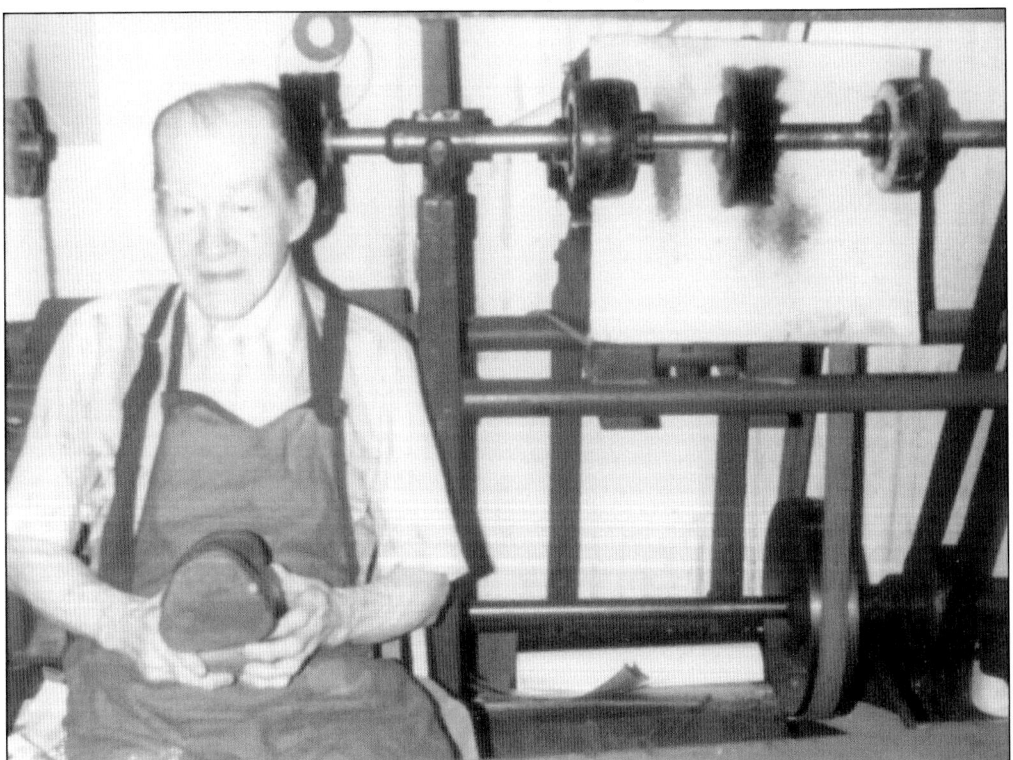

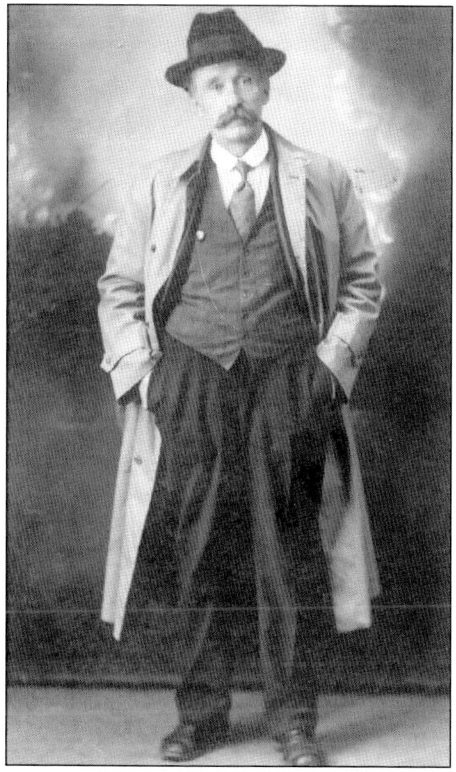

Casper Ott. A native of Switzerland, Ott immigrated to the United States in 1880 with his wife, Margaret, and two children. In 1885, he established himself in the general merchandise business and opened Ott's Groceries on Union Street, considered one of the finest stores in the borough. He was affiliated with Acacia Lodge No. 579, Ancient Free and Accepted Masons of Taylor, and many more organizations. When his barn burned in 1894, Ott and others in the borough realized the need for fire protection. Up until that time, the only water used to put out fires came from deep wells. Ott organized a fire company from among the Swiss and German residents, and he was made the first president of Taylor Hose Company No. 1. Ott came to Taylor in the 1800s and never left; the people of the community held him in the highest regard. (Both, courtesy of Margaret Greco.)

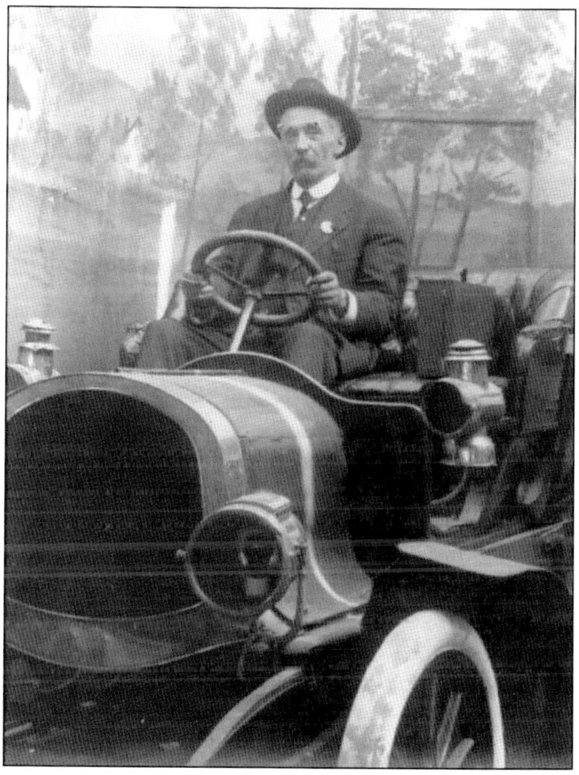

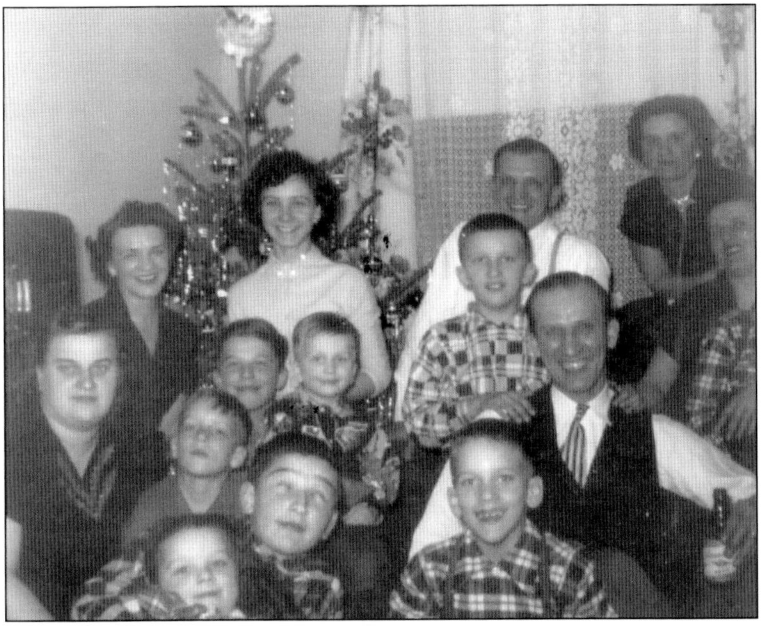

Russian Christmas Eve. The Hordich family of the Lincoln Heights section in Taylor follows the Julian calendar, and they are pictured celebrating the Russian Orthodox holiday. (Courtesy of Barbara Hordich Togher.)

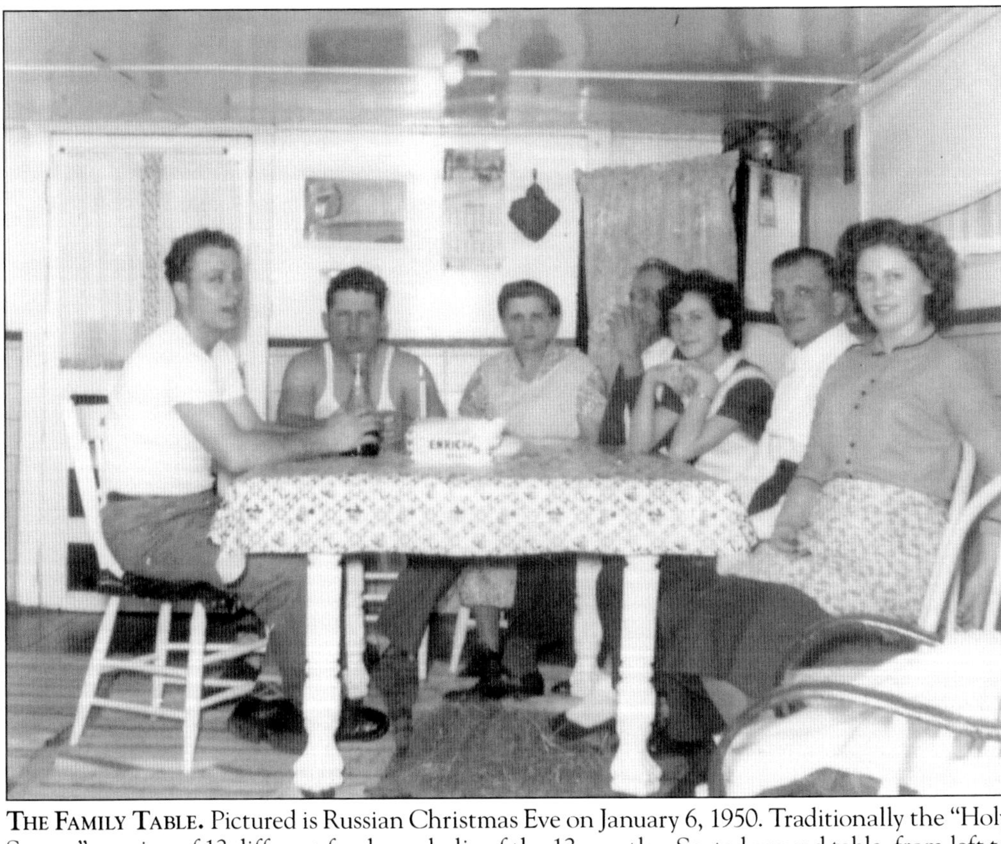

The Family Table. Pictured is Russian Christmas Eve on January 6, 1950. Traditionally the "Holy Supper" consists of 12 different foods symbolic of the 12 apostles. Seated around table, from left to right, are Steve Wozniak, William Wozniak, Mary Wozniak, Matthew Wozniak, Barbara Hordich, Walter Hordich, and Olga Hordick. (Courtesy of Barbara Hordich Togher.)

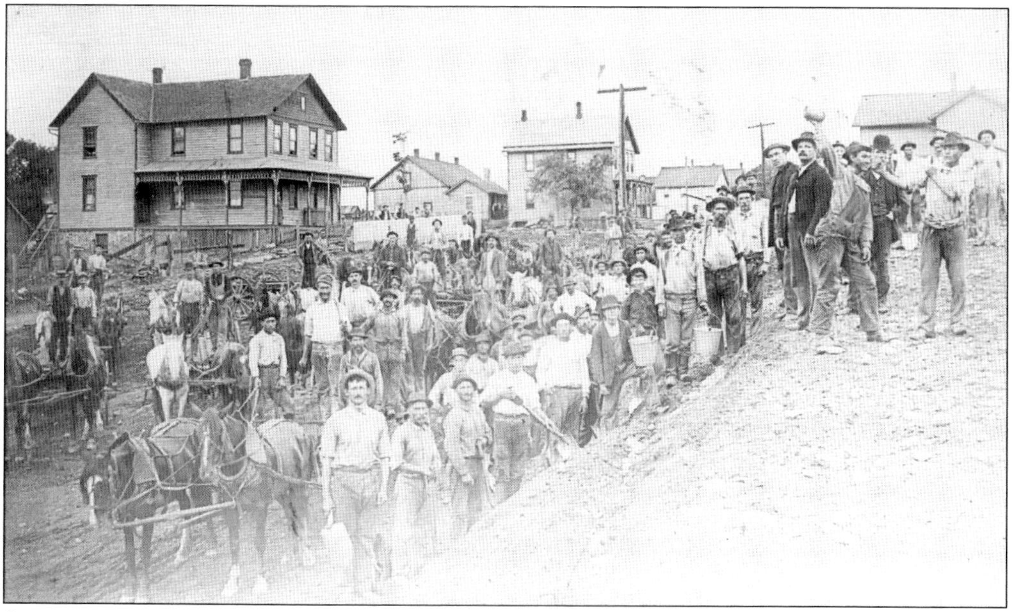

STREETCAR TRACKS. Workers are grading for streetcar tracks on South Main and Hospital Streets in the Rendham section, near the present-day Taylor Post Office. (Courtesy of Shawn Murphy.)

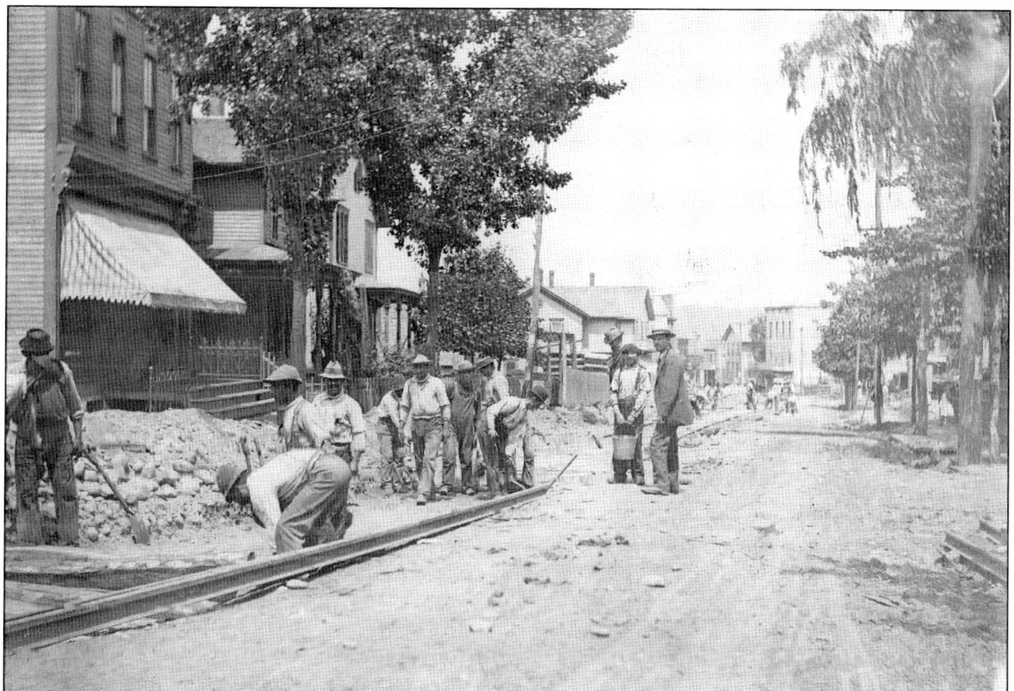

MAKING TRACKS IN TAYLOR. Seen here is the laying of the trolley tracks in the business district on Main Street. (Courtesy of Nancy and Bob Thomas.)

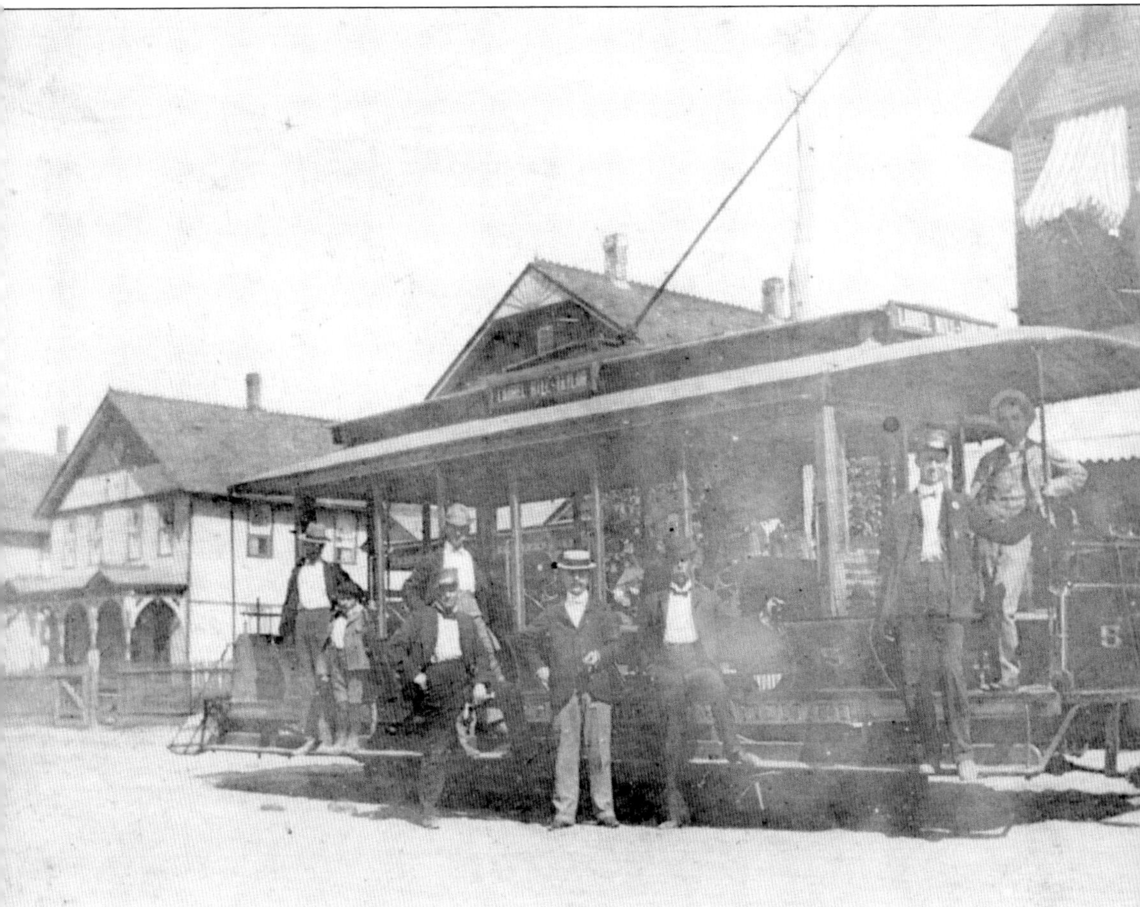

First Streetcar. In the late 1800s, an electric streetcar company received a franchise to enter Taylor due to the efforts of Dr. J. W. Houser, president of the corporation. The very first electric streetcar to run through Taylor took place on December 16, 1893. (Courtesy of Nancy and Bob Thomas.)

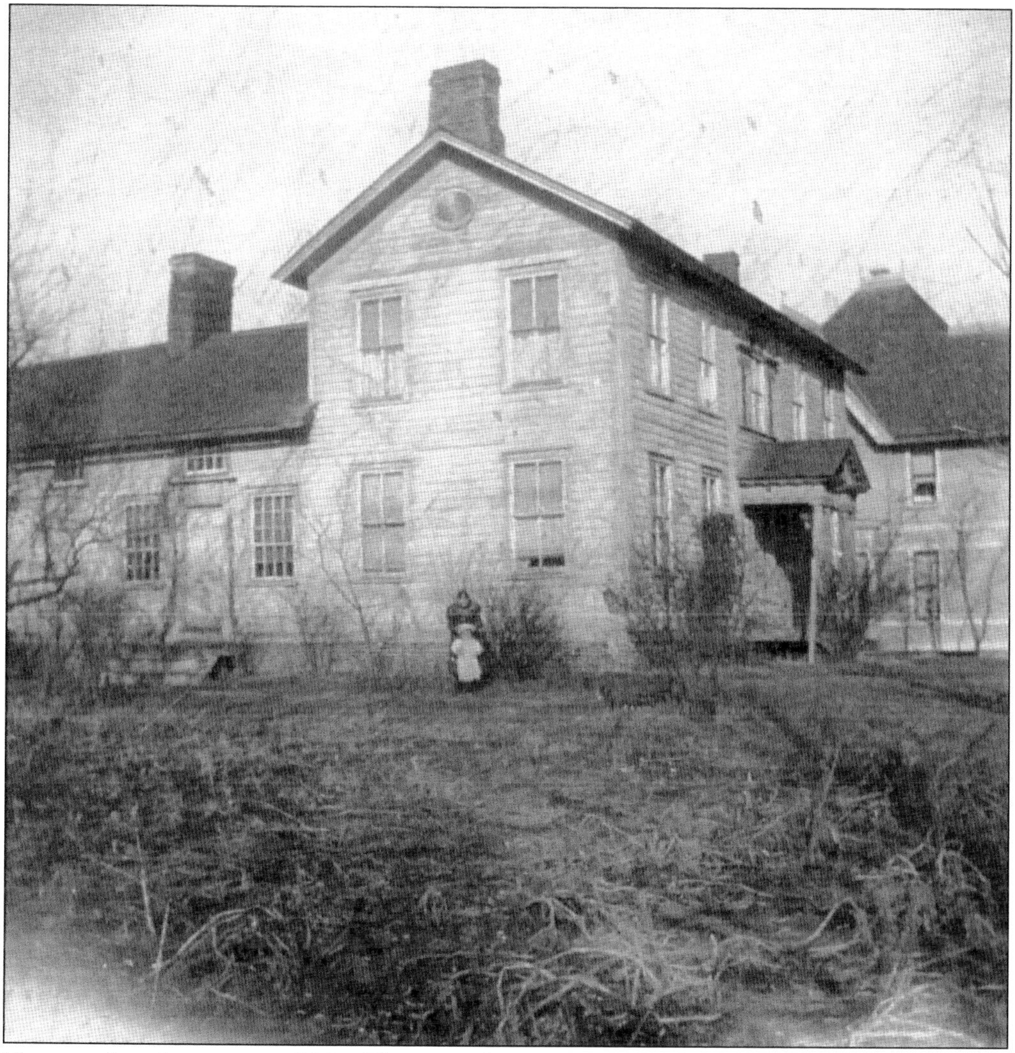

HOME OF IRA ATHERTON, 1870S. The second generation of Taylor's pioneer family, Ira was the father of John D. and Willard Atherton, who opened Atherton Brothers' store on the main thoroughfare in 1896. This is the current site of the Jacob Davis Funeral Home at 422 South Main Street. The original home was built by Willard Atherton. (Courtesy of Shawn Murphy.)

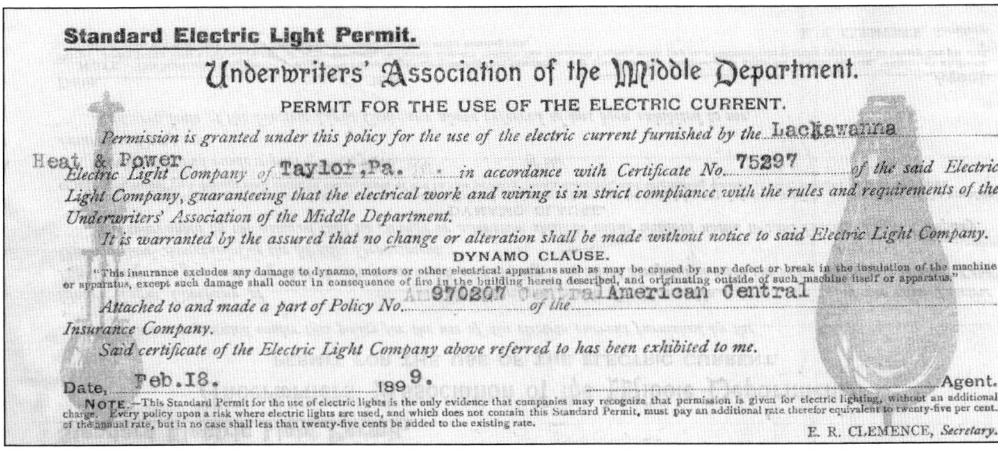

Standard Electric Light Permit.

Underwriters' Association of the Middle Department.

PERMIT FOR THE USE OF THE ELECTRIC CURRENT.

Permission is granted under this policy for the use of the electric current furnished by the Lackawanna Heat & Power *Electric Light Company of* Taylor, Pa. *in accordance with Certificate No.* 75297 *of the said Electric Light Company, guaranteeing that the electrical work and wiring is in strict compliance with the rules and requirements of the Underwriters' Association of the Middle Department.*

It is warranted by the assured that no change or alteration shall be made without notice to said Electric Light Company.

DYNAMO CLAUSE.

"This insurance excludes any damage to dynamo, motors or other electrical apparatus such as may be caused by any defect or break in the insulation of the machine or apparatus, except such damage shall occur in consequence of fire in the building herein described, and originating outside of such machine itself or apparatus."

Attached to and made a part of Policy No. 970207 *of the* American Central *Insurance Company.*

Said certificate of the Electric Light Company above referred to has been exhibited to me.

Date, Feb. 18. 1899. .... Agent.

NOTE.—This Standard Permit for the use of electric lights is the only evidence that companies may recognize that permission is given for electric lighting, without an additional charge. Every policy upon a risk where electric lights are used, and which does not contain this Standard Permit, must pay an additional rate therefor equivalent to twenty-five per cent. of the annual rate, but in no case shall less than twenty-five cents be added to the existing rate.

E. R. CLEMENCE, *Secretary.*

TAYLOR'S ELECTRIC COMPANY. This was a standard electric light permit dated February 18, 1899. It states permission is granted under this policy for the use of the electric current furnished by the Lackawanna Heat and Power Light Company of Taylor. (Courtesy of Shawn Murphy and Taylor Community Library.)

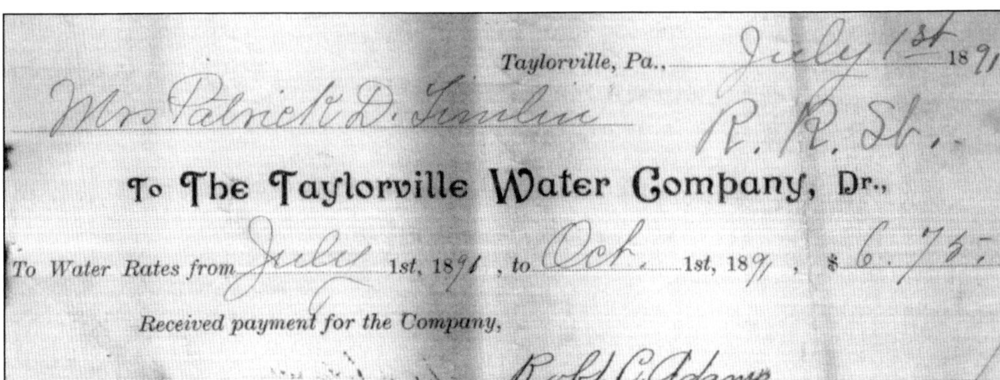

Taylorville, Pa., July 1st 1891

Mrs Patrick D. Timlin R. R. St.

To The Taylorville Water Company, Dr.,

To Water Rates from July *1st, 18*91*, to* Oct. *1st, 18*91*,* $6.75

Received payment for the Company,

Robt. C. Adams

TAYLOR'S WATER COMPANY. This bill dated July 1, 1891, indicates Mrs. Patric D. Timlin paid the Taylorville Water Company the water rate from July 1, 1891, through October 1, 1891, in the amount of $6.75. (Courtesy of Shawn Murphy and Taylor Community Library.)

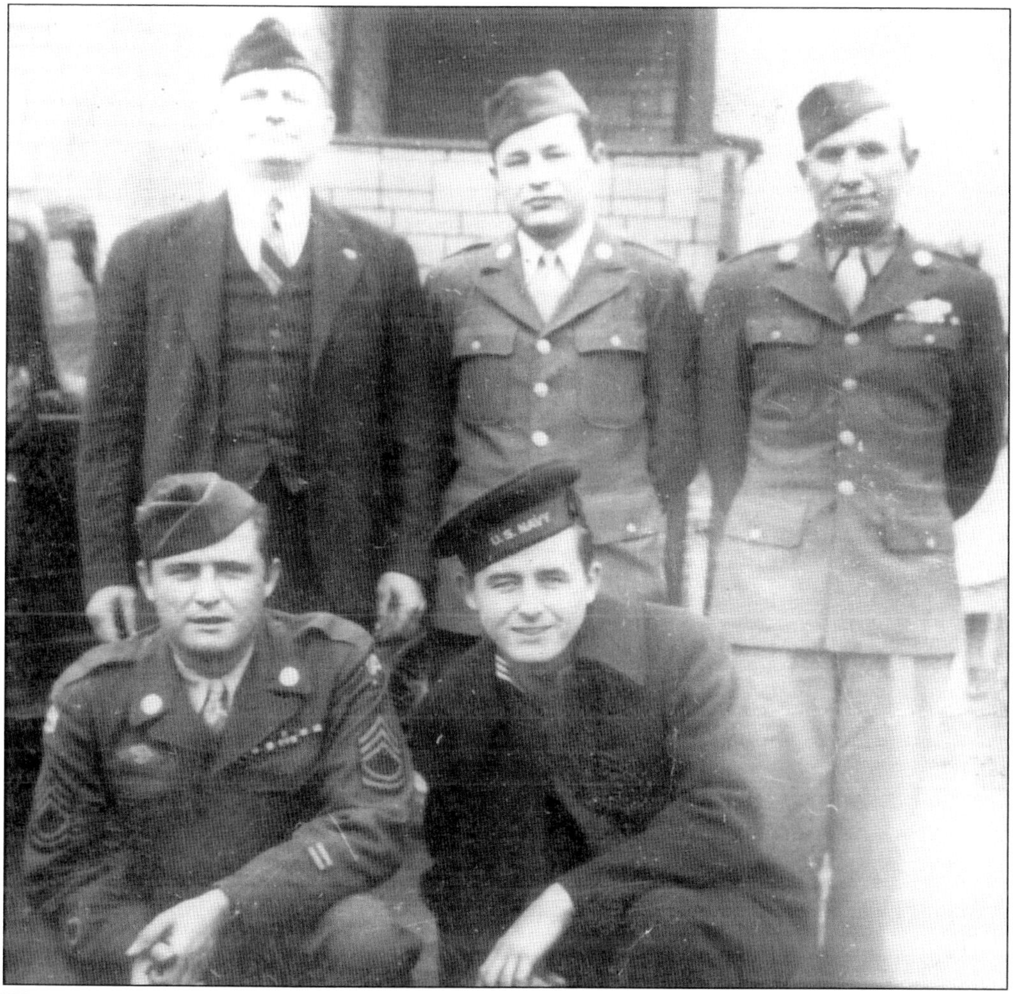

Wartime. Various veterans posed for this picture. They are, from left to right, (first row) John Gable Jr., Patton's Third Army staff sergeant, World War II; Albert Gable, seaman first class, World War II; (second row) John Gable, World War I; Edward Gable, sergeant, World War II; and Joseph Gable, private first class First Army Battle of the Bulge and No. 3 in the front line. John Gable entered World War I at the age of 16. He was stationed in Panama from 1911 to 1918. All of these men are all members of American Legion Post No. 306. (Courtesy of Shawn Murphy.)

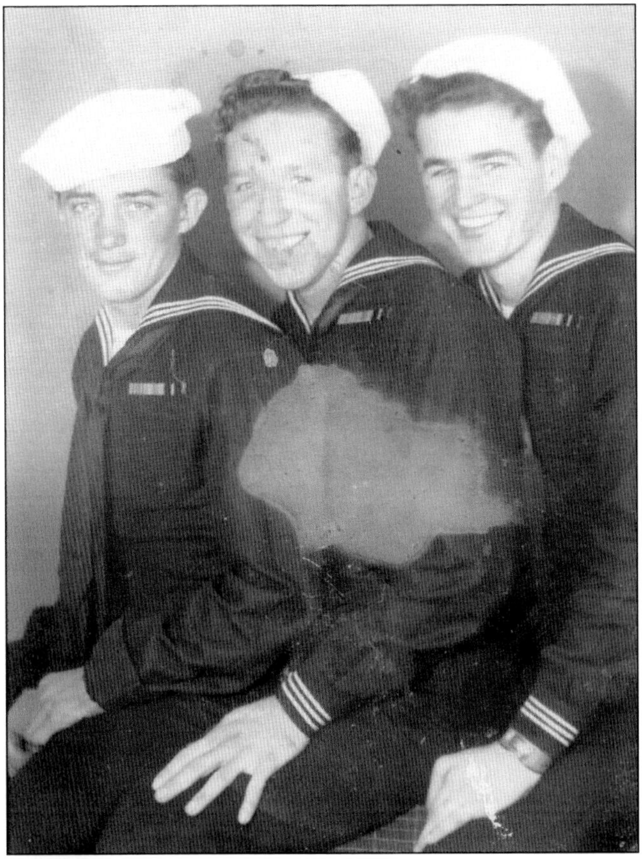

Taylor's Sailors. Three local boys pose for a picture while on leave. The only one identified is Michael Dorin, seen on the right. (Courtesy of the Gawel family.)

Salute the Flag. The soldiers holding the flag are the sons of Andrew and Mary Dorin, who lived on Fourth Street in Feltsville. Pictured from left to right are Michael, Andrew, Mary, and John (J. D.) Dorin. (Courtesy of the Gawel family.)

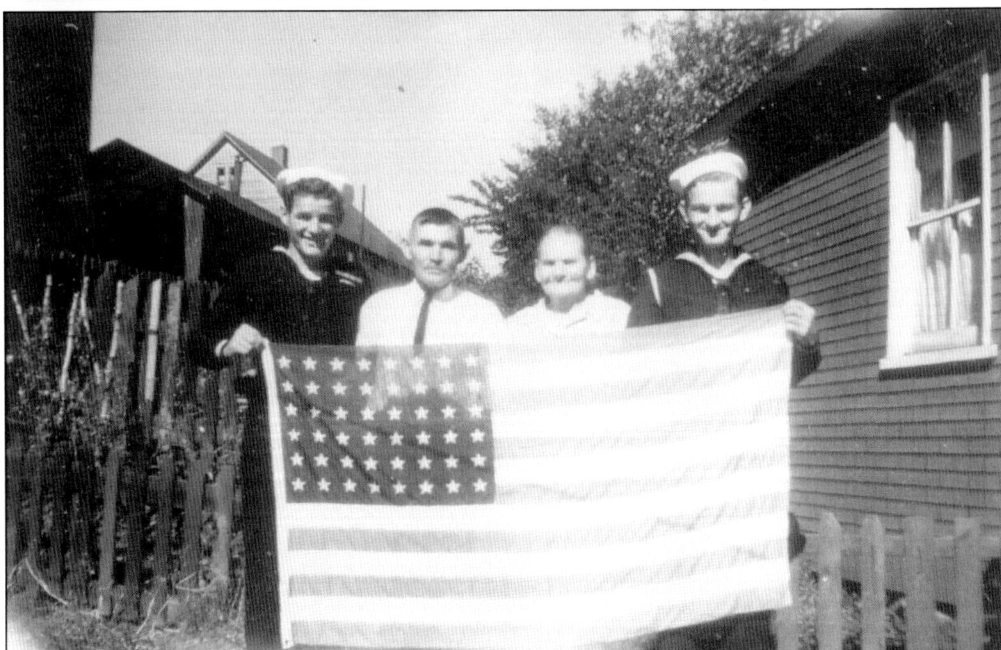

Mary Timlin Lally. In this *c.* 1917 photograph, Mary is posing with her son, Patrick A. Lally, before he leaves for France in World War I. The Lally family lived on Taylor's Main Street. (Courtesy of Richard Snyder.)

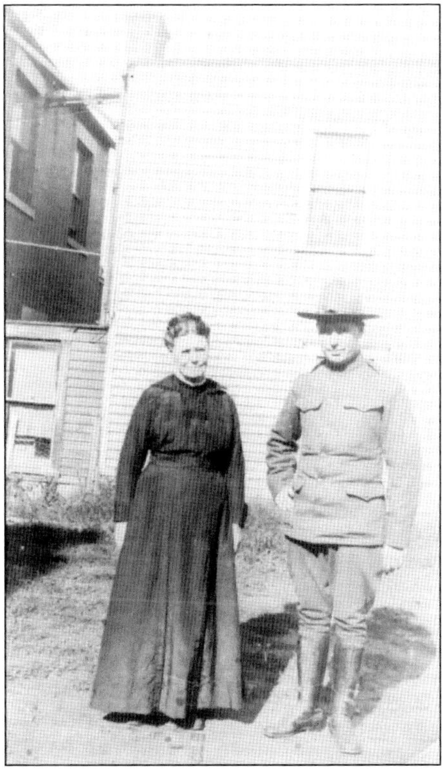

Vietnam War Wall. The wall lists the names of Taylor's Vietnam War casualties. They are as follows: Thomas Hefferman, James Scherer, and Walter Smith. (Courtesy of Shawn Murphy and Taylor Community Library.)

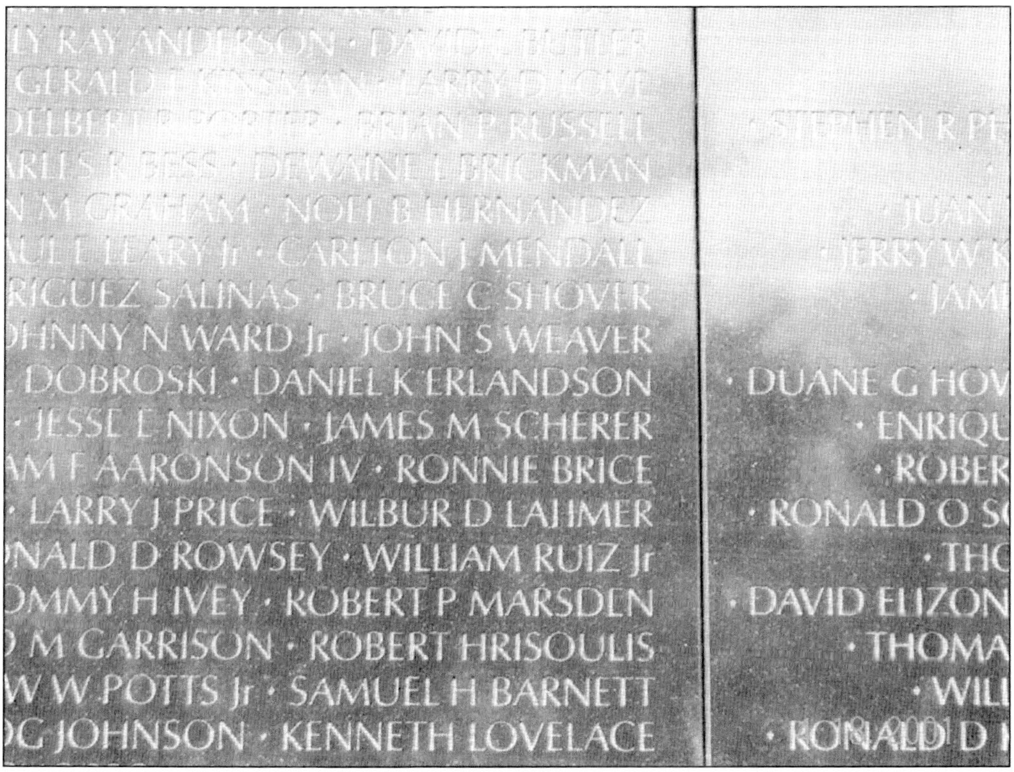

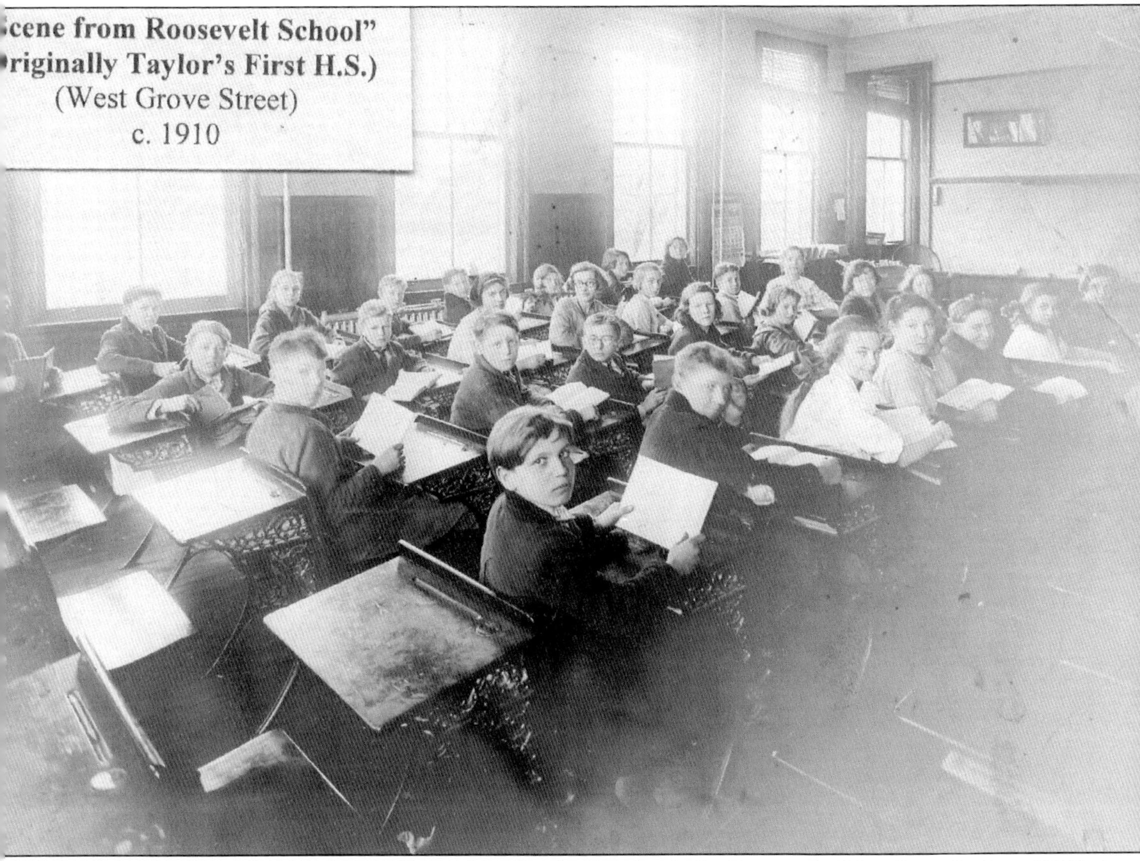

ROOSEVELT SCHOOL. Originally Taylor's first high school, the Roosevelt School was built in 1905. A little-known fact is that the school's gymnasium was in the attic. Later it was made into an elementary school. The school was located on West Grove Street. (Courtesy of Shawn Murphy.)

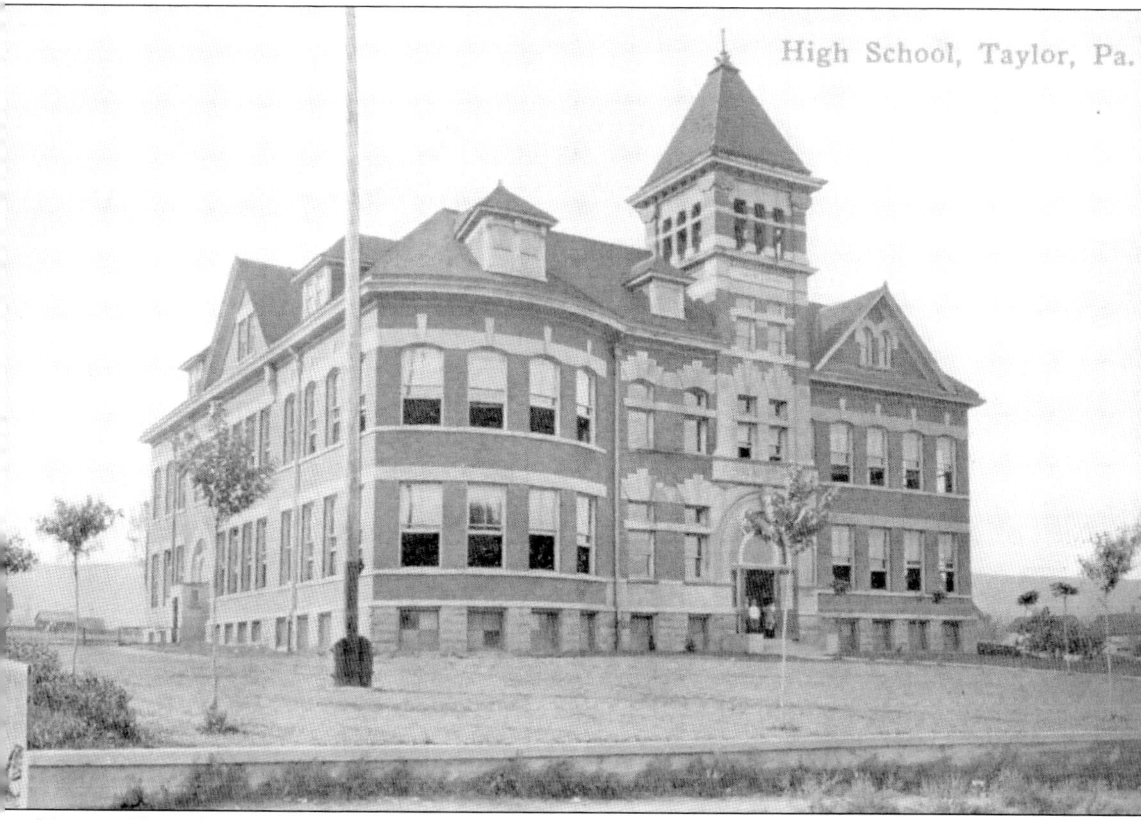

Taylor High School. The new high school was built on Main Street in 1926 and replaced Roosevelt High School (pictured), which was then made into an elementary school. The first graduating class was in 1927. Dorothy Decker, who still resides in Taylor, was a member of that original graduating class; she just recently celebrated her 100th birthday. (Author's collection.)

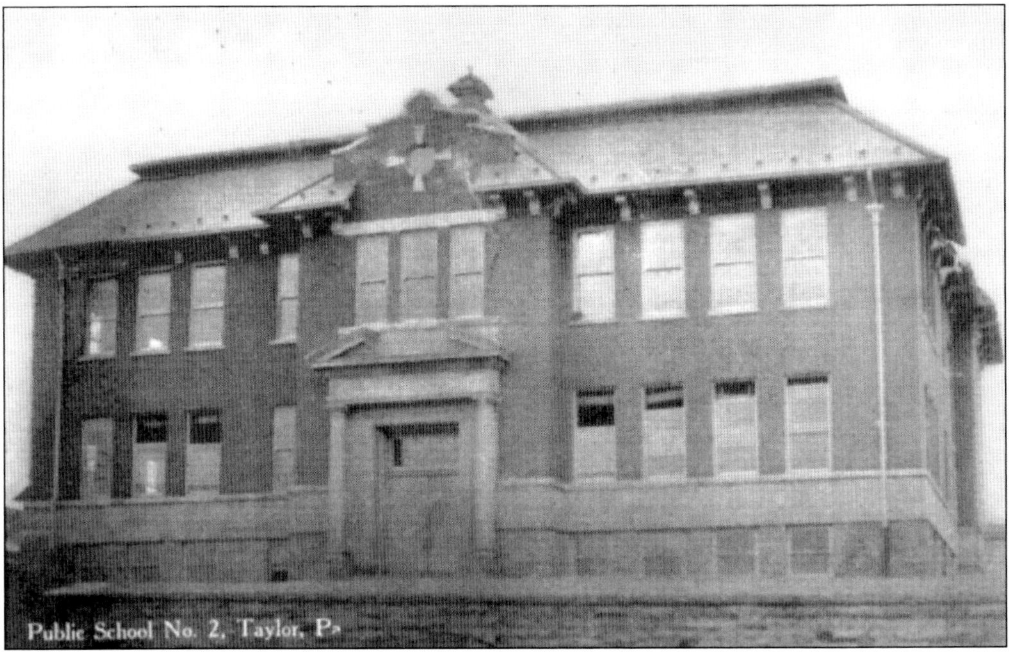

PUBLIC SCHOOL NO. 2. Also known as Washington School, this school was located on Grove Street. It was used as an elementary school. (Courtesy of Nancy and Bob Thomas.)

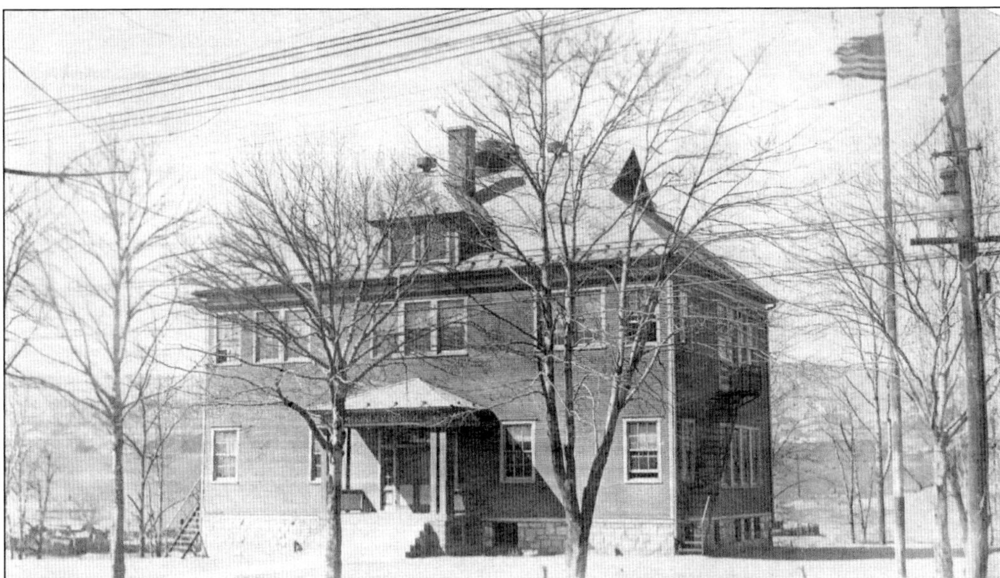

MCKINLEY SCHOOL. Located on North Main Avenue across from St. John the Baptist Church, McKinley School was torn down some time ago and was used for lumber. (Courtesy of Nancy and Bob Thomas.)

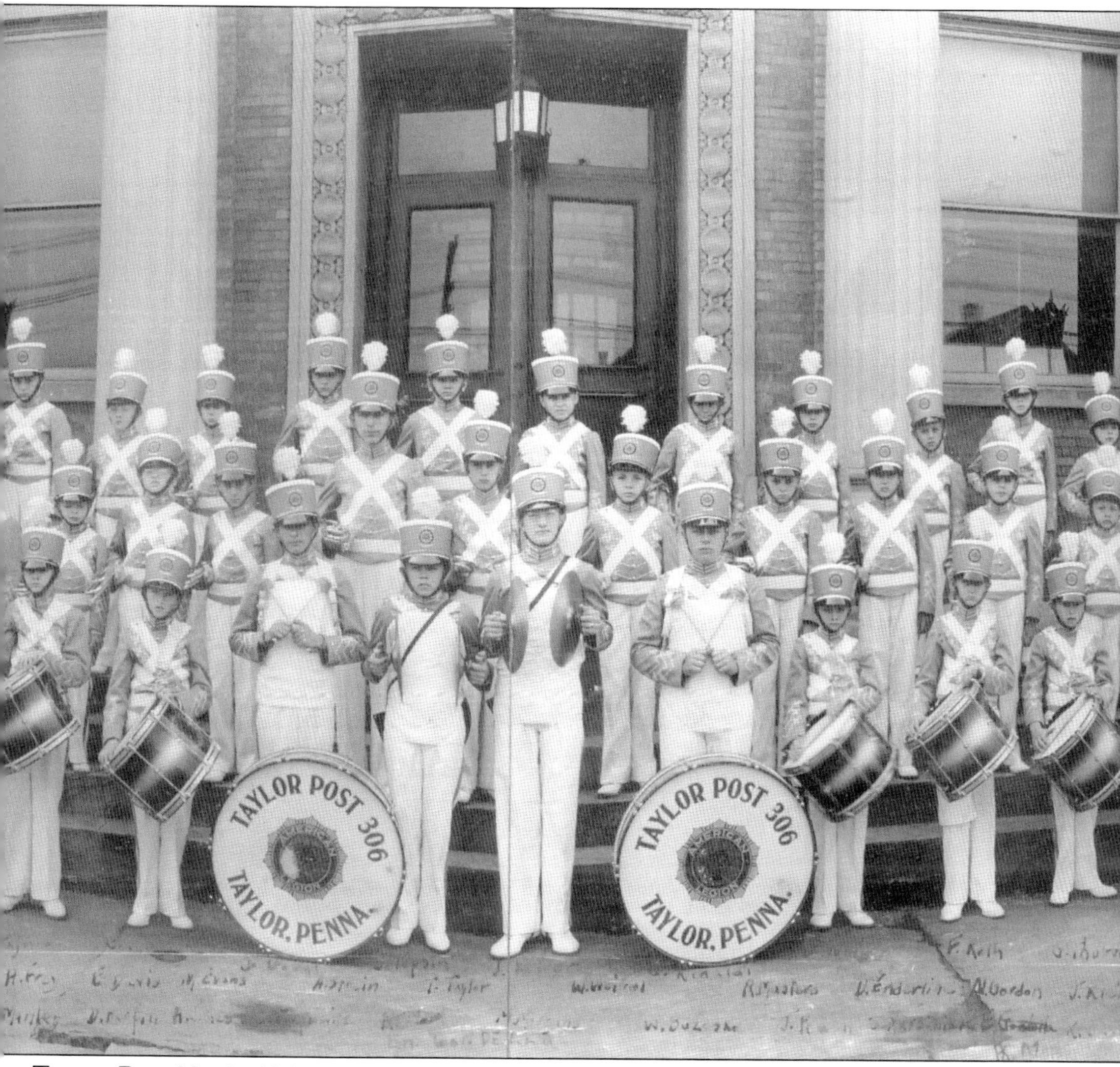

TAYLOR POST NO. 306 MARCHING BAND. The band of boys poses in front of Taylor High School while waiting to perform in the annual Memorial Day parade in May 1935. (Courtesy of Nancy and Bob Thomas.)

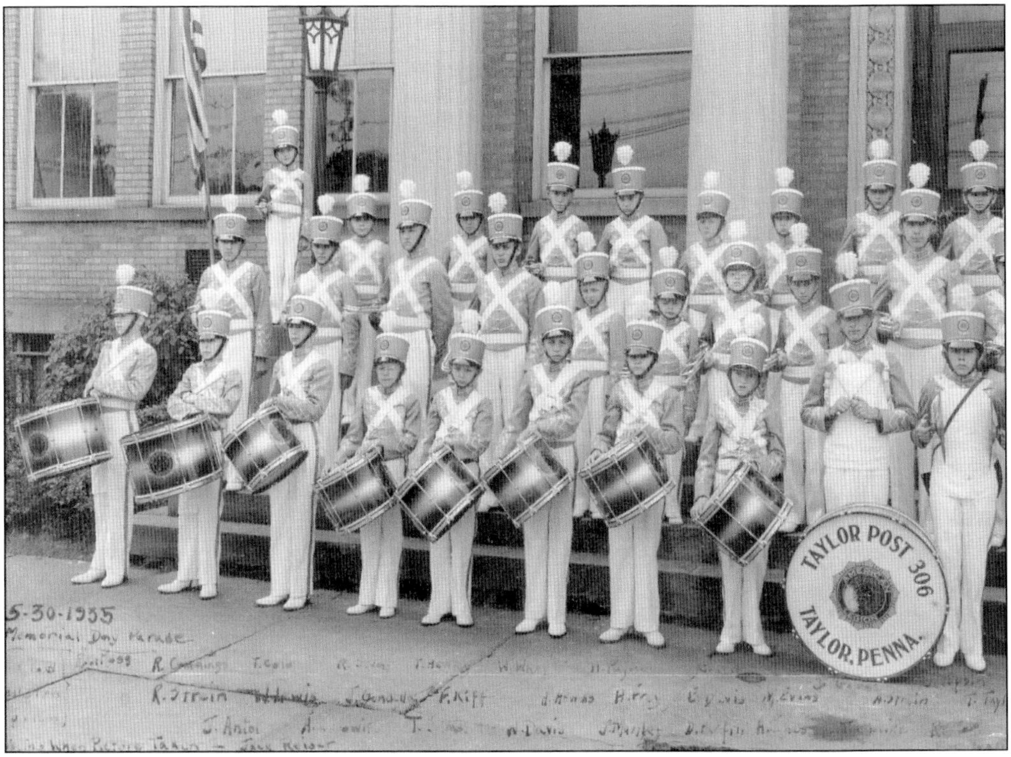

TAYLOR POST NO. 306. American Legion Post No. 306 is still located in Taylor on Main Street. (Courtesy of Nancy and Bob Thomas.)

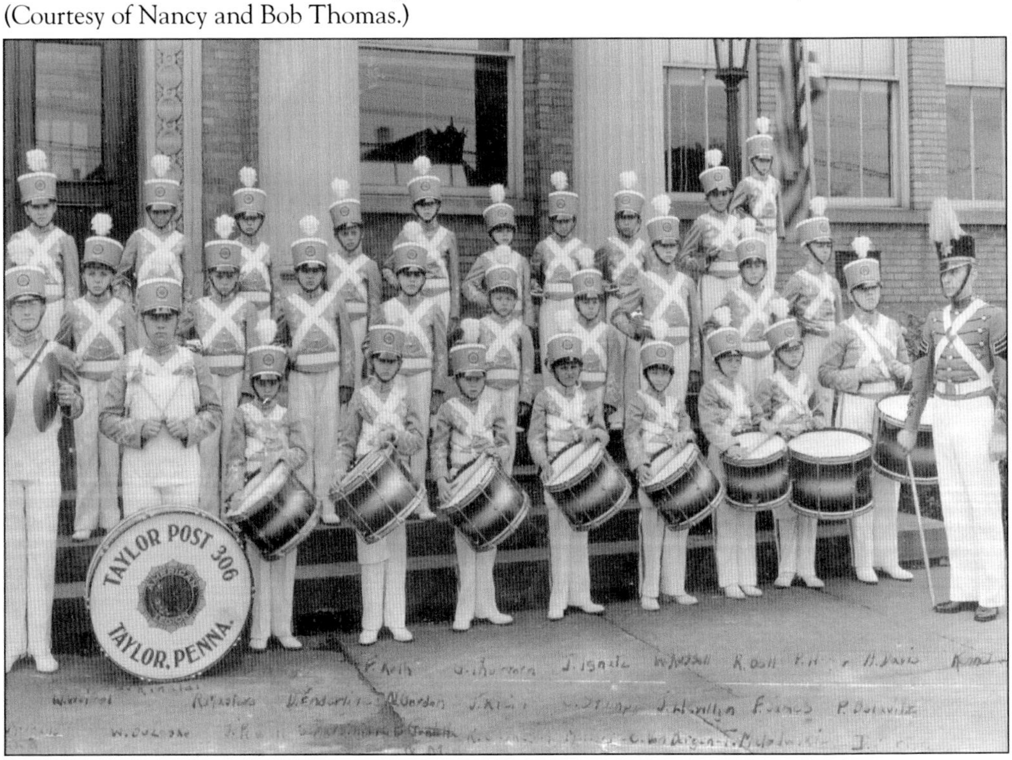

The New School. This is a dedication program from the new Taylor High School, which was built in 1926. Taylor High School took the place of Roosevelt High School. (Courtesy of Shawn Murphy and Taylor Community Library.)

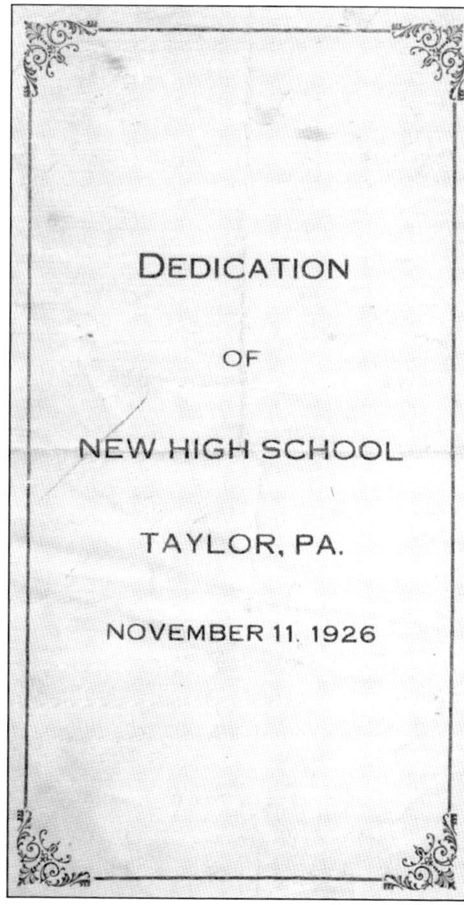

DEDICATION

OF

NEW HIGH SCHOOL

TAYLOR, PA.

NOVEMBER 11, 1926

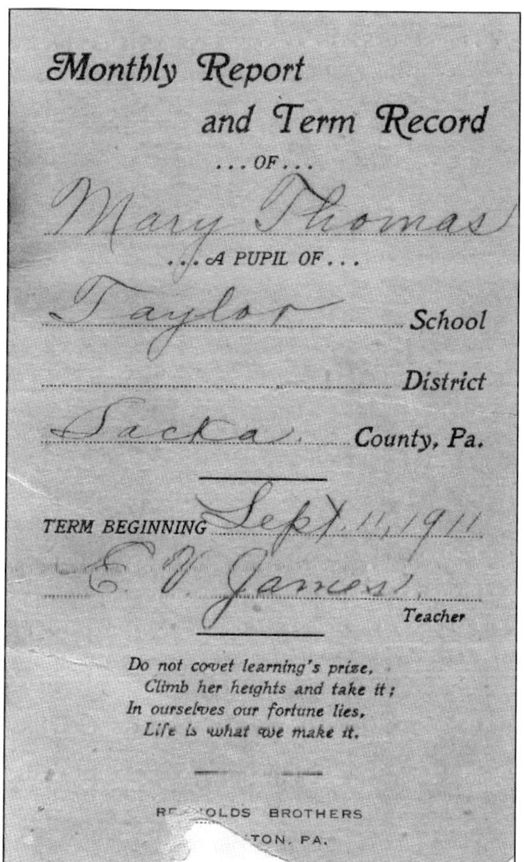

Monthly Report and Term Record

...OF...

Mary Thomas

...A PUPIL OF...

Taylor School

District

Lacka. County, Pa.

TERM BEGINNING Sept. 11, 1911

E. V. James

Teacher

Do not covet learning's prize,
Climb her heights and take it;
In ourselves our fortune lies,
Life is what we make it.

Report Card. This postcard is dated September 11, 1911, and belonged to pupil Mary Thomas. Her teacher was E. V. James. In 1911, teachers sent monthly report cards. According to her high grades, Mary was an excellent student. She was ranked No. 1 in her class with a monthly average grade of 98.6. (Courtesy of Shawn Murphy and Taylor Community Library.)

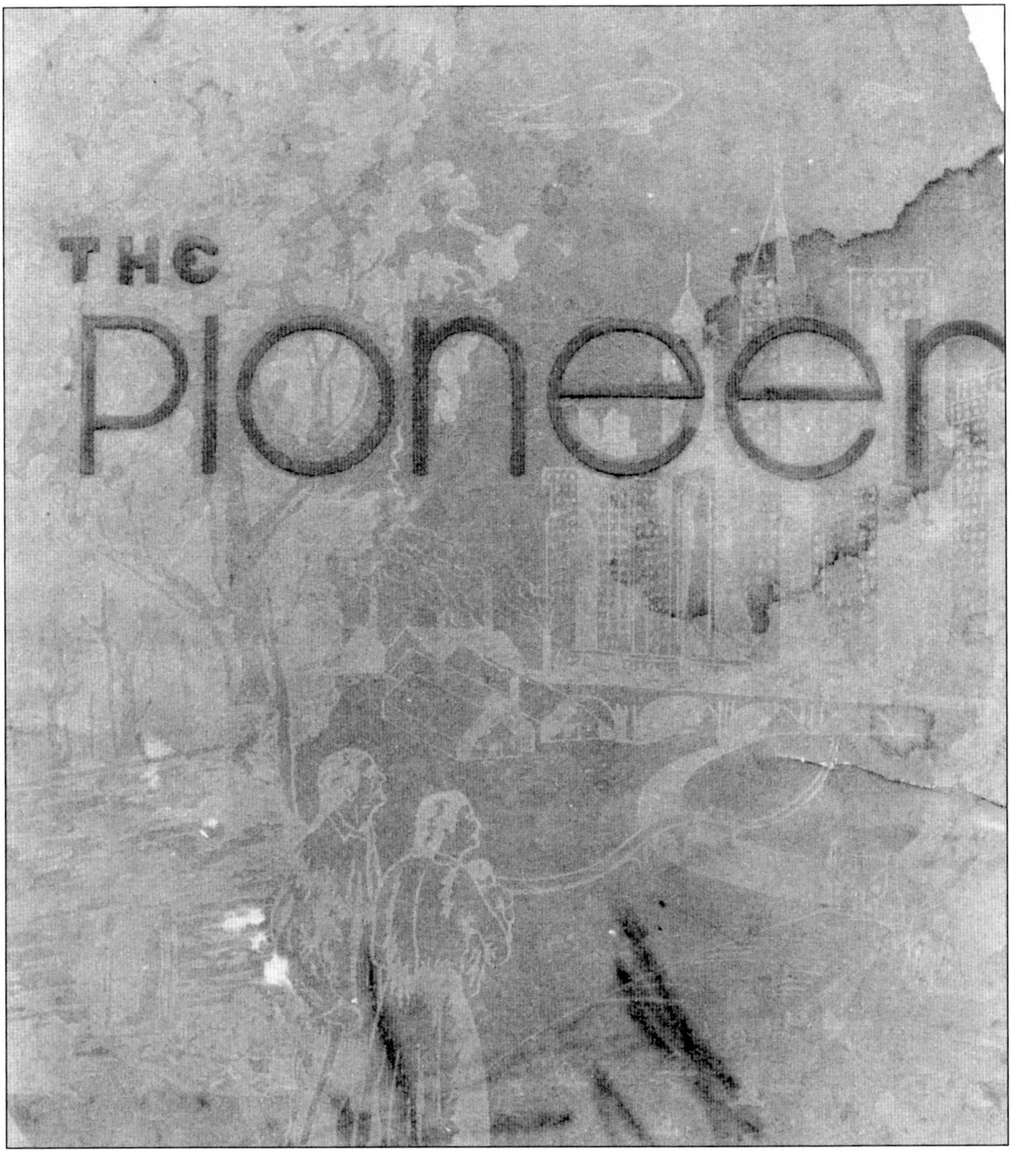

The Pioneer. This is volume one of the Taylor High School yearbook. The 1939 senior class presents *The Pioneer*, which delineates in pictorial and narrative form the history of the school year in seven chapters. The yearbook for that year was dedicated to Reba Griffith, a teacher and the woman responsible for helping to raise funds to open a public library in Taylor. (Courtesy of Shawn Murphy and Taylor Community Library.)

The 1939 Senior Class. Here is a program of the commencement exercises for the Taylor High School senior class. The graduation ceremony was held in the auditorium on June 23, 1939. (Courtesy of Shawn Murphy and Taylor Community Library.)

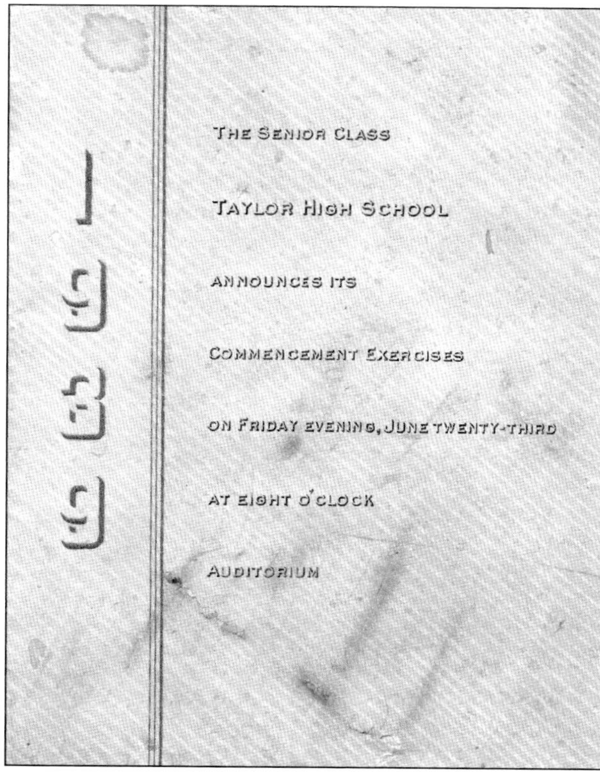

1939

THE SENIOR CLASS

TAYLOR HIGH SCHOOL

ANNOUNCES ITS

COMMENCEMENT EXERCISES

ON FRIDAY EVENING, JUNE TWENTY-THIRD

AT EIGHT O'CLOCK

AUDITORIUM

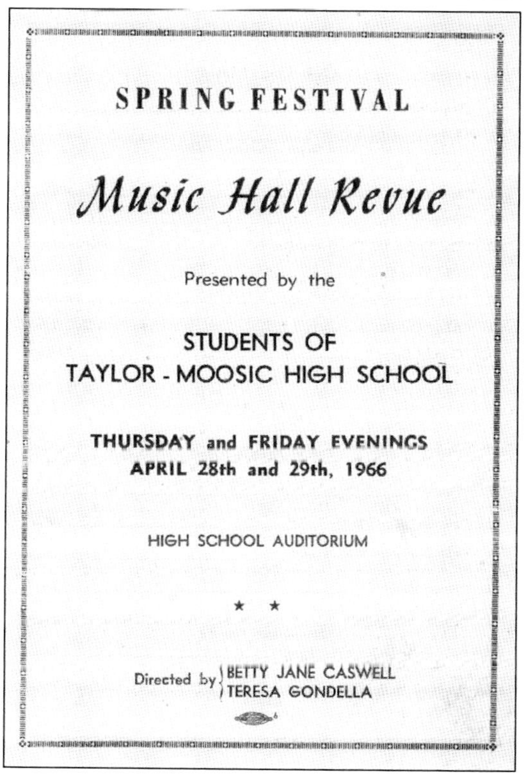

SPRING FESTIVAL

Music Hall Revue

Presented by the

STUDENTS OF
TAYLOR - MOOSIC HIGH SCHOOL

THURSDAY and FRIDAY EVENINGS
APRIL 28th and 29th, 1966

HIGH SCHOOL AUDITORIUM

★ ★

Directed by BETTY JANE CASWELL
TERESA GONDELLA

Spring Festival. Presented by the students of Taylor High School, this year's program was called *Music Hall Revue*, a performance of songs from the Gay Nineties and Roaring Twenties. Broadway melodies such as *Sixteen Going on Seventeen* and *Camelot* were sung by the students. (Courtesy of Shawn Murphy and Taylor Community Library.)

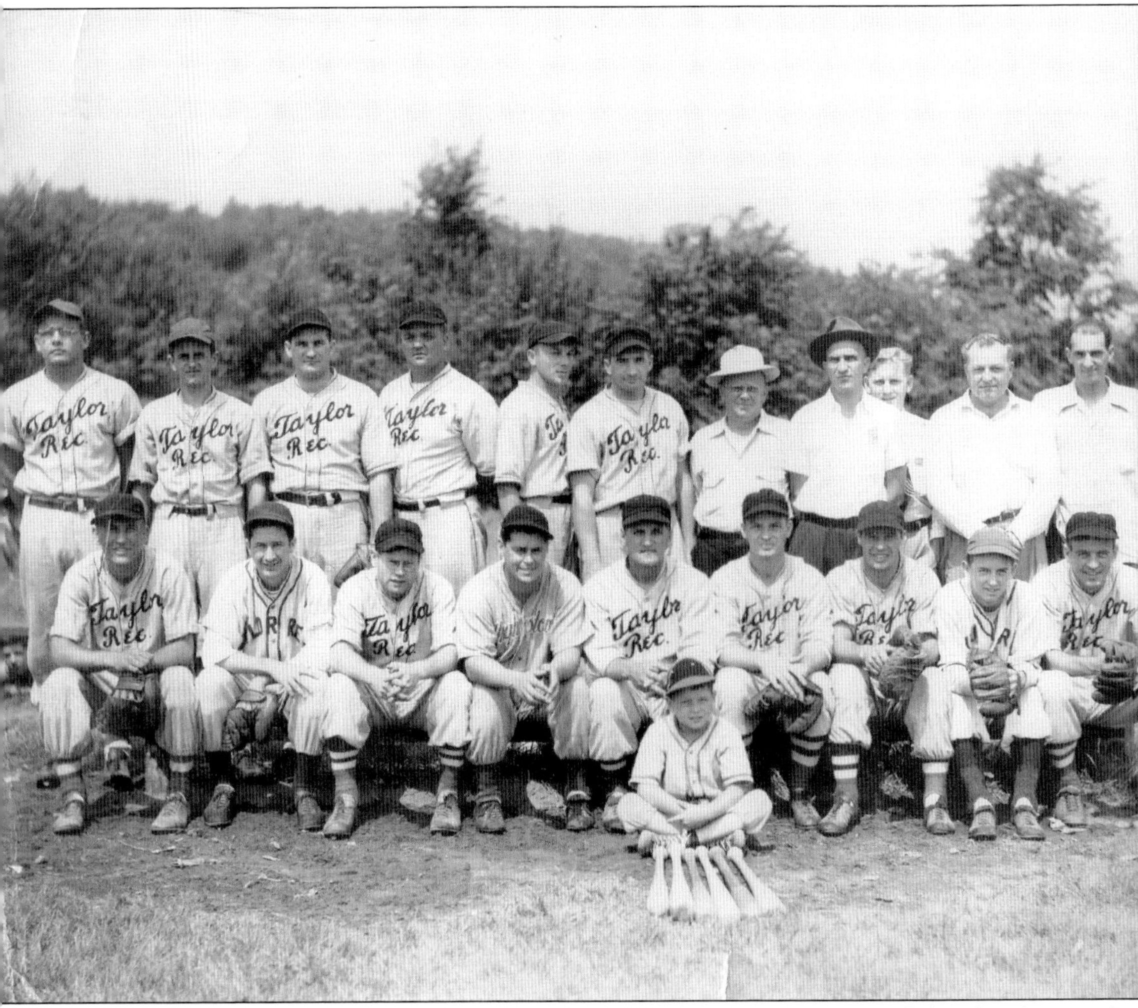

Taylor Baseball Team. The Taylor Recreation team formed in the 1940s and played at the top of Union Street, where Derenick Park is located today. In the center of picture is Joseph Wincovich, Taylor's chief of police and sheriff of Lackawanna County. (Courtesy of Kathleen Olekszulin.)

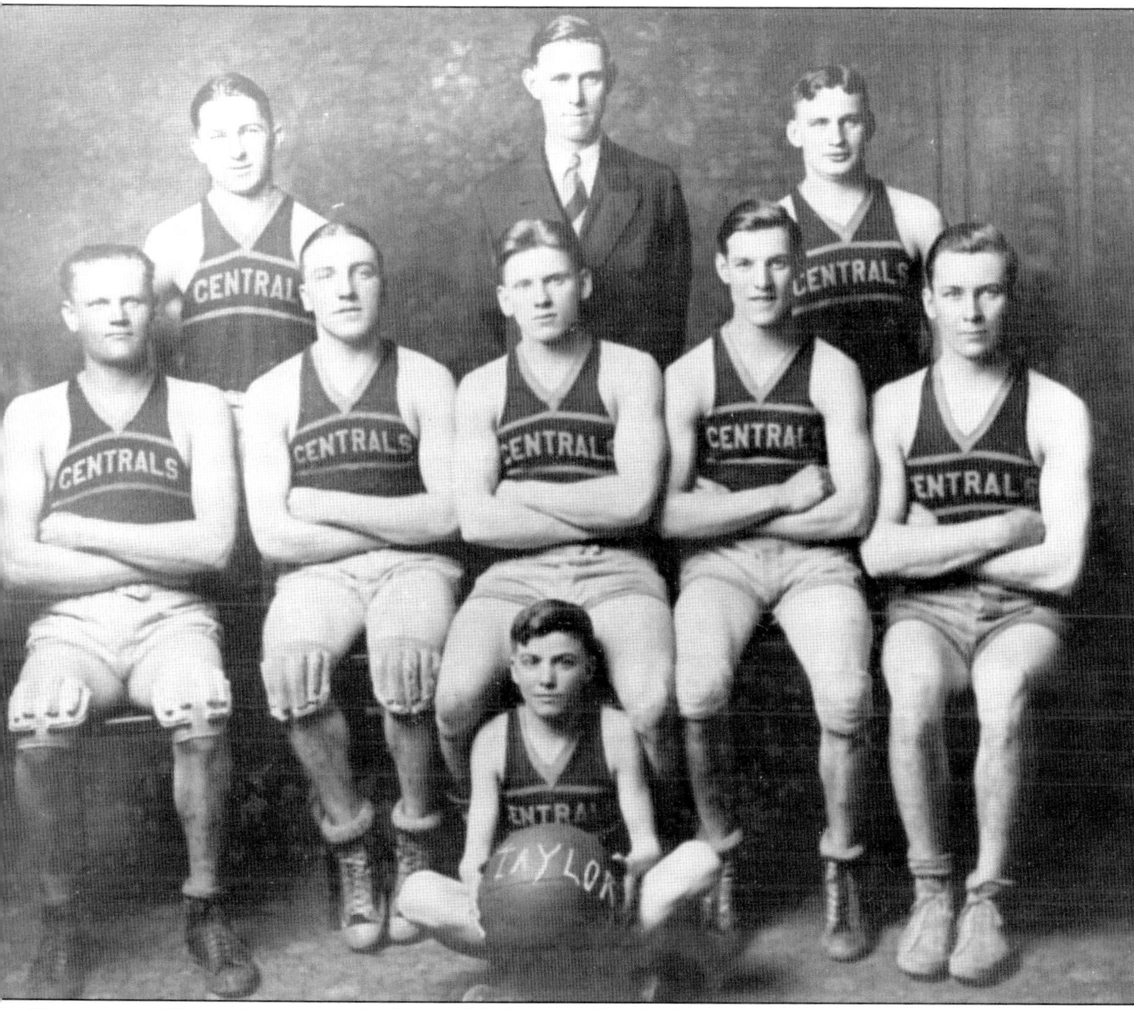

Basketball Team. Pictured is the Taylor High School basketball team in an undetermined year, possibly around the late 1920s or early 1930s. Seated in the second row, center, is Howard (Red) Powell, whose family owned and operated Powell's Grocery Store. (Courtesy of Marie Eskra.)

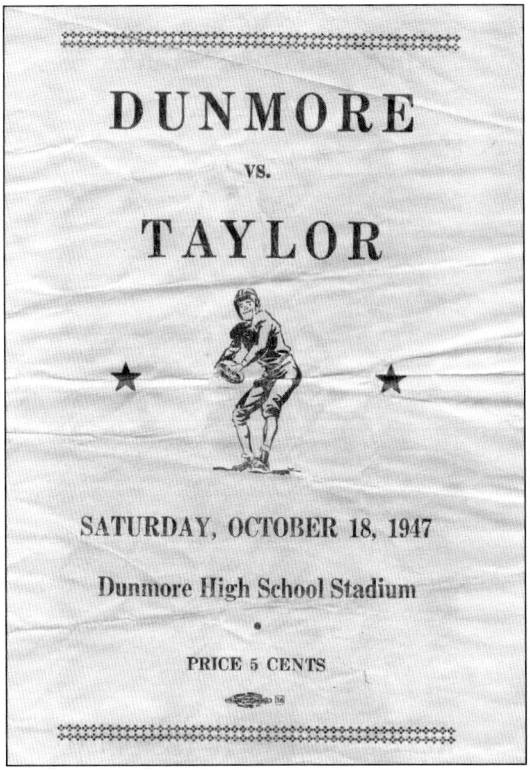

DUNMORE VS. TAYLOR. Taylor's football team is the Trojans. This game was played on October 18, 1947. The cost of the program was only a nickel. (Courtesy of Shawn Murphy.)

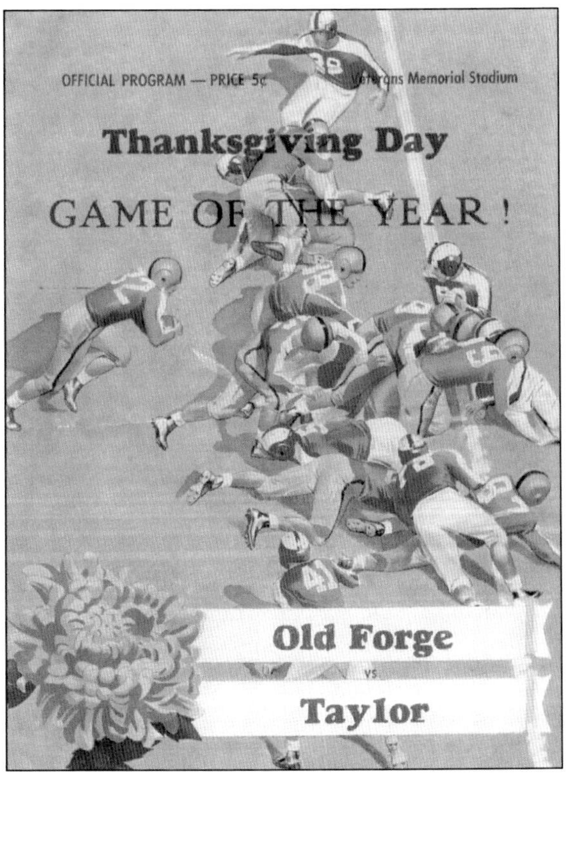

THANKSGIVING DAY GAME. The Old Forge Blue Devils played the Taylor Trojans in the biggest game of the year. It was played traditionally on Thanksgiving Day. The program is dated 1949. (Courtesy of Shawn Murphy.)

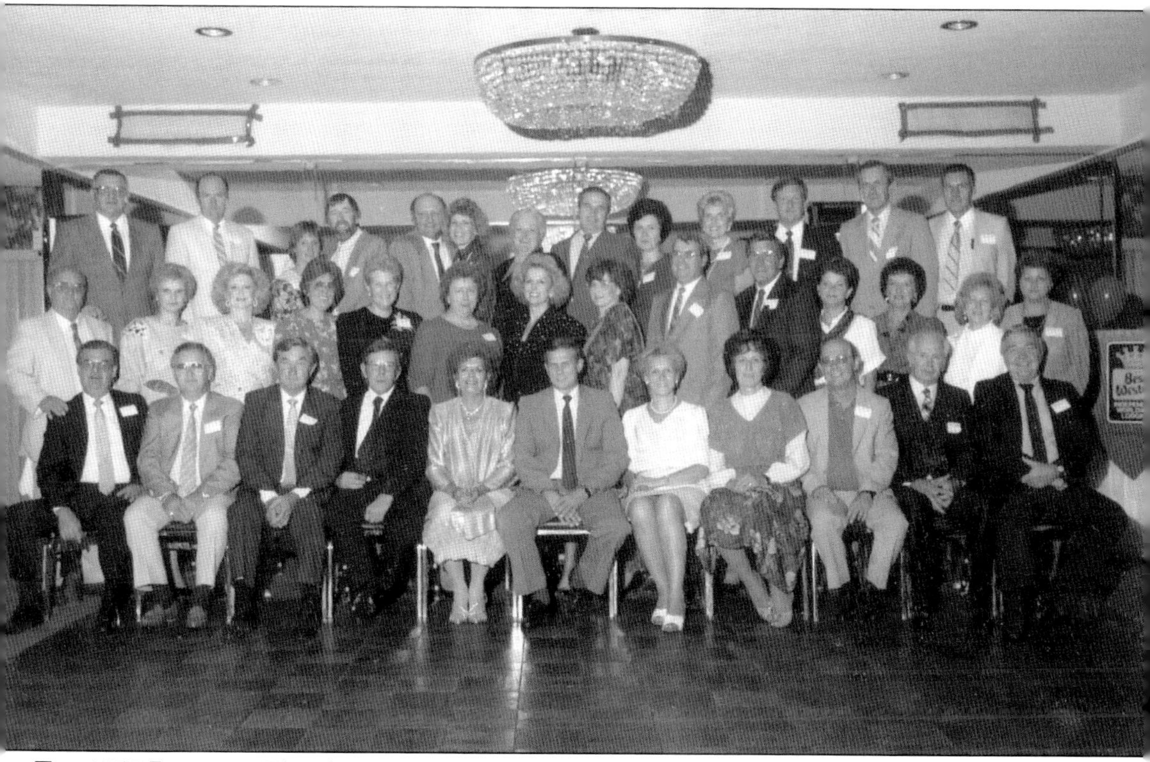

The 1957 Reunion. The class reunion for Taylor High School's class of 1957 is pictured here. (Courtesy of Barbara Togher.)

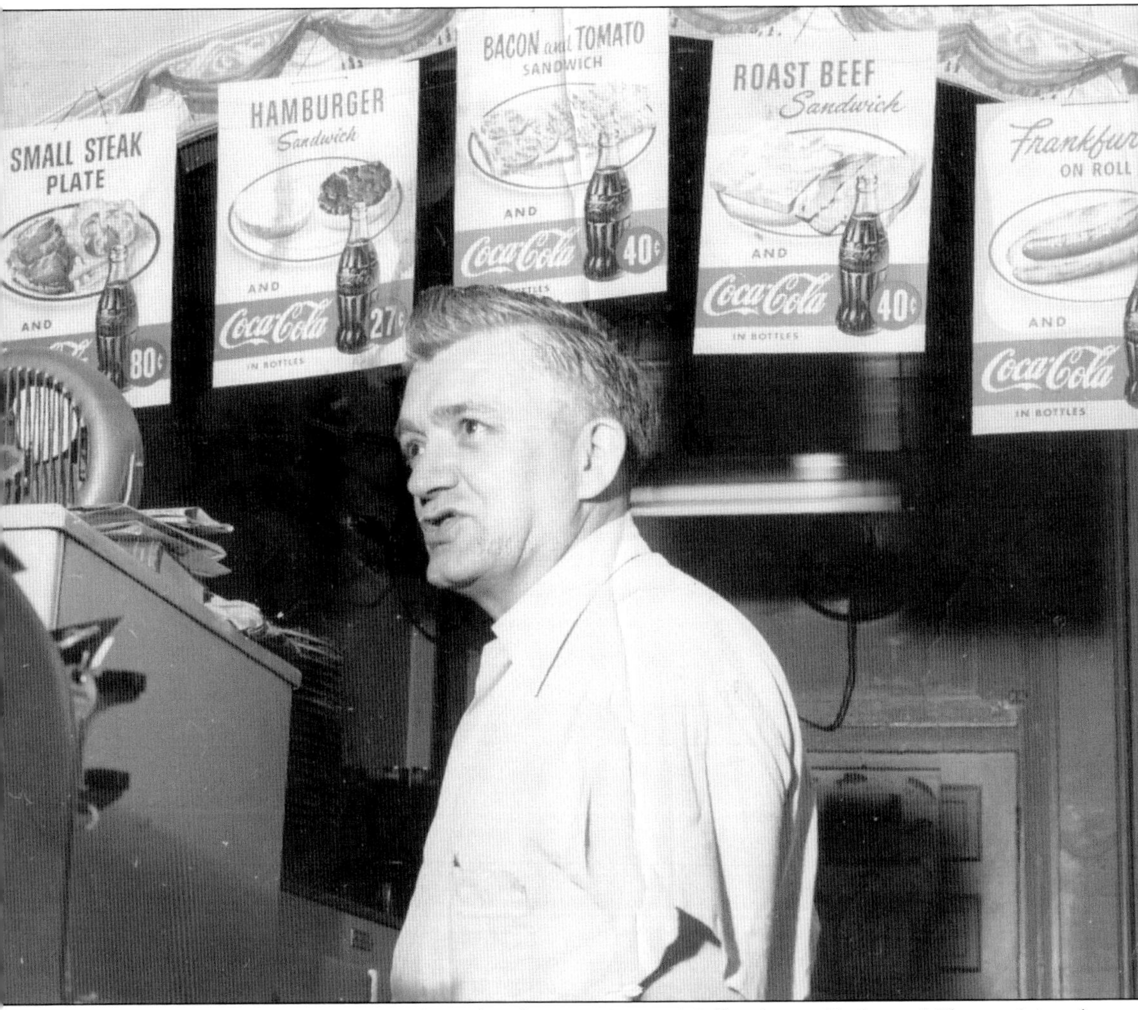

LOUIS MALKA. Keeping up the school spirit, Louis Malka (grandfather of Shawn Murphy, elementary school teacher and Taylor historian) sold hot dogs and other concession-type foods out of the back of a school bus during Taylor High School ball games in the 1940s. When's the last time you paid 27¢ for a hamburger and Coke? (Courtesy of Shawn Murphy.)

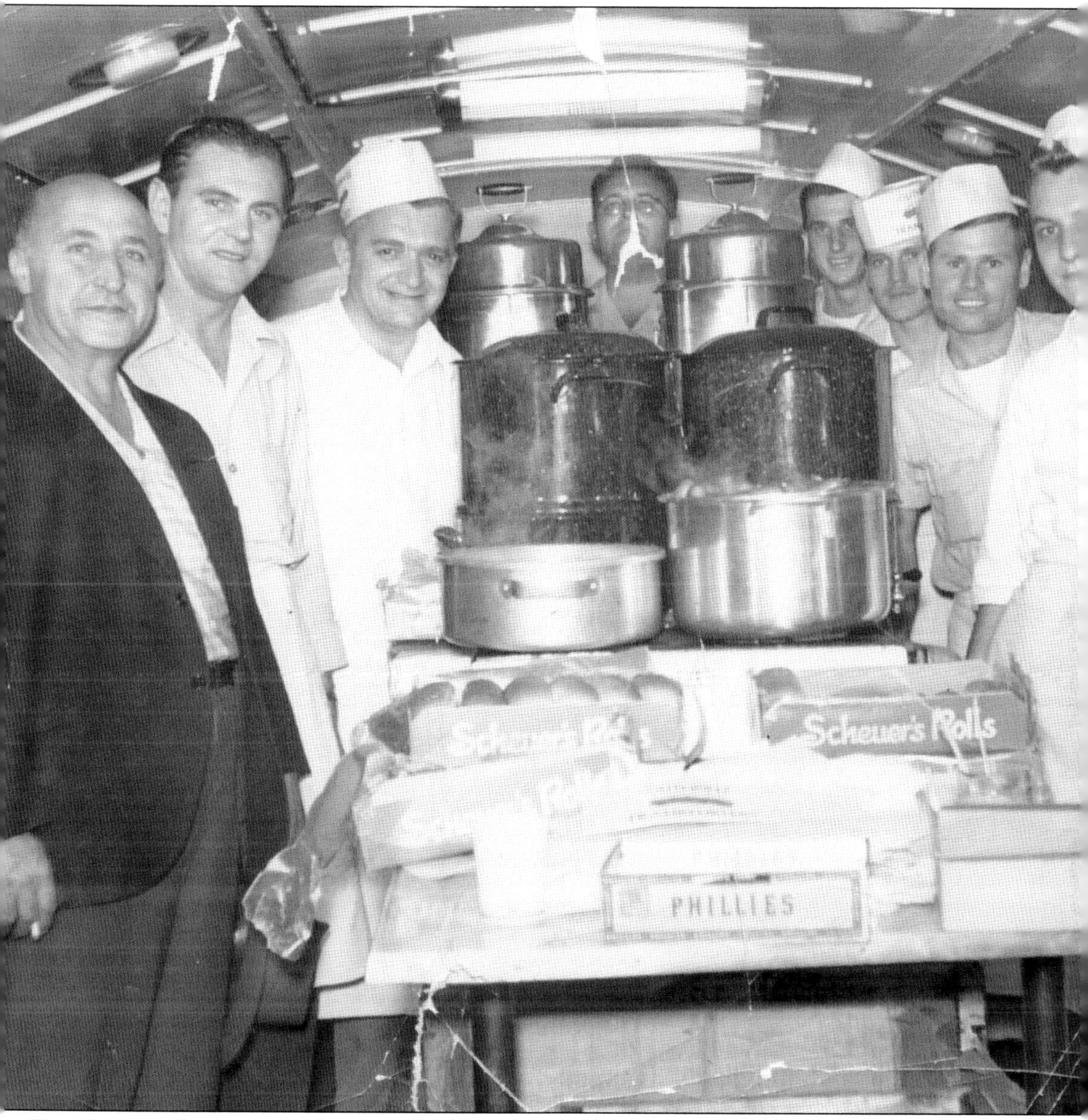

THE CENTRAL LUNCHROOM. Louis Malka (third from left) and Hensie Ott (first on the left) were co-owners of The Central Lunchroom, located on Union Street next door to the Thomas Theatre Hensie Ott was the son of Casper Ott, the first president of the Taylor No. 1 Hose Company. (Courtesy of Shawn Murphy.)

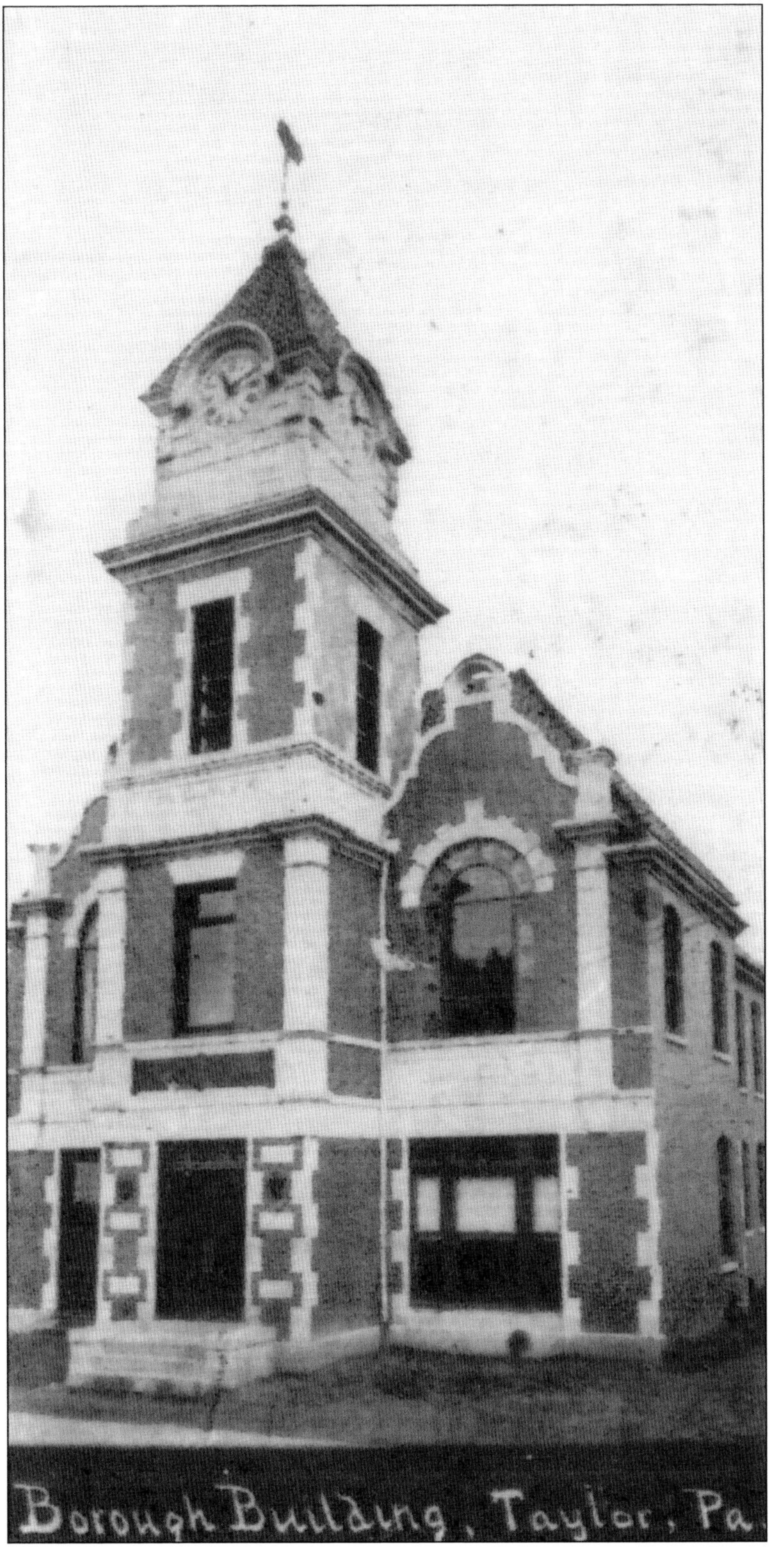

ORIGINAL BOROUGH BUILDING. Constructed in 1909, the building sat among many of the company houses that lined Union Street. It housed the police station, library, mayor's office, and public meeting rooms. The beautiful architectural design was admired by all; many of Taylor children relied on the huge clock located in the steeple to remind them of their curfew. The building was destroyed by fire in 1973, and many valuable and important records were lost, including a major part of Taylor's history. What was left of the burned-out structure was torn down, and a new building was built. Taylor's current borough building resides on the same site. (Courtesy of Nancy and Bob Thomas.)

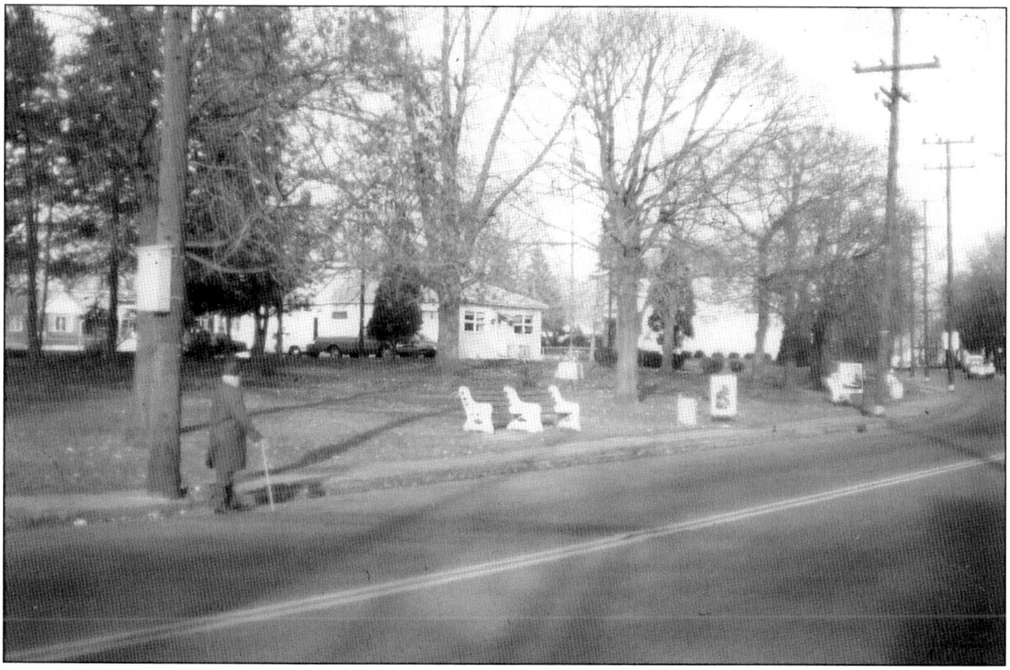

The Park. Erected in 1919, the blue building was the field house where people would compete in table tennis tournaments. The flagpole in front of the building was to honor the veterans of World War I. After the borough building was destroyed by fire, the police station resided here for several years. Below is currently the site of the Taylor Community Center, home to many different organizations and activities. Take note, the flagpole to honor the veterans still stands proudly outside its doors. (Courtesy of Shawn Murphy.)

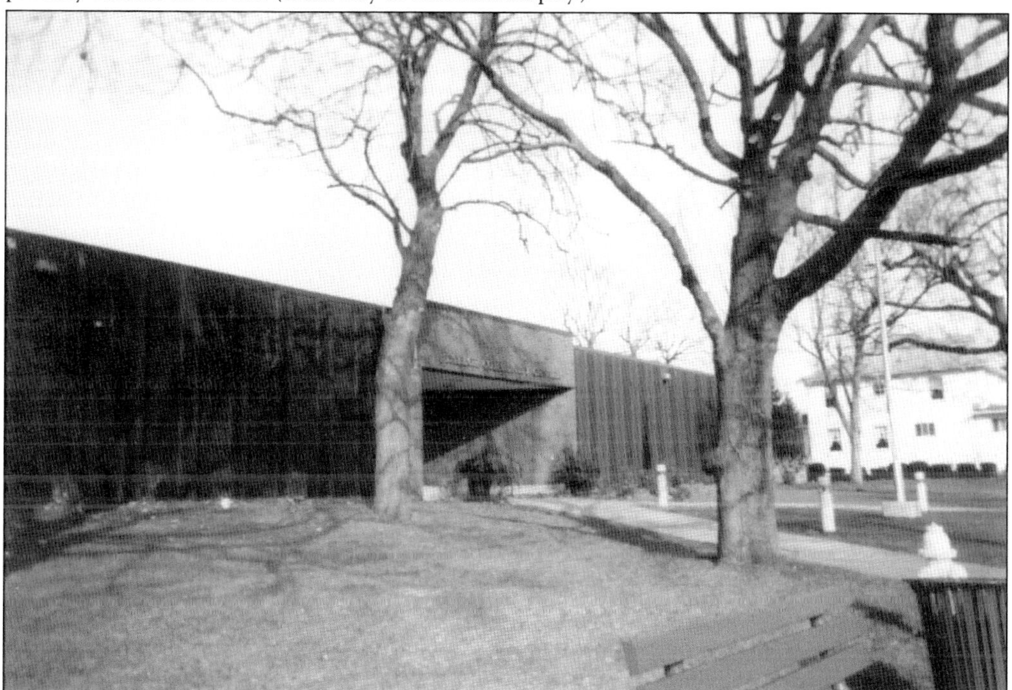

Members of the Historical Society of the Taylor High School

EXECUTIVE COMMITTEE

Veronica Florek
Wilfred Anderson
Wm. Francis
Gertrude Dunlap
Harry Armstrong

Mary Connolly
Anna Florek
Wm. Francis
Aaron Weissberger
Wilfred Anderson
Emil Tkachuke
Alvin Neiger
Veronica Florek
Ralph Winkler
Mabel Edwards
Girard Summerhill
Roy Powell
Steven Ritsko
Ruth Coombs
Gertrude Dunlap
Ben Huggler
Andrew Rickwalder

Thomas Corcoran
Walter Ilchuk
Evyleen Frutiger
Ruth Williams
Dorothy Schield
Harry Armstrong
William Gould
William Powell
George Kutney
Gertrude Strein
Joseph Llewellyn Jr.
George Maline
John Kapral
Ann Edwards
Hannah Fraley
Walter Lanyon
Edward Moyes

SOCIETY SPONSOR - MELVILLE DAVIS

Contributors to the Parley Hughes Memorial Fund. (One Dollar and Over)

Junior O. U. A. M.	$100.00
American Legion (Poppy Sale)	97.49
Public Schools (Tags)	37.26
Polish Falcons	50.00
D. A. R.	10.00
Masons	10.00
Eastern Star	10.00
Woodlawn Farm Dairy	10.00
Daughters of America	5.00
David W. Phillips	5.00
Mildred Davis	5.00
Frank Hildebrand	5.00
J. A. Powell	5.00
Dr. D. E. Jones	5.00
W. G. Watkins	5.00
E. G. Watkins	5.00
David F. Davis	5.00
Martha Powell	3.00
Walter Balcerewicz	2.50
Benjamin J. Davis	2.00
Dr. Collins	2.00
George J. Powell	2.00
W. S. Robinson	2.00
W. J. Powell	2.00
Burschel Dairy Co.	2.00
Veronica Florek	$ 1.00
Anna Florek	1.00
Mary Connolly	1.00
John Zahornacky	1.00
Oliver Thomas	1.00
Gertrude Dunlap	1.00
Hilda Becker	1.00
Jennie Nicholls	1.00
Dr. C. H. Nicholls	1.00
Kate Olmstead	1.00
Anna Phillips	1.00
Hilda Thomas	1.00
Benjamin Jenkins	1.00
Rachel Thomas	1.00
Morgan Gwyn	1.00
Winfield Masters	1.00
Otto Gersteneker	1.00
Merwyn Howells	1.00
Maude Evans	1.00
Mrs. D. M. Davis	1.00
Fernell Bichler	1.00
Joseph Llewellyn	1.00
Fred Wilson	1.00
Mrs. Charles Pfaff	1.00
Mrs. William James	1.00

TAYLOR HISTORICAL SOCIETY. In the 1920s, the historical society was part of the high school. It was responsible for erecting the new tombstone for Revolutionary War veteran Parley Hughes in the Taylor Memorial Cemetery. The list seen here includes names of all the members. The current Taylor Historical Society was formed on January 9, 2007. The meetings are held at the Taylor Community Library and a variety of historical programs are presented monthly. Christine Schaefer is the president, and Jeanie Sluck is the vice president. (Courtesy of Taylor Community Library.)

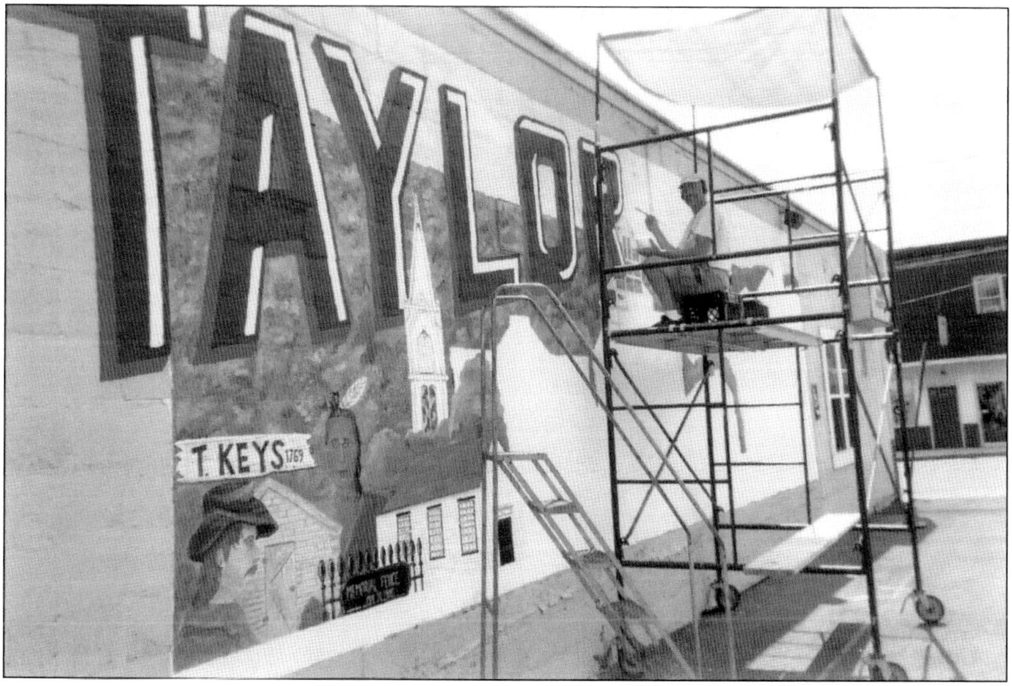

TAYLOR MURAL. Local artist and teacher Mark Ciocca is shown here preserving Taylor's history with every stroke of his brush. The mural incorporates Taylor's past with its future. Images of its coal-mining heritage are blended with current images, such as the library and community center. The completion of the mural took one month and was dedicated to the community in the summer of 2007. (Above, courtesy of Shawn Murphy and Taylor Community Library; below, courtesy author's collection.)

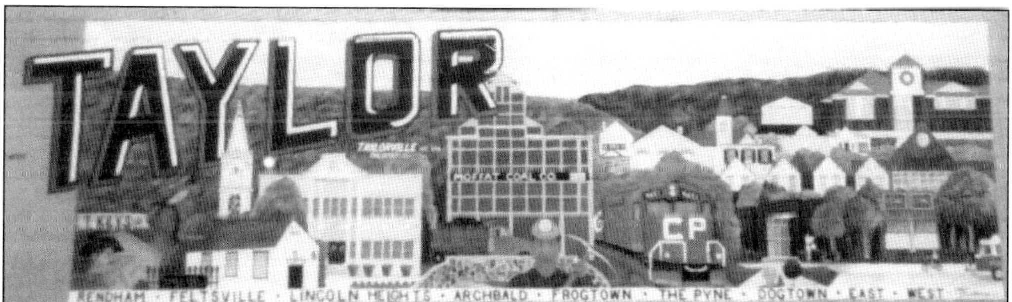

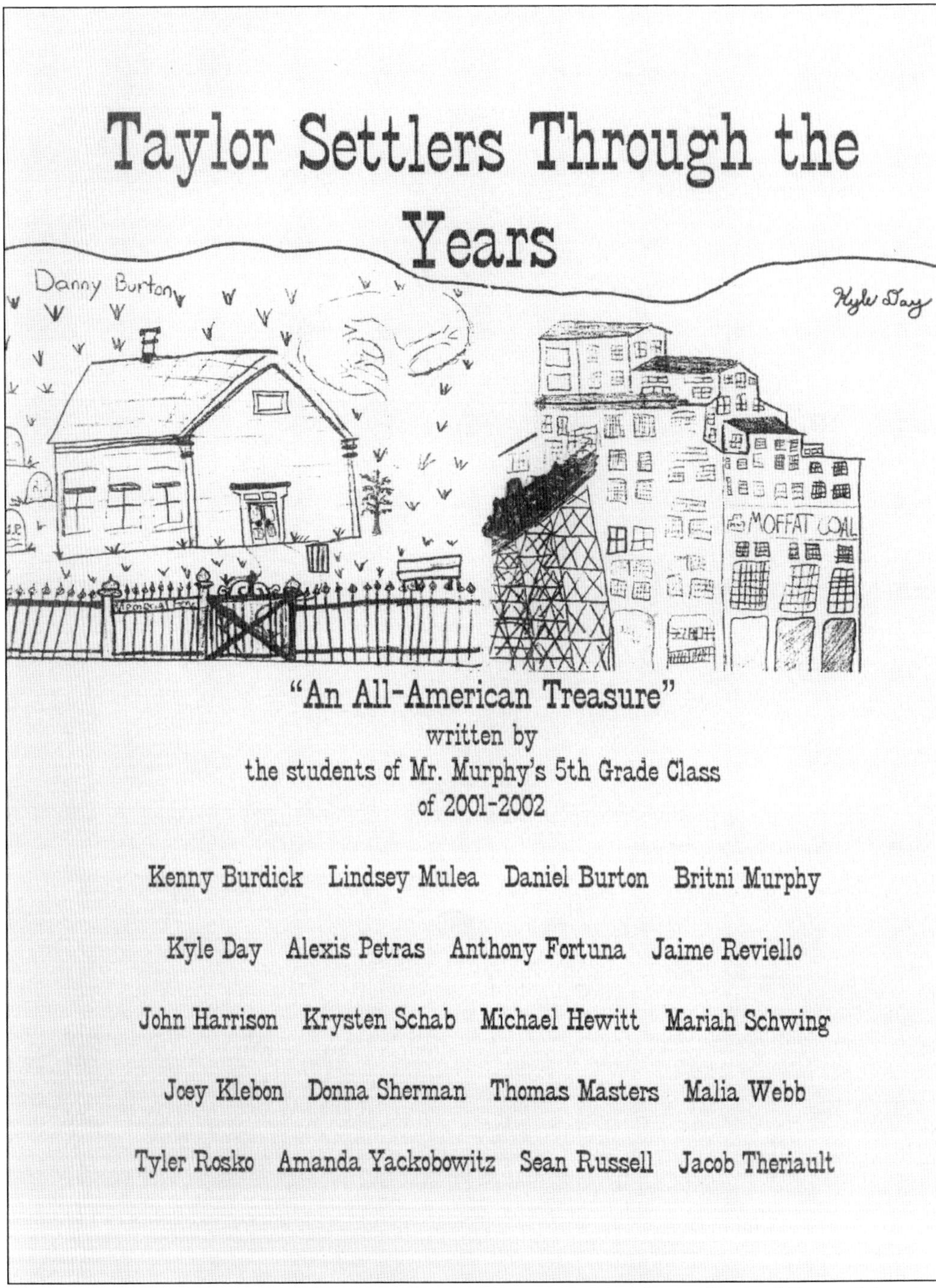

Taylor Settlers Through the Years

"An All-American Treasure"

written by
the students of Mr. Murphy's 5th Grade Class
of 2001-2002

Kenny Burdick Lindsey Mulea Daniel Burton Britni Murphy

Kyle Day Alexis Petras Anthony Fortuna Jaime Reviello

John Harrison Krysten Schab Michael Hewitt Mariah Schwing

Joey Klebon Donna Sherman Thomas Masters Malia Webb

Tyler Rosko Amanda Yackobowitz Sean Russell Jacob Theriault

TAYLOR SETTLERS THROUGH THE YEARS. This is a play written by the students of Shawn Murphy's fifth-grade class of 2001–2002. It takes residents on a very enjoyable journey of Taylor's history in four acts: 1771–1779, Native American Massacre; 1780s, Farming Years; 1800s, Anthracite Coal is Discovered; and 1902, Taylor's Patch Section. Each May the play is performed by the students of Murphy's fourth-grade class at the historical First Presbyterian Church. The event is a community favorite. (Courtesy of Shawn Murphy.)

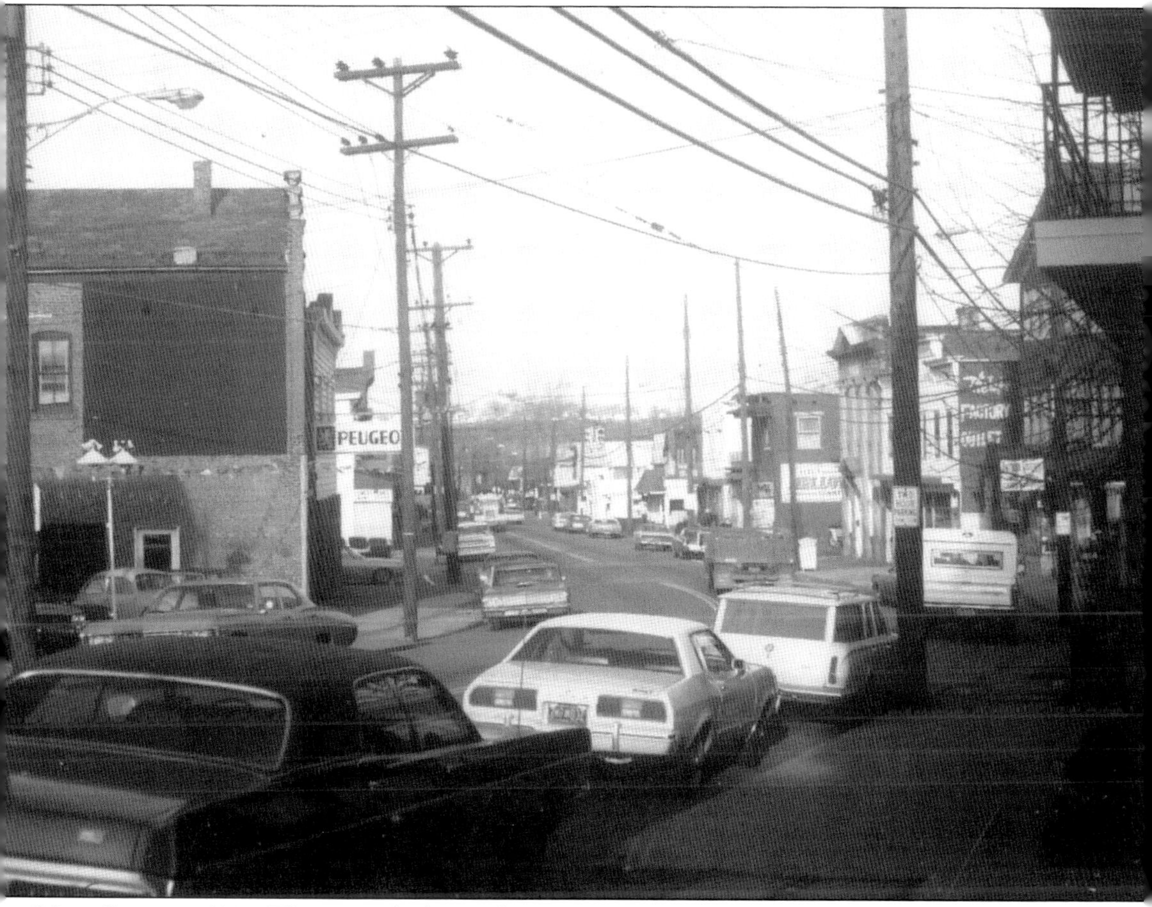

Main Street, 1970s. This image looks north on Main Street at the intersection of Union Street as seen in the 1970s. This was taken from the same angle as the 1911 photograph. (Courtesy of Shawn Murphy.)

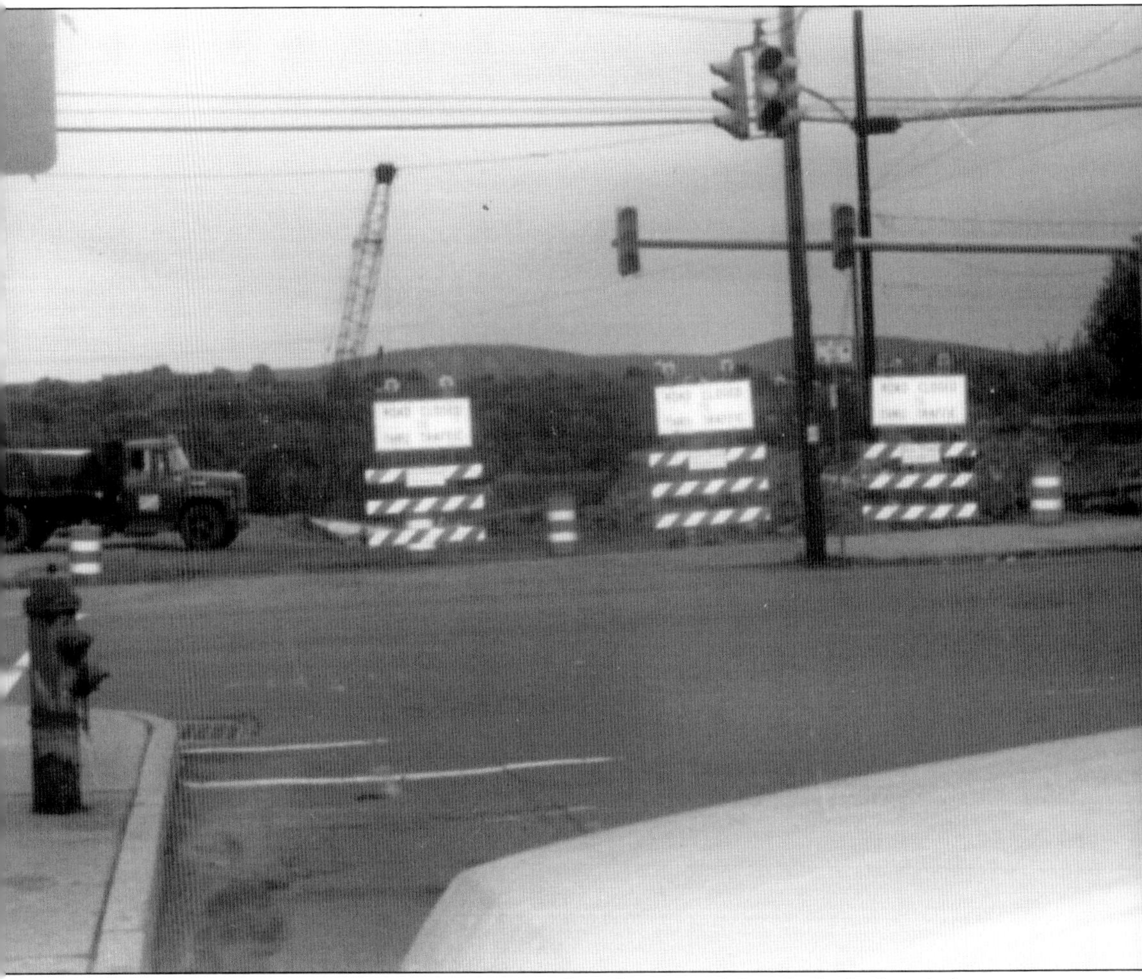

Construction of the Veteran's Bridge. Though proposed decades beforehand, the construction of the Veteran's Bridge did not begin until the early 1990s. Located at the intersection of Main and Union Streets, the bridge links Taylor to the Minooka section of Scranton. (Courtesy of Barbara Hordich Togher.)

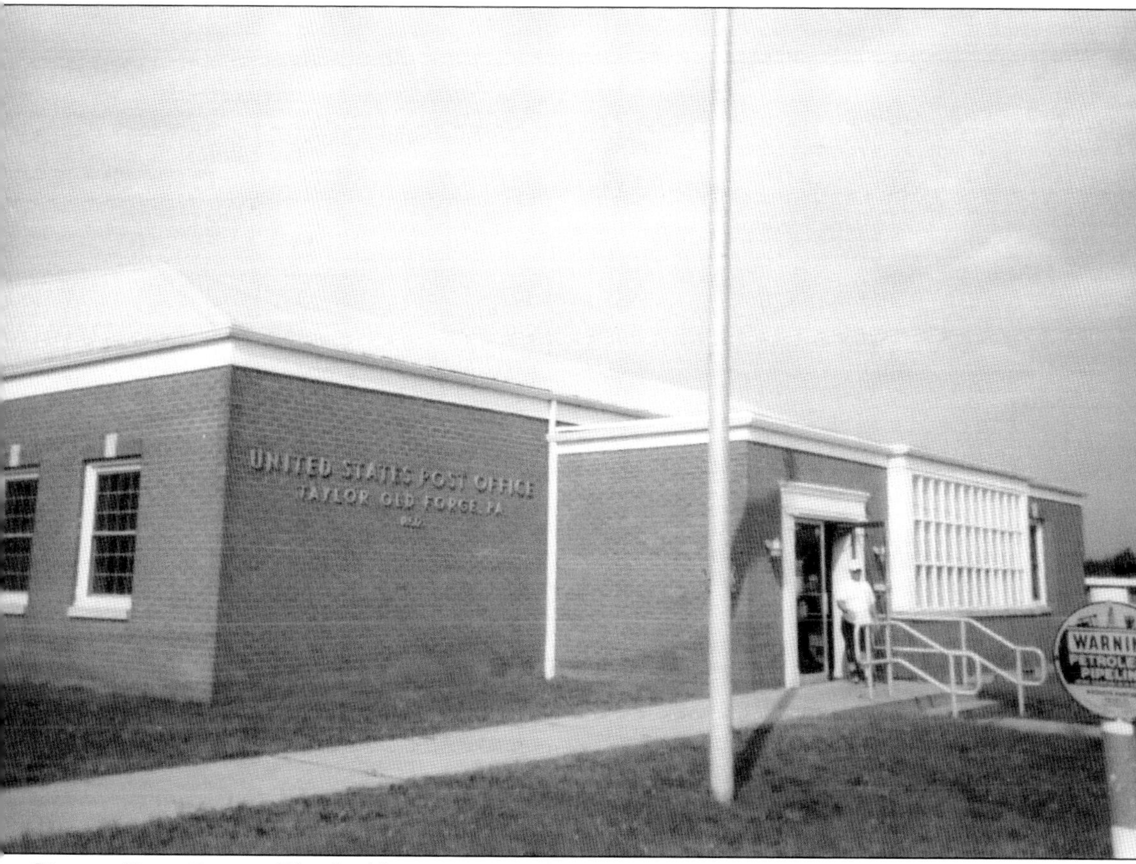

TAYLOR POST OFFICE. This building was opened in 1961 and provides services for both Taylor and Old Forge communities. The first postmaster was J. Edward Day. An article dated 1913 states that Taylor will be getting mail service for the first time. Before that year, people would have to walk to the post office to pick up their mail. The U.S. Post Office was responsible for abbreviating Taylorville to Taylor. (Author's collection.)

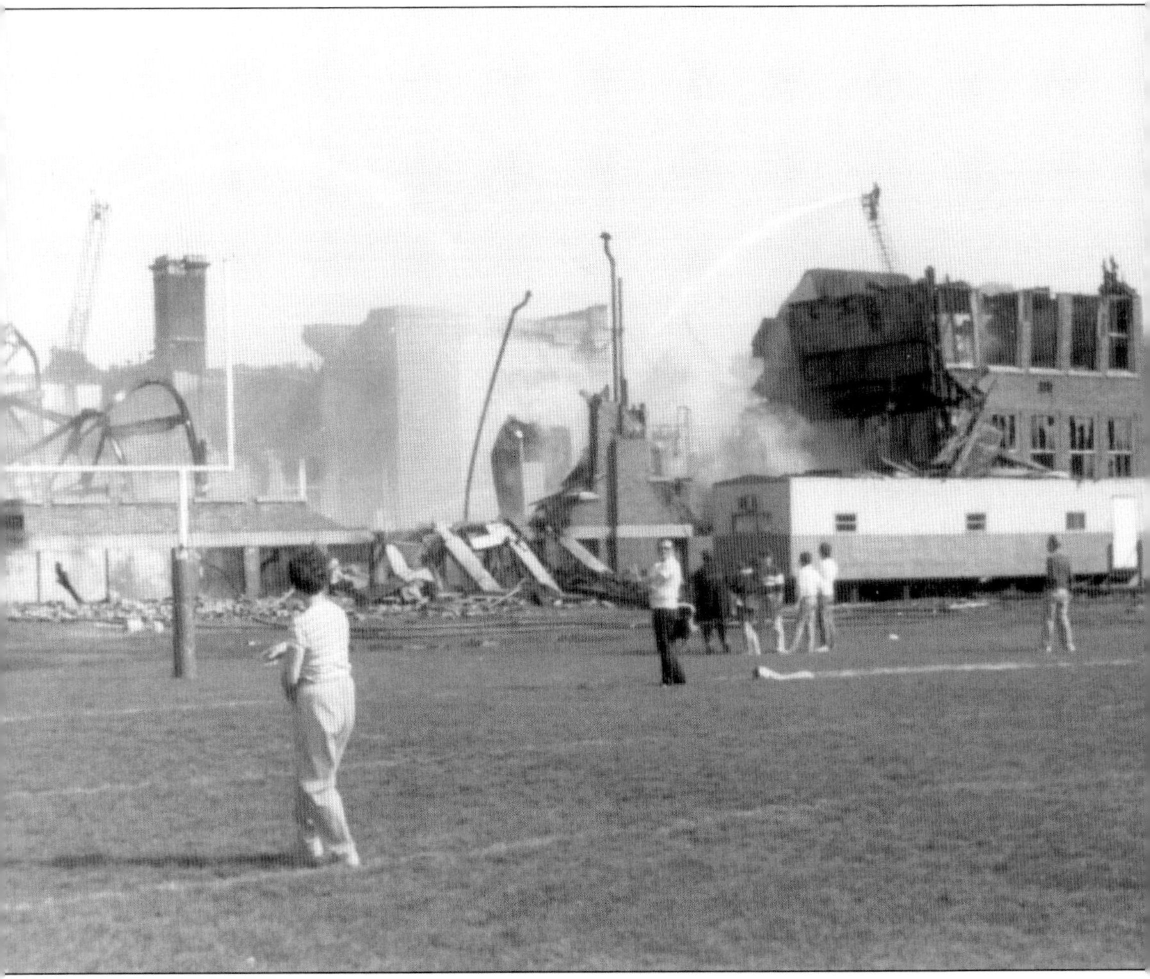

Burning of Taylor High School. The old Taylor Elementary School, which served the community for generations first as a high school and later as an elementary school, was destroyed by fire in 1989. The building was closed at the time. Little could be done to save the school, as the fire was so intense; cars on Union Street blocks away were covered in ash. In the early 1980s, the school was transformed into a Hollywood set for the taping of the movie *That Championship Season* written by the late Jason Miller, who chose the school for the film because it maintained the characteristics of a high school from the 1940s and 1950s. (Courtesy of Barbara Hordich Togher.)

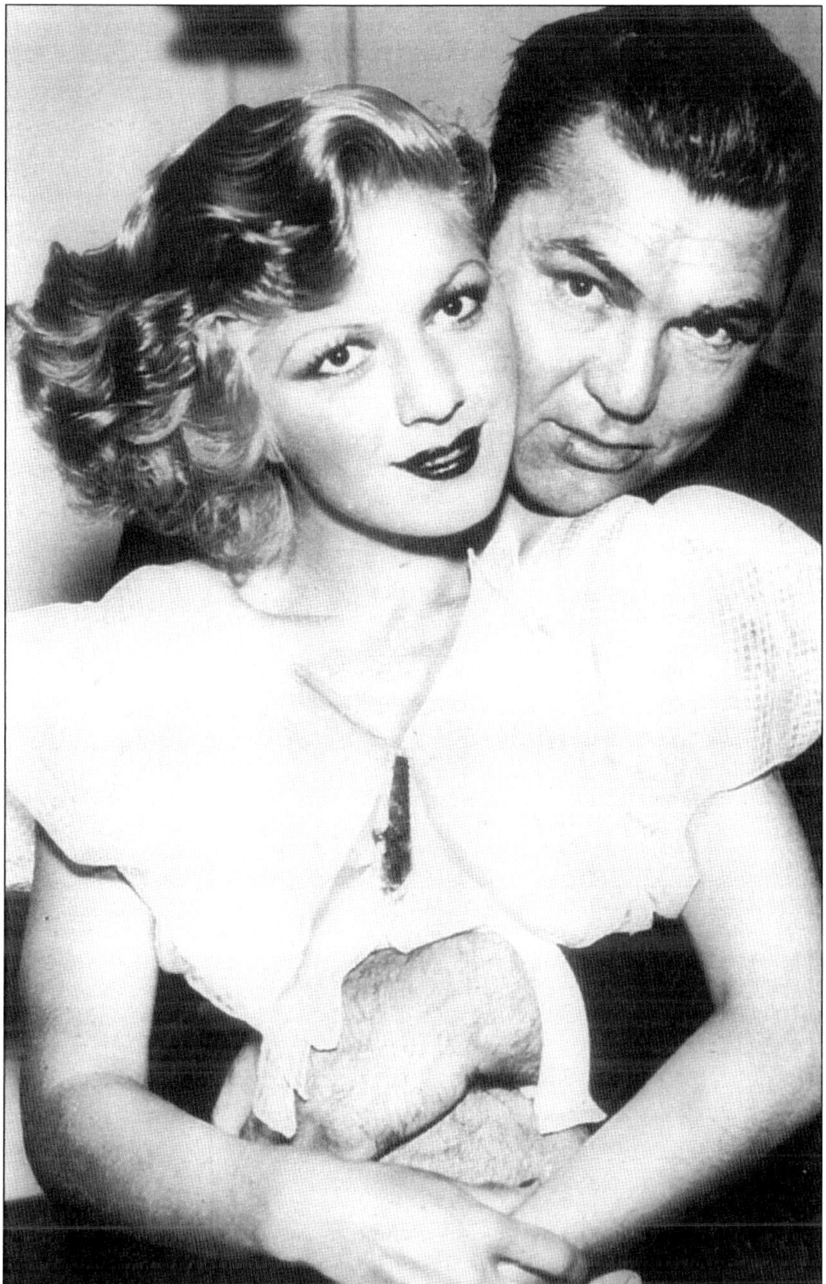

The William Sisters. The three sisters, Leona, Dorothy, and Hannah, were all born in Taylor between 1905 and 1911. Leona, the eldest, was not a performer, unlike her two siblings. Dorothy and Hannah entered show business at a young age. They performed in Vaudeville stage shows in New York and Chicago and sang with the Paul Whiteman Orchestra at the old Crystal Palace at Rocky Glen in the early 1920s. Eventually the sister act broke up. Hannah danced at a New York City nightclub where she popularized the tune "Hard-Hearted Hannah, the Vamp from Savannah." In the 1930s, Hannah wed Jack Dempsey, the boxer (pictured); they would later divorce. Hannah passed away in 1973 at the age of 62. (Courtesy of Cecile B. Champagne.)

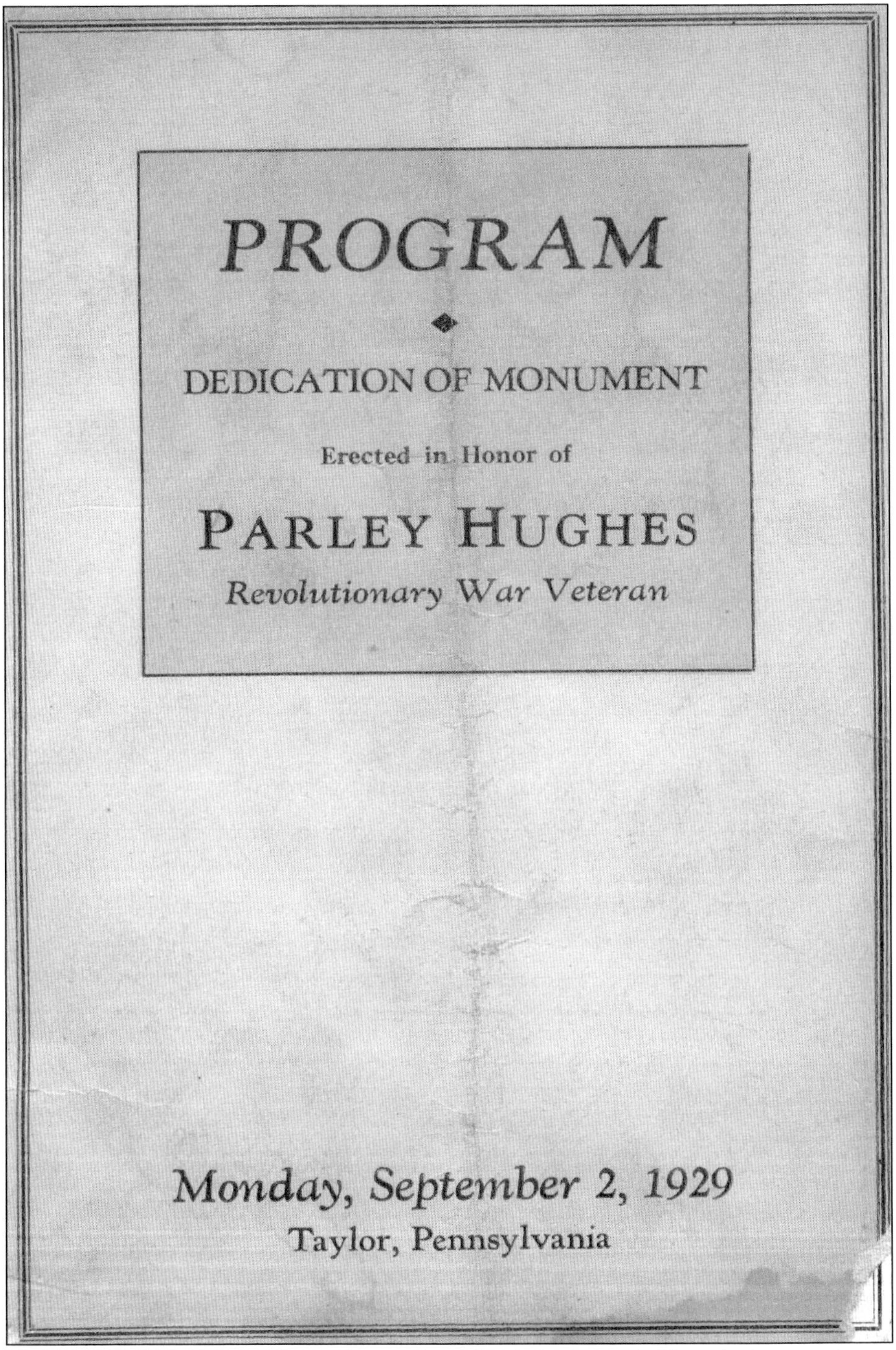

PROGRAM

DEDICATION OF MONUMENT

Erected in Honor of

PARLEY HUGHES

Revolutionary War Veteran

Monday, September 2, 1929

Taylor, Pennsylvania

PARLEY HUGHES DEDICATION. The program is from the dedication, which took place on September 22, 1929, in honor of the new monument erected for the Revolutionary War veteran Parley Hughes. The Taylor High School Historical Society of that year was responsible for gathering the funds for the new stone. Parley's original stone slab is still located in the rear of the Taylor Memorial Cemetery. (Courtesy of Shawn Murphy.)

PROGRAM

Opening Song .... *America*

Introductory Address .... *D. F. Davis*
Town Historian

Historical Sketch .... *Thomas Murphy*

Musical Number

Presentation of Stone .... *Veronica Florek*

Acceptance .... *John D. Atherton*

Taps .... *Edwin Harris*

Musical Number

Address .... *Judge George W. Maxey*

Closing Song .... *Star Spangled Banner*

GUESTS

JUDGE GEORGE W. MAXEY	
THOMAS MURPHY	Lackawanna County Historian
HAROLD HEFFER	American Legion
THOMAS LISOWSKI	Polish Falcons
MRS. EVAN J. DAVIS	D. of A.
OLIVETTE HOSKINS	Eastern Star
ALBERT J. HODGE	Jr. O. U. A. M.
MRS. J. M. CAIRNS	D. A. R.
ALBERT SULZER	Masons
BURTON WATKINS	Masons
W. J. POWELL	Principal of Taylor High School
WILLIAM G. WATKINS	County Controller
WILLIAM REPP	Cemetery Board
T. J. STEWART	Cemetery Board
HON. ALBERT DAVIS	State Senator 22nd District
S. FLETCHER WEYBURN	Secretary Lackawanna County Historical Society
EDWIN HARRIS	Clerk of the Courts
SAMUEL HARLOS	Cemetery Board
JOHN D. ATHERTON	Cemetery Board
M. J. LLOYD	Retired Principal of Taylor High School
DR. D. E. JONES	Supervisor of Music Taylor Schools
J. A. POWELL	Burgess of Taylor

List of Guests. The actual dedication to Parley Hughes took place in the cemetery, where many of the townsfolk gathered as spectators. Some of the prominent guests in attendance were Taylor historian D. F. Davis, who presented the introductory address; Thomas Murphy, historian and author of the *History of Lackawanna County*; Thomas Lisowski, Polish Falcons; John D. Atherton; and J. A. Powell, burgess of Taylor. (Courtesy of Shawn Murphy.)

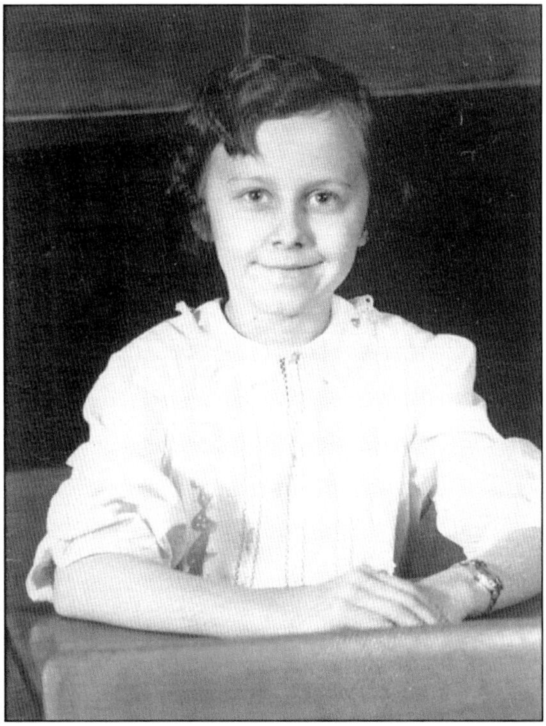

GERALDINE MATSKO GRADE SCHOOL. This *c.* 1950 grade school photograph shows Geraldine Matsko, the daughter of Anna Matician Matsko and Michael Matsko. She attended Washington School on Grove Street. (Courtesy of Geraldine Matsko Kashuba.)

NATURALIZATION PAPERS. Like many immigrants, Anna Demjan Matician became a naturalized citizen of the United States. Her naturalization paper, shown here, is dated November 24, 1925. (Courtesy of Mary Ann Matsko.)

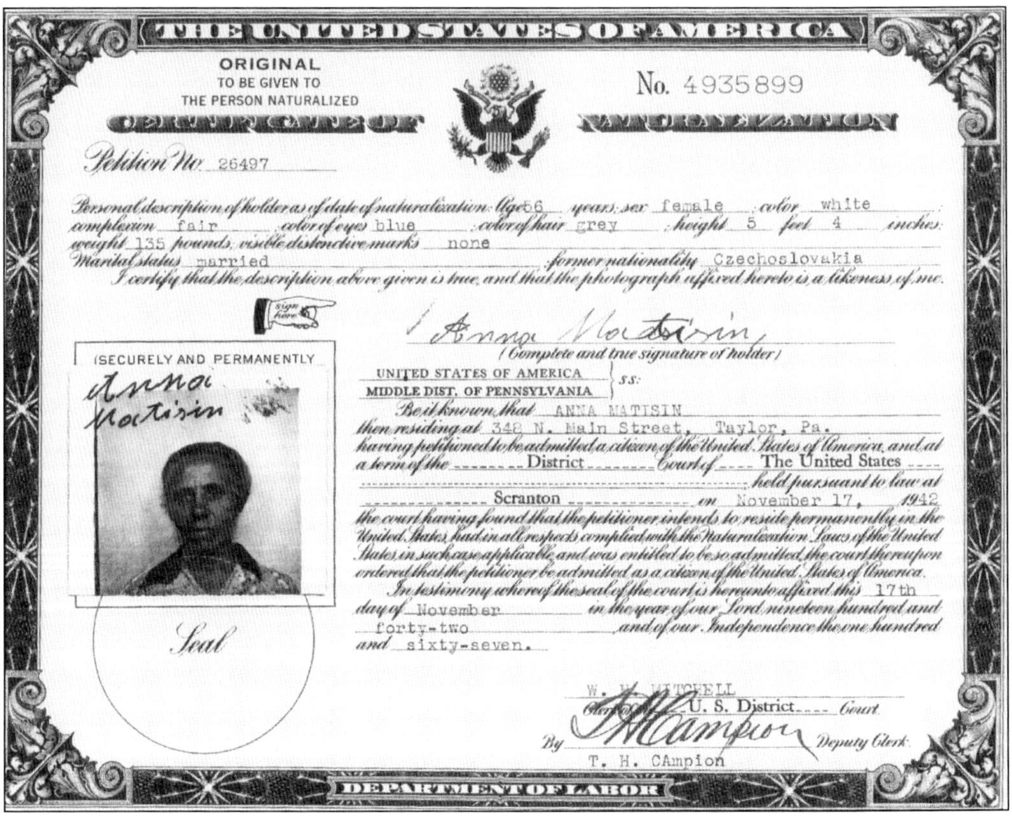

THE UNITED STATES OF AMERICA

ORIGINAL
TO BE GIVEN TO
THE PERSON NATURALIZED

No. 4935899

CERTIFICATE OF NATURALIZATION

Petition No. 26497

Personal description of holder as of date of naturalization: Age 56 years; sex female color white complexion fair color of eyes blue color of hair grey height 5 feet 4 inches; weight 135 pounds; visible distinctive marks none
Marital status married former nationality Czechoslovakia
I certify that the description above given is true, and that the photograph affixed hereto is a likeness of me.

Anna Matisin
(Complete and true signature of holder)

(SECURELY AND PERMANENTLY

Anna Matisin

UNITED STATES OF AMERICA
MIDDLE DIST. OF PENNSYLVANIA } SS:

Be it known, that ANNA MATISIN then residing at 348 N. Main Street, Taylor, Pa. having petitioned to be admitted a citizen of the United States of America, and at a term of the District Court of The United States held pursuant to law at Scranton on November 17, 1942 the court having found that the petitioner intends to reside permanently in the United States, had in all respects complied with the Naturalization Laws of the United States in such case applicable, and was entitled to be so admitted, the court thereupon ordered that the petitioner be admitted as a citizen of the United States of America.

In testimony whereof the seal of the court is hereunto affixed this 17th day of November in the year of our Lord nineteen hundred and forty-two and of our Independence the one hundred and sixty-seven.

Seal

W. W. MITCHELL
Clerk of the U. S. District Court.
By T.H. Campion Deputy Clerk.
T. H. CAmpion

DEPARTMENT OF LABOR

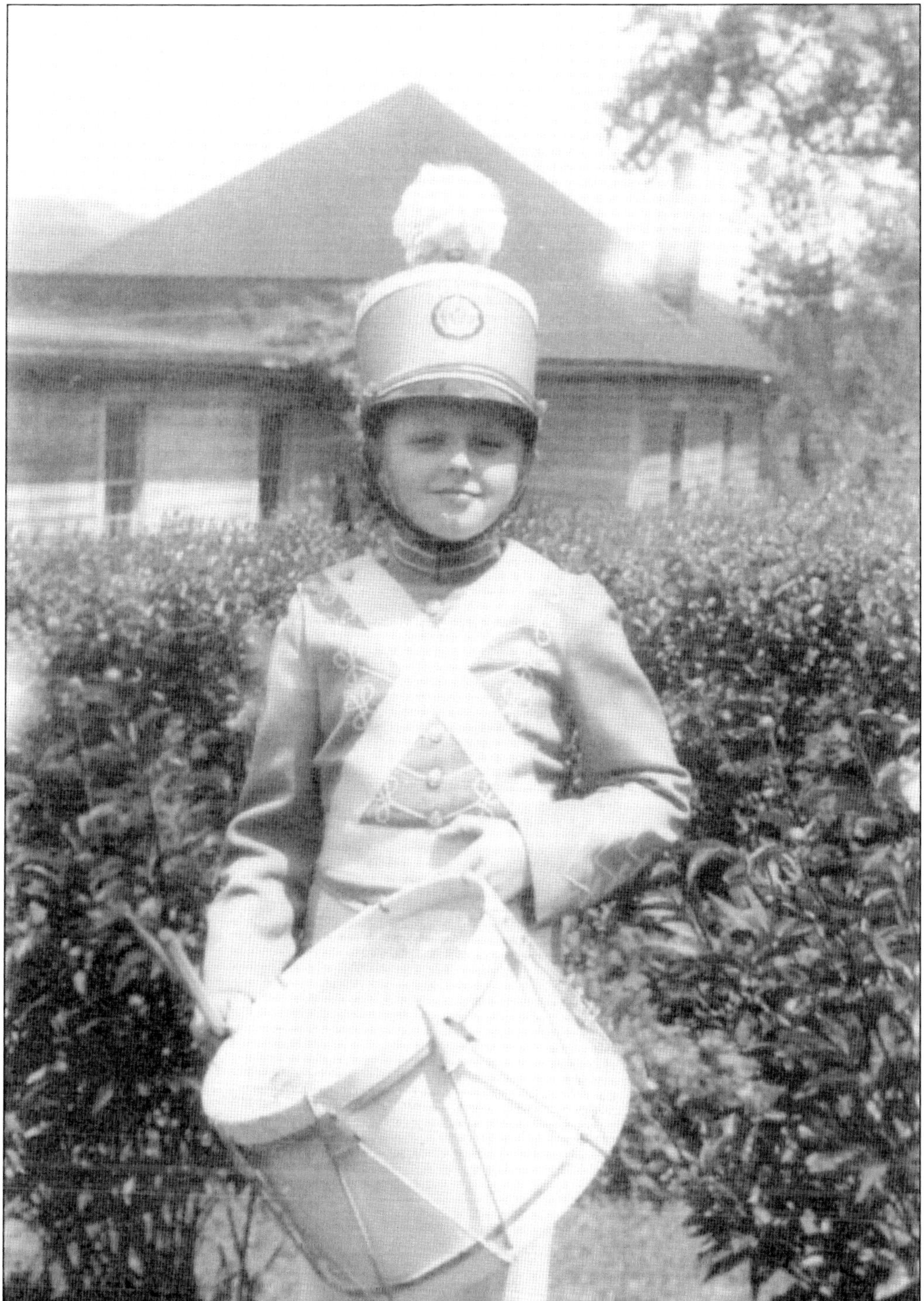

WILLIAM MORGAN. Seen here in his band uniform, William Morgan graduated from Taylor High School in 1952. His great-grandfather, Morgan B. Morgan, was burgess of Taylor as well as the justice of the peace for four terms. (Courtesy of Joyce Morgan.)

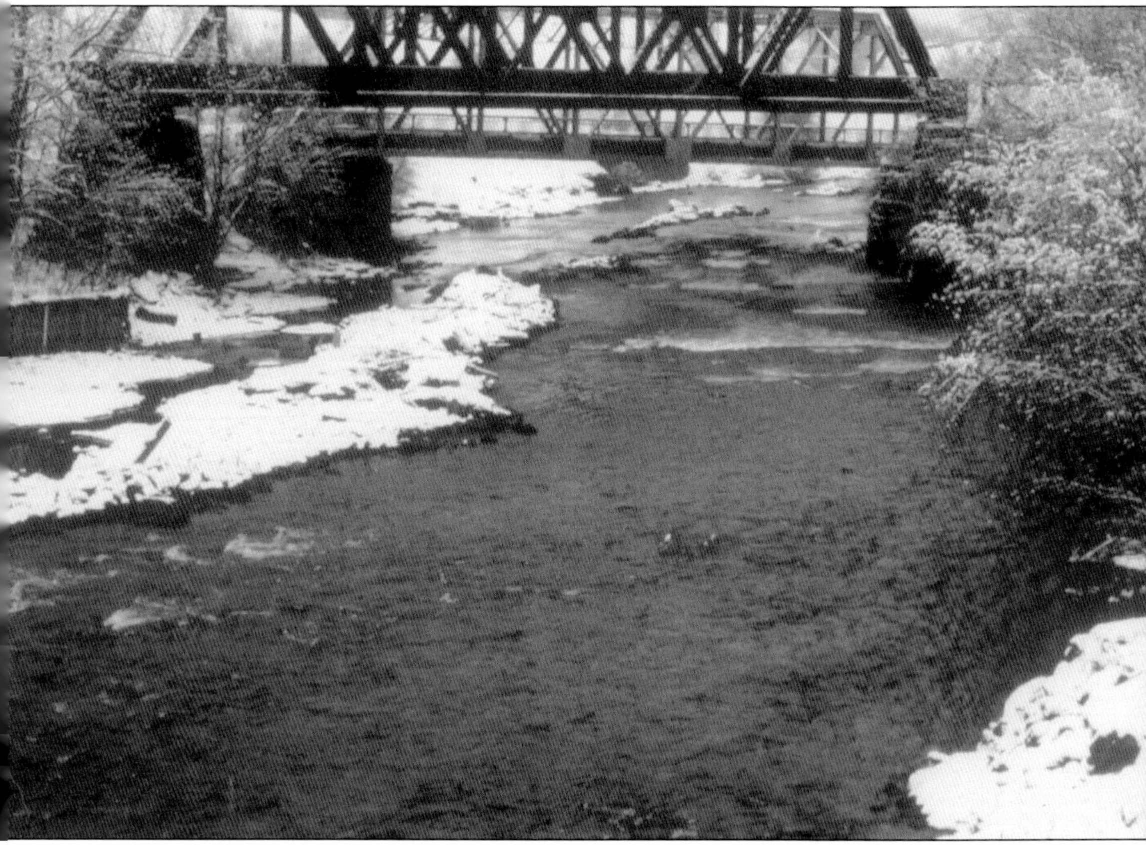

The Black Bridge. The Black Bridge connects Moosic to Taylor and is located behind the Forest Home Cemetery. For generations people have been walking across the bridge. (Courtesy of Shawn Murphy.)

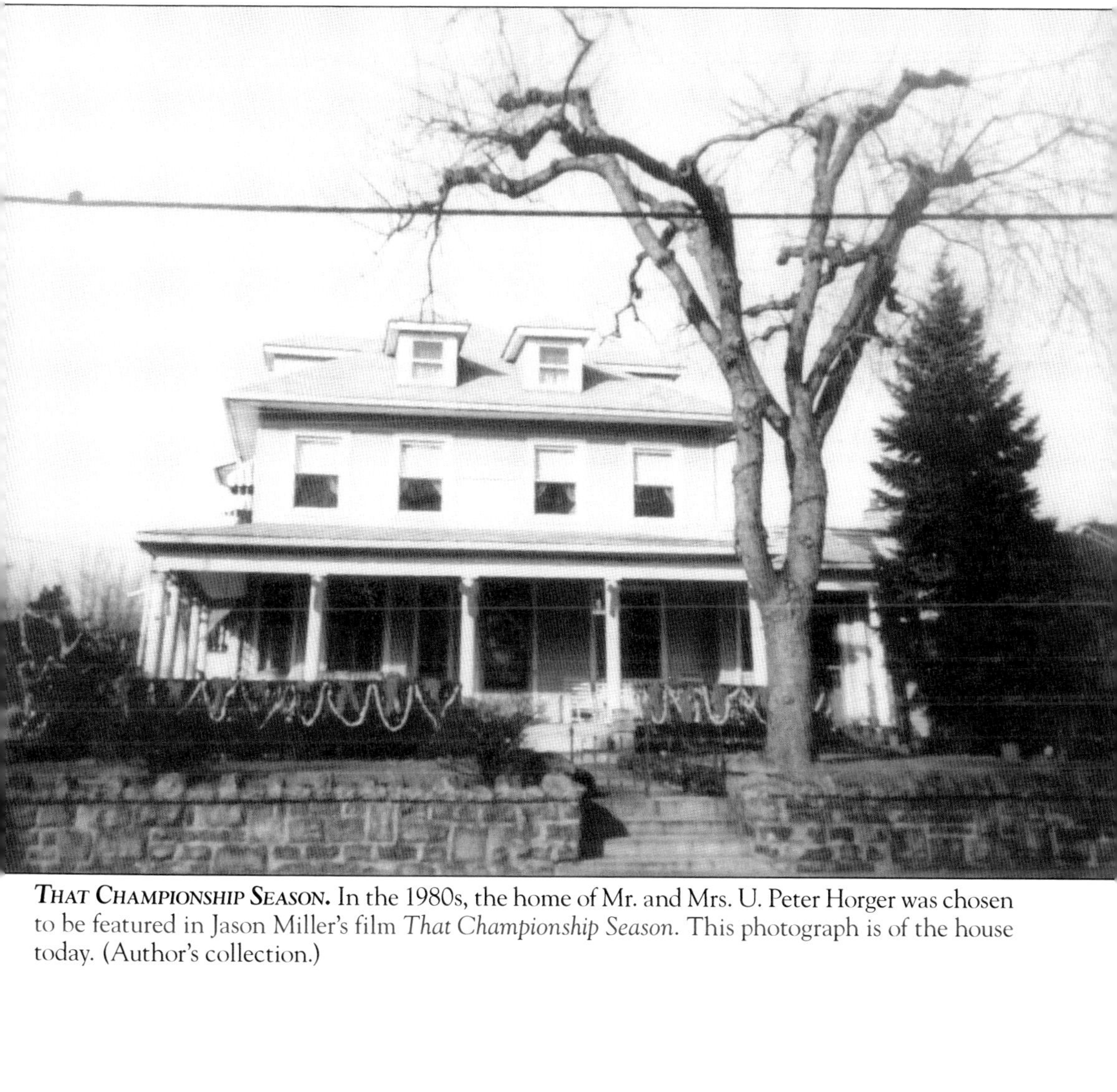

THAT CHAMPIONSHIP SEASON. In the 1980s, the home of Mr. and Mrs. U. Peter Horger was chosen to be featured in Jason Miller's film *That Championship Season*. This photograph is of the house today. (Author's collection.)

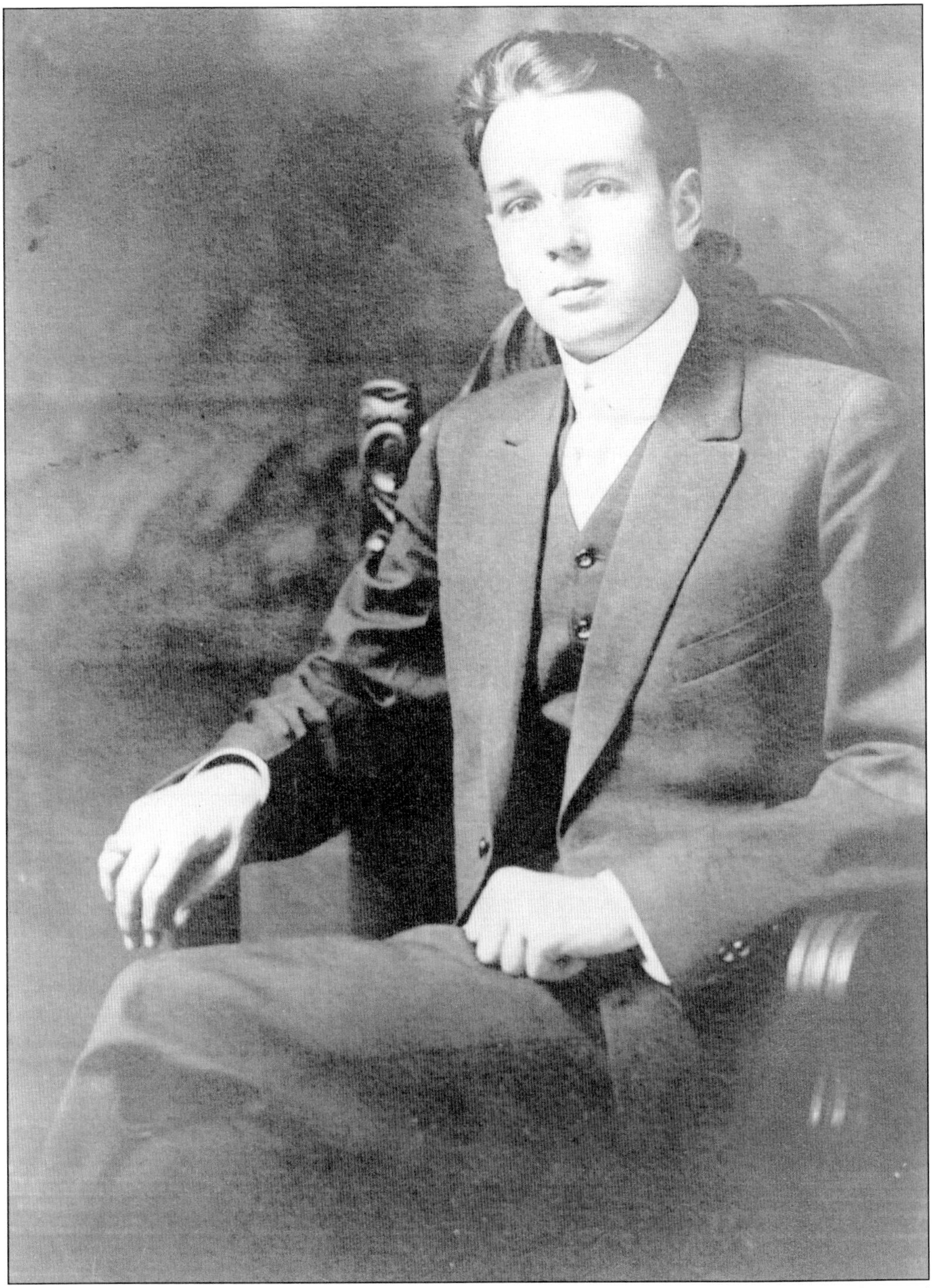

Dr. W. H. Olmstead. For more than 30 years, Dr. Olmstead had a medical practice in Taylor, and he was ranked among the leading physicians and surgeons of Lackawanna County. During World War I, he volunteered for service and was sent to France with the 116th Sanitary Train Medical Corp. He died during the 1918 influenza epidemic and is buried at the American Cemetery in France. This photograph is of him as a young man. (Author's collection.)

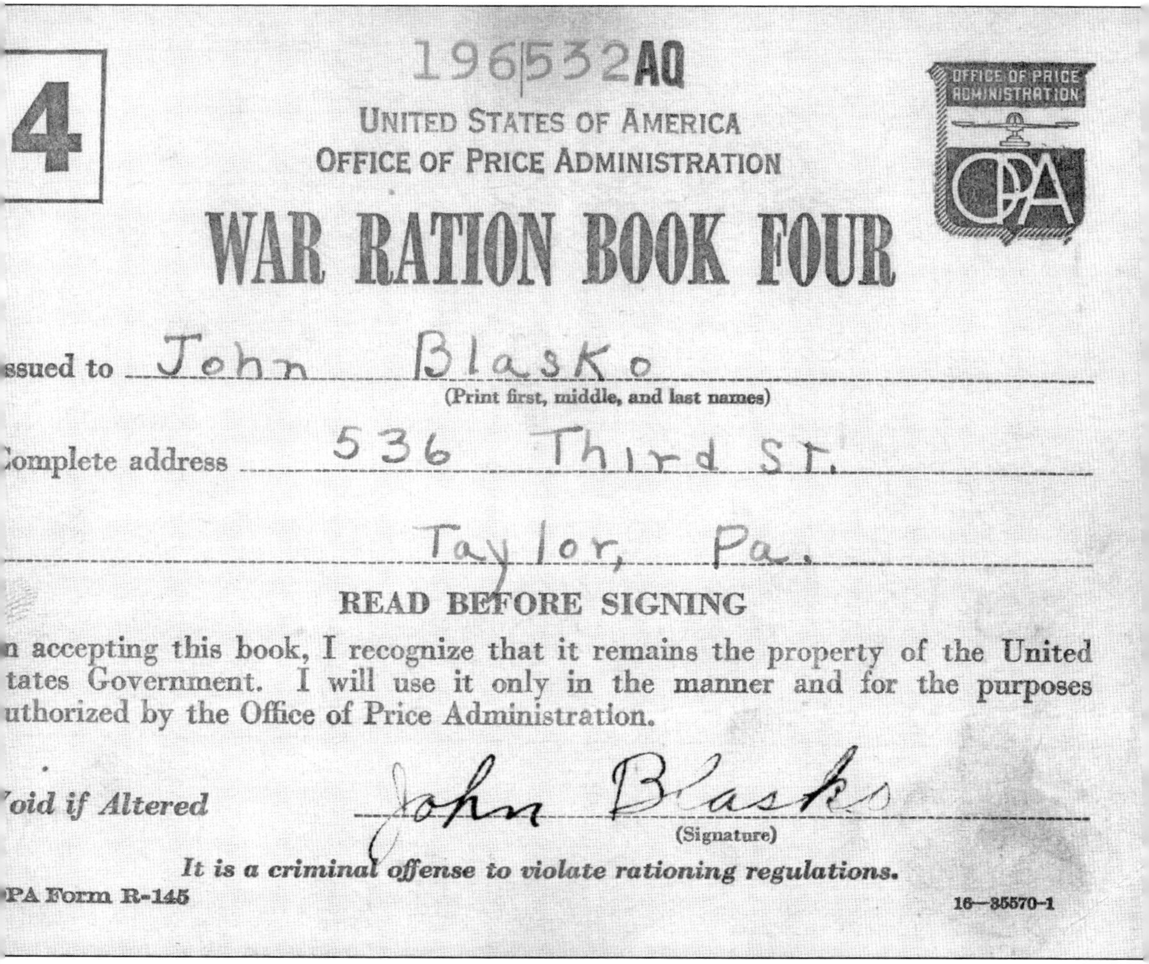
4

196532AQ

UNITED STATES OF AMERICA
OFFICE OF PRICE ADMINISTRATION

OFFICE OF PRICE ADMINISTRATION
OPA

WAR RATION BOOK FOUR

[I]ssued to John Blasko
(Print first, middle, and last names)

[C]omplete address 536 Third St.

Taylor, Pa.

READ BEFORE SIGNING

[I]n accepting this book, I recognize that it remains the property of the United [S]tates Government. I will use it only in the manner and for the purposes [a]uthorized by the Office of Price Administration.

[V]oid if Altered John Blasko
(Signature)

It is a criminal offense to violate rationing regulations.

[O]PA Form R-145 16—35570-1

WAR RATION BOOK. During World War II, nationwide food rationing was instituted in the spring of 1942. War ration books contained stamps and gave precise details of the amounts of certain food people were allowed. This book belonged to John Blasko of 536 Third Street of Taylor. (Courtesy of Dan Zeleniak.)

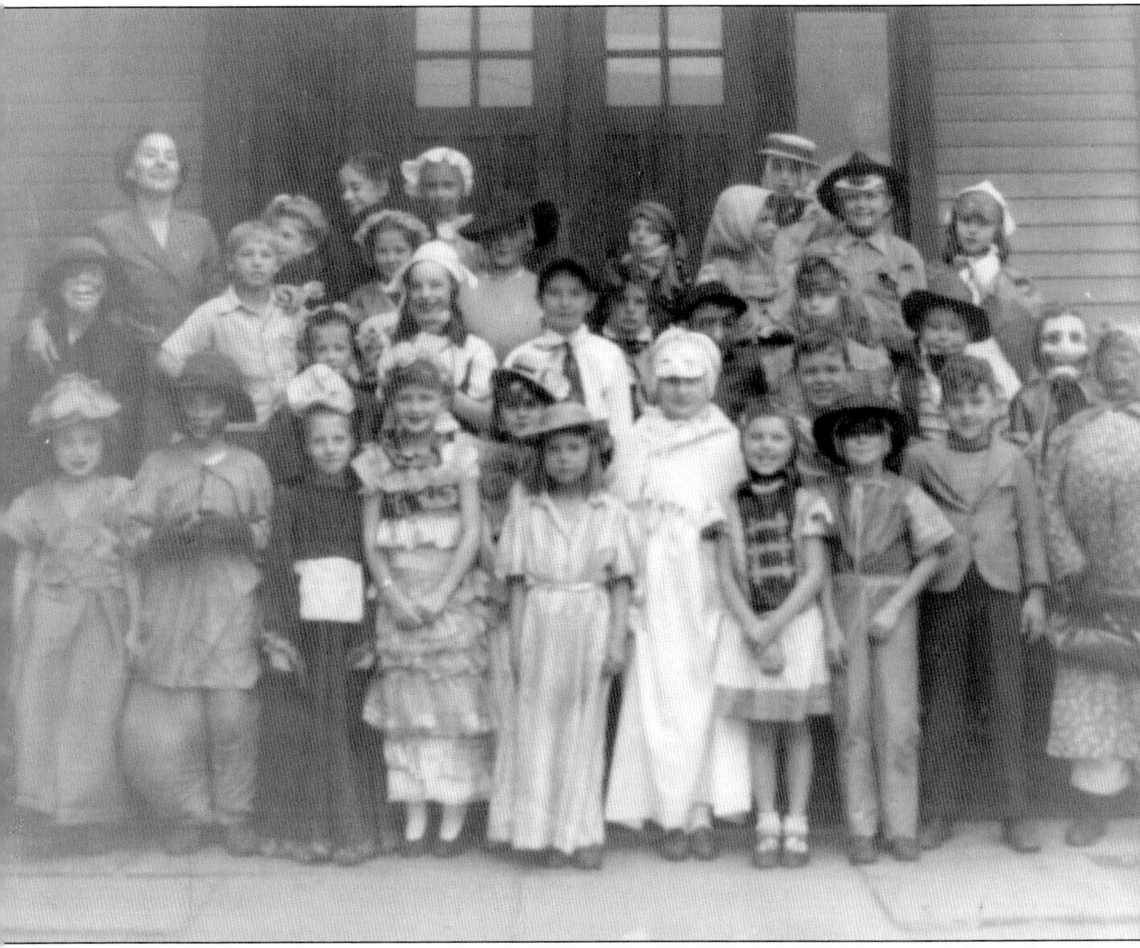

HALLOWEEN 1946. This photograph is of Miss Harris's class at Lincoln School, located in the Lincoln Heights Section of Taylor. The children are posing in their Halloween costumes. (Courtesy of Dan Zeleniak.)

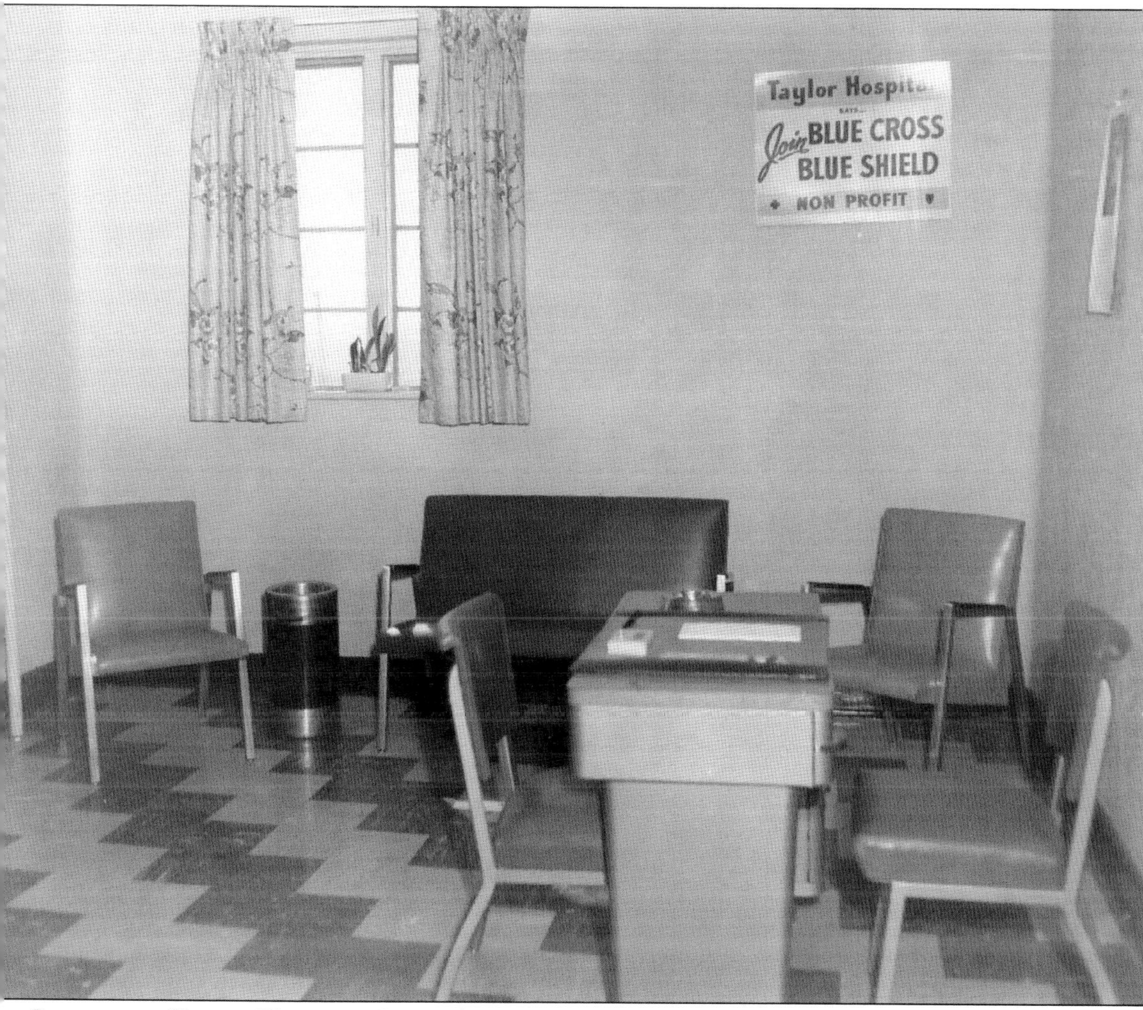

Interior of Taylor Hospital. Pictured is a waiting area of the Taylor Hospital. Note the large ashtray in the seating area and the other one on the desk for people to use while they waited. (Courtesy of Dan Zeleniak.)

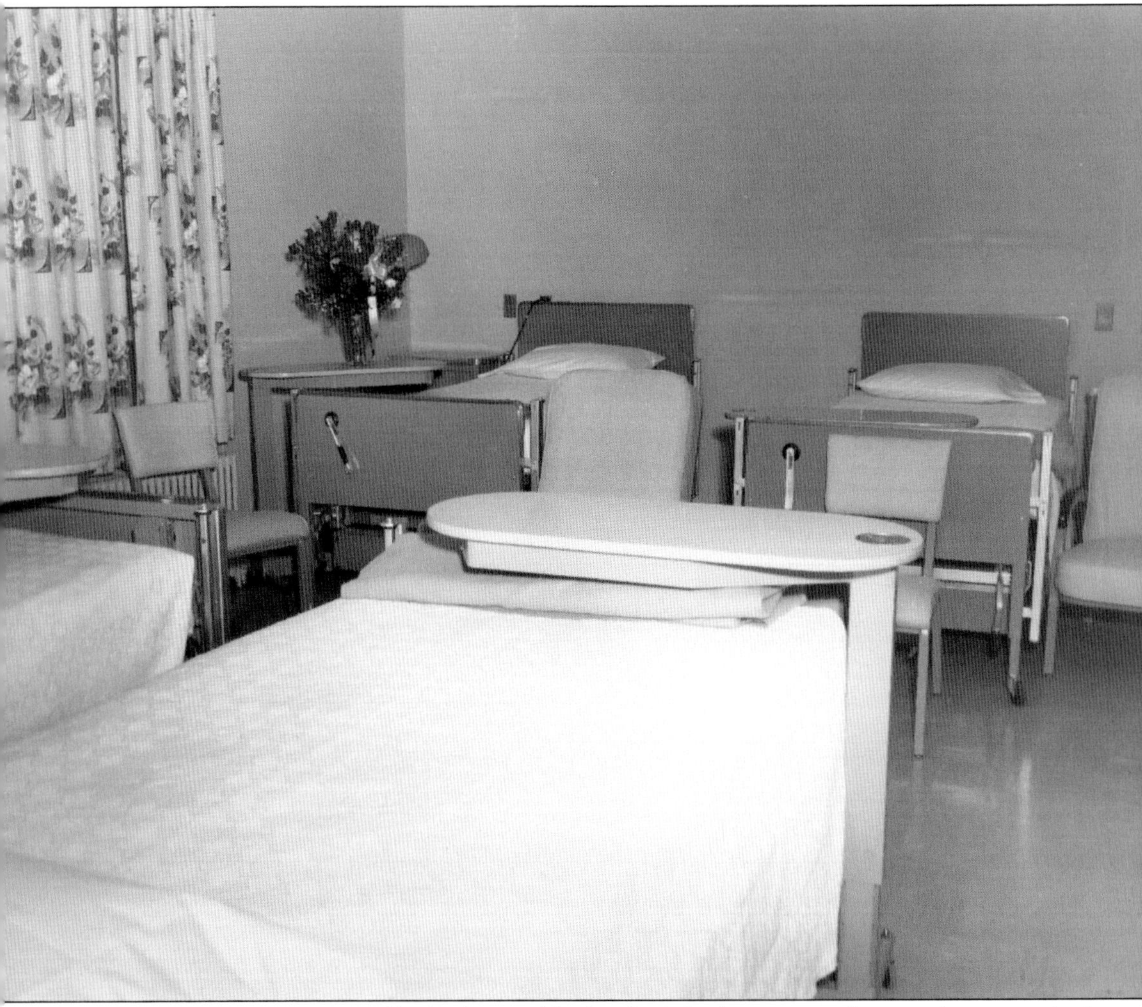

Hospital Rooms. Originally the hospital had only 50 beds—not nearly enough to provide the care that was needed for the community. With the many mines in the vicinity, the volume of accidents was high, and eventually the hospital expanded. (Courtesy of Dan Zeleniak.)

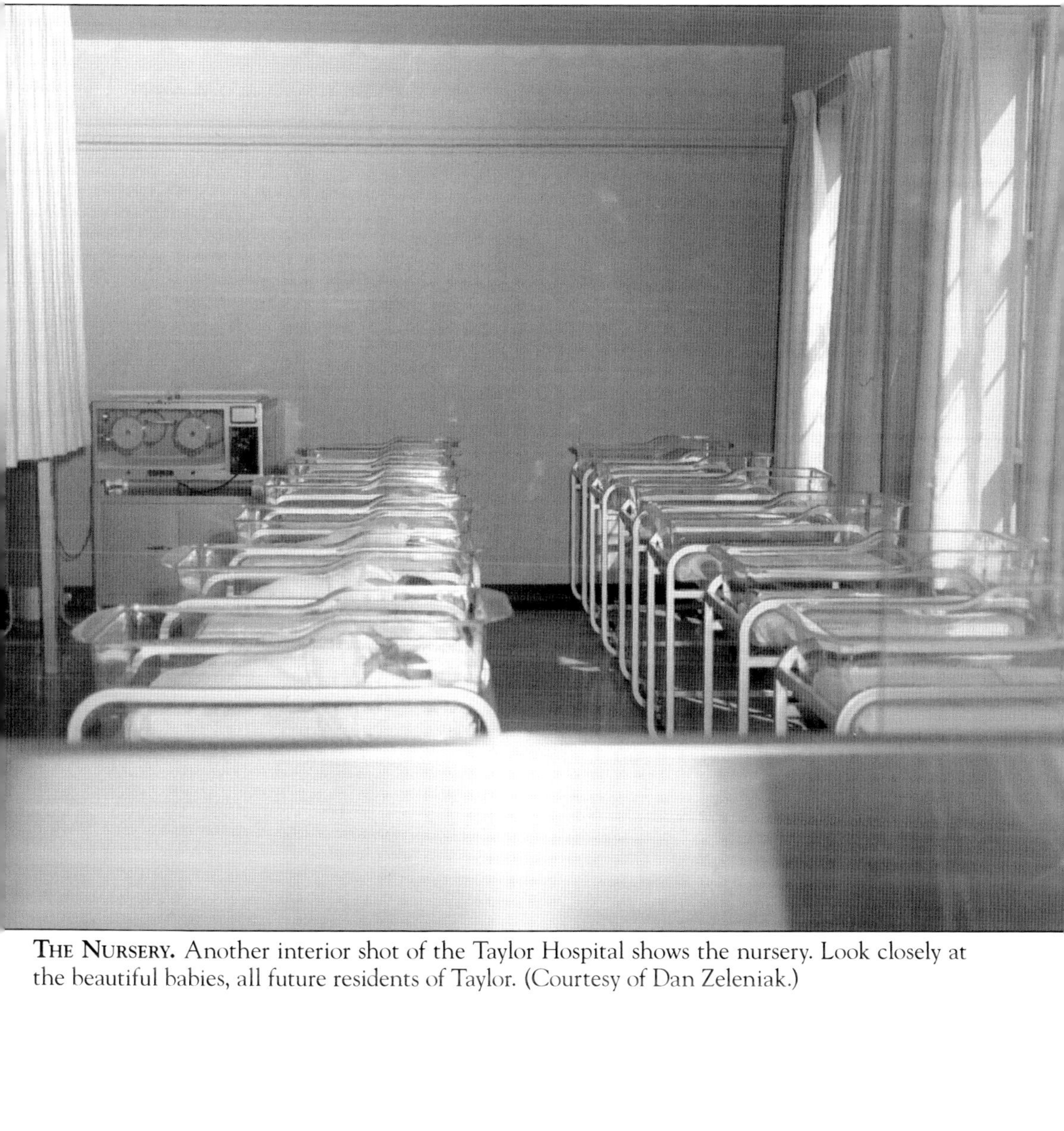

THE NURSERY. Another interior shot of the Taylor Hospital shows the nursery. Look closely at the beautiful babies, all future residents of Taylor. (Courtesy of Dan Zeleniak.)

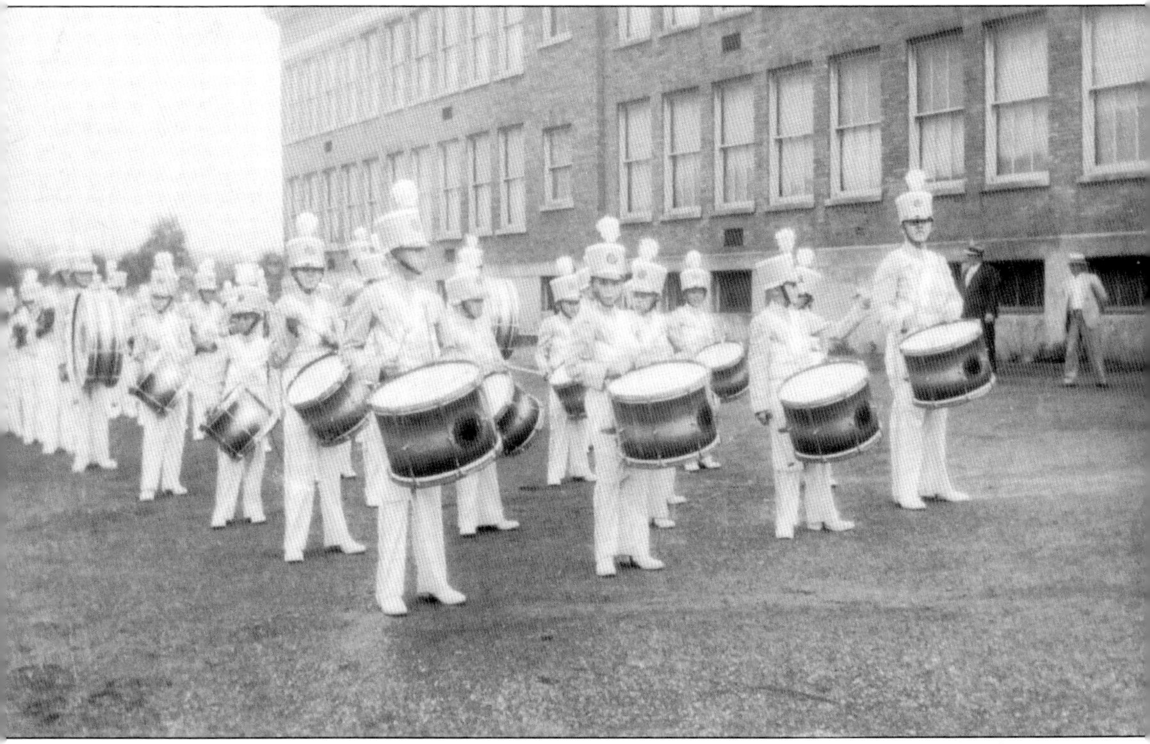

MARCHING BAND. The Taylor High School marching band is seen in front of the school practicing before the annual Memorial Day parade. (Author's collection.)

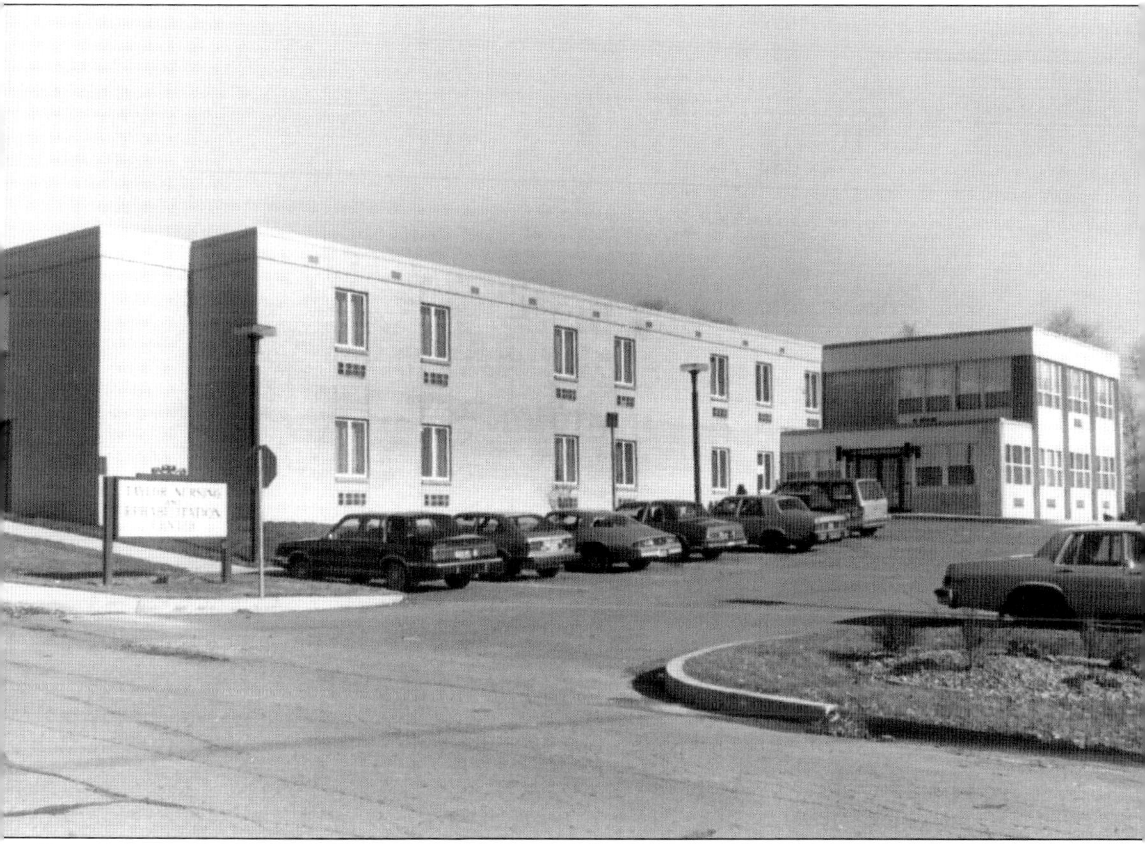

TAYLOR NURSING AND REHABILITATION CENTER. The Taylor Nursing and Rehabilitation Center is located on Hospital Street, the site of the former Taylor Hospital. The facility caters to the needs of the elderly and disabled. (Courtesy of Lackawanna Historical Society.)

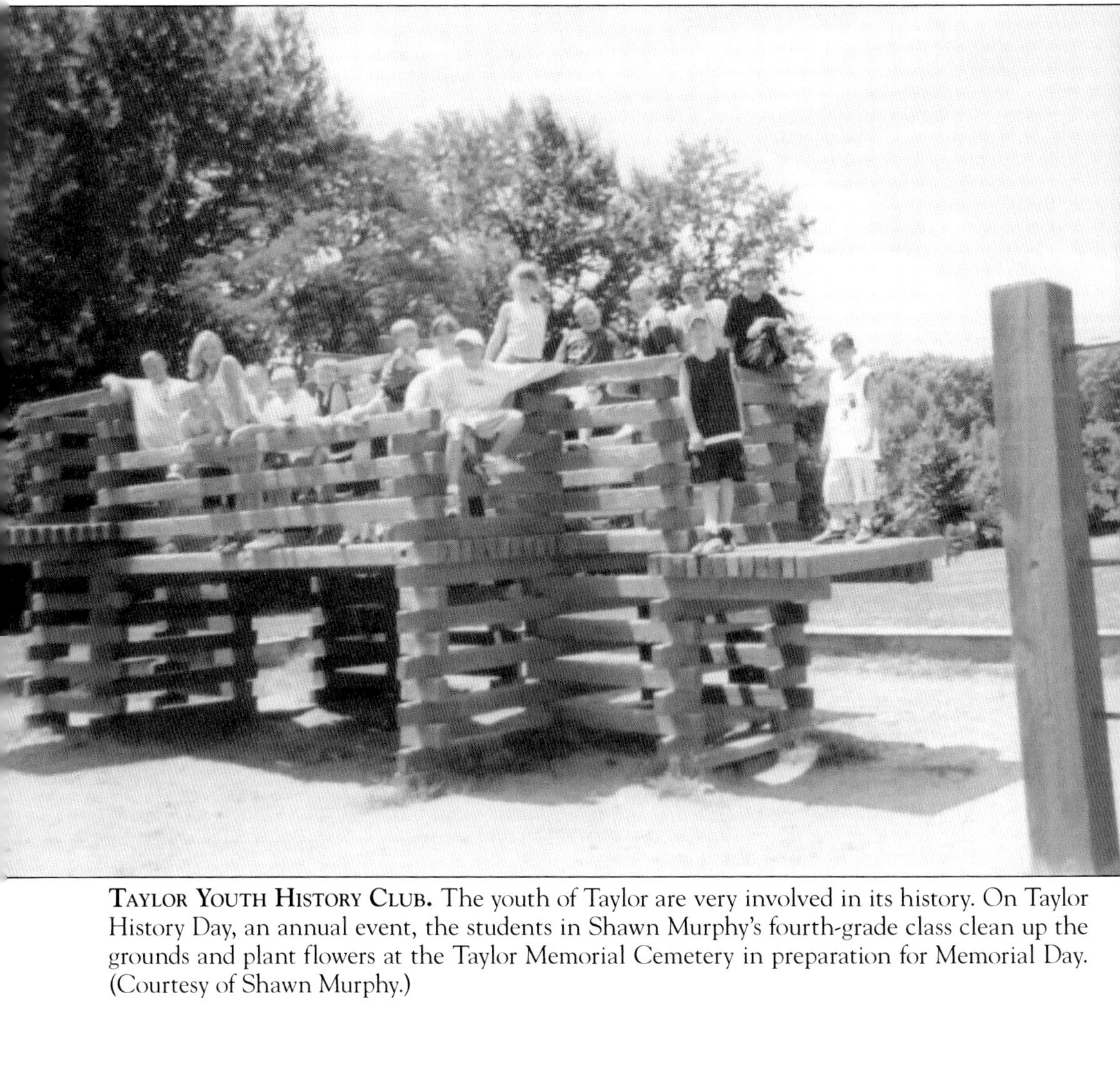

TAYLOR YOUTH HISTORY CLUB. The youth of Taylor are very involved in its history. On Taylor History Day, an annual event, the students in Shawn Murphy's fourth-grade class clean up the grounds and plant flowers at the Taylor Memorial Cemetery in preparation for Memorial Day. (Courtesy of Shawn Murphy.)

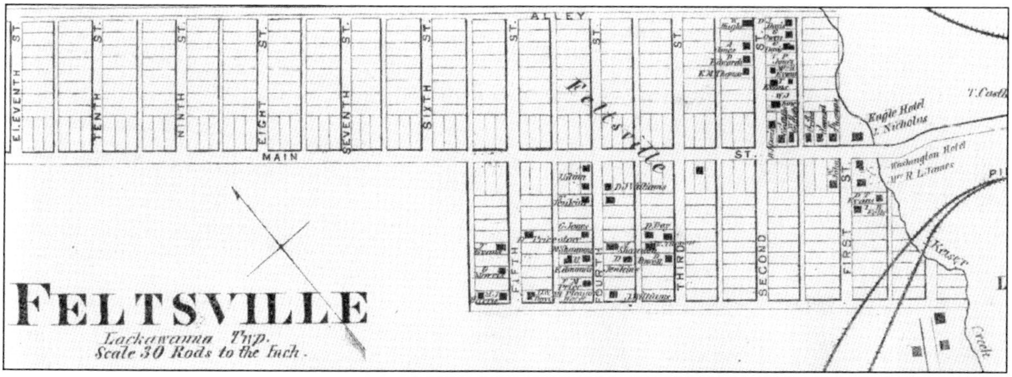

FELTSVILLE MAP. Seen here is the map of the Patch showing all the street names. It was taken from actual surveys by and under the direction of D. G. Beers. The map is from the Atlas of Luzerne County. (Courtesy of Lackawanna Historical Society.)

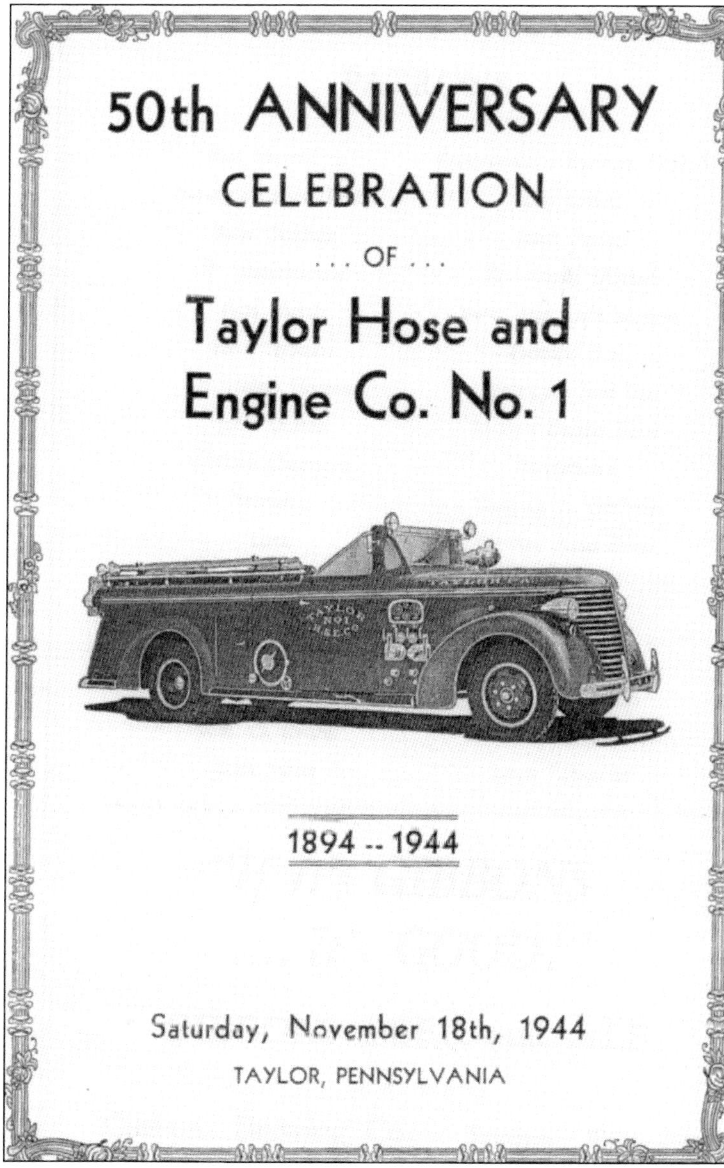

50th ANNIVERSARY

CELEBRATION

. . . OF . . .

Taylor Hose and Engine Co. No. 1

1894 -- 1944

Saturday, November 18th, 1944

TAYLOR, PENNSYLVANIA

TAYLOR HOSE AND ENGINE COMPANY NO. 1. The organization was formed on December 7, 1894, when community members realized the urgent need for fire protection, as the only water piped into Taylor came from a long distance and they had to rely on deep wells to put out fires. (Courtesy of Shawn Murphy.)

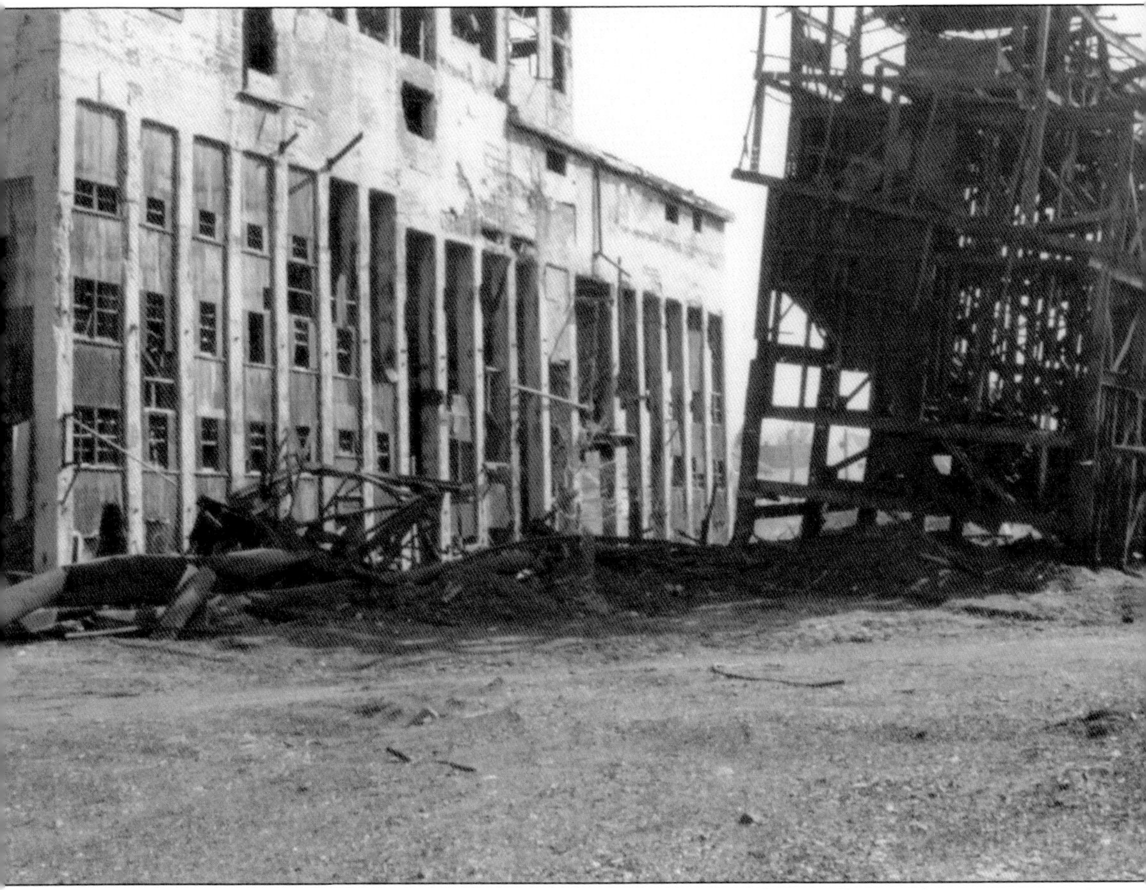

Moffat Coal Company Demise. Shown is what became of the Moffat Coal Company in the 1970s, when it fell victim to arson. (Courtesy of Dan Zeleniak.)

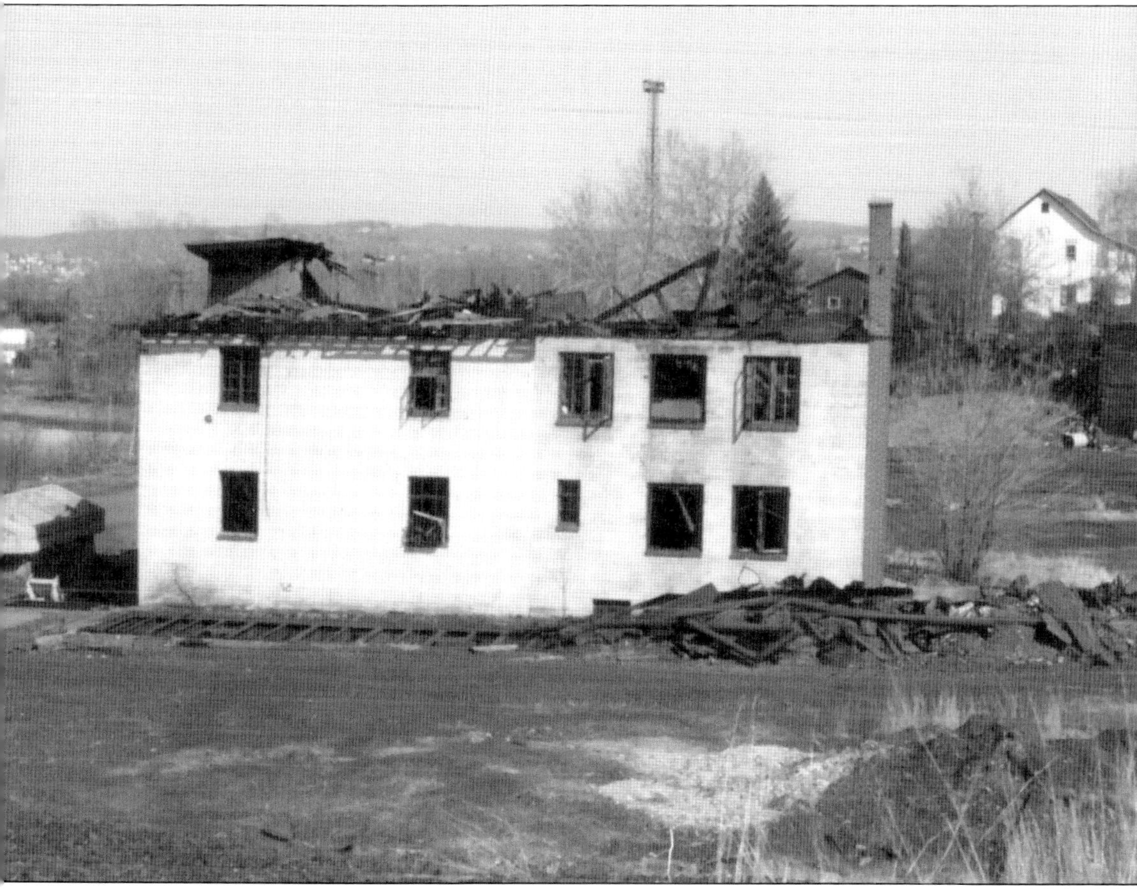

VICTIM OF ARSON AND VANDALISM. Here is another image of a building owned by the Moffat Coal Company after it was set ablaze in the 1970s. The fire department had to be dispatched several times to put out fires. Although the breaker was made of concrete, it did still contain lumber. (Courtesy of Dan Zeleniak.)

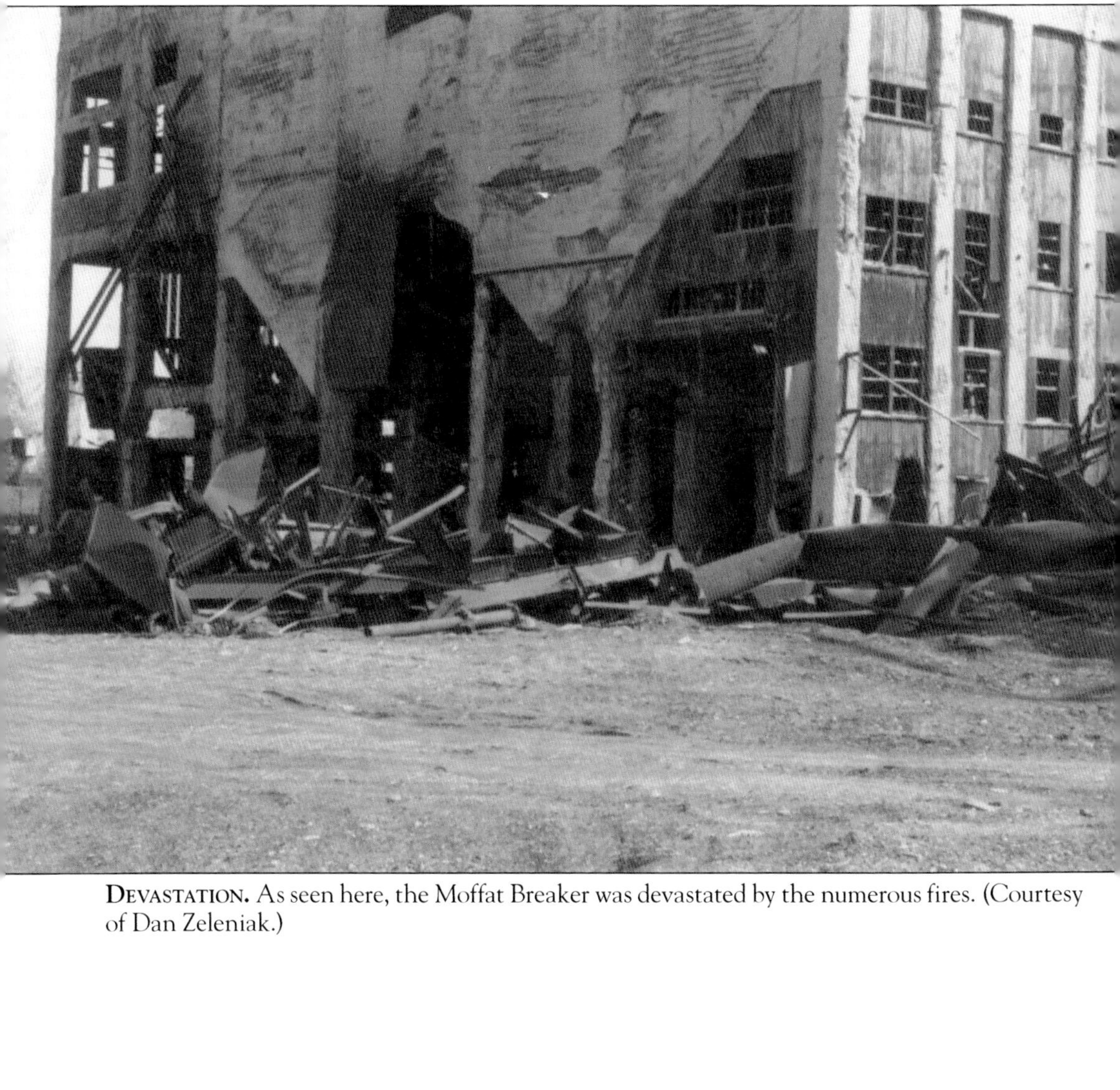

DEVASTATION. As seen here, the Moffat Breaker was devastated by the numerous fires. (Courtesy of Dan Zeleniak.)

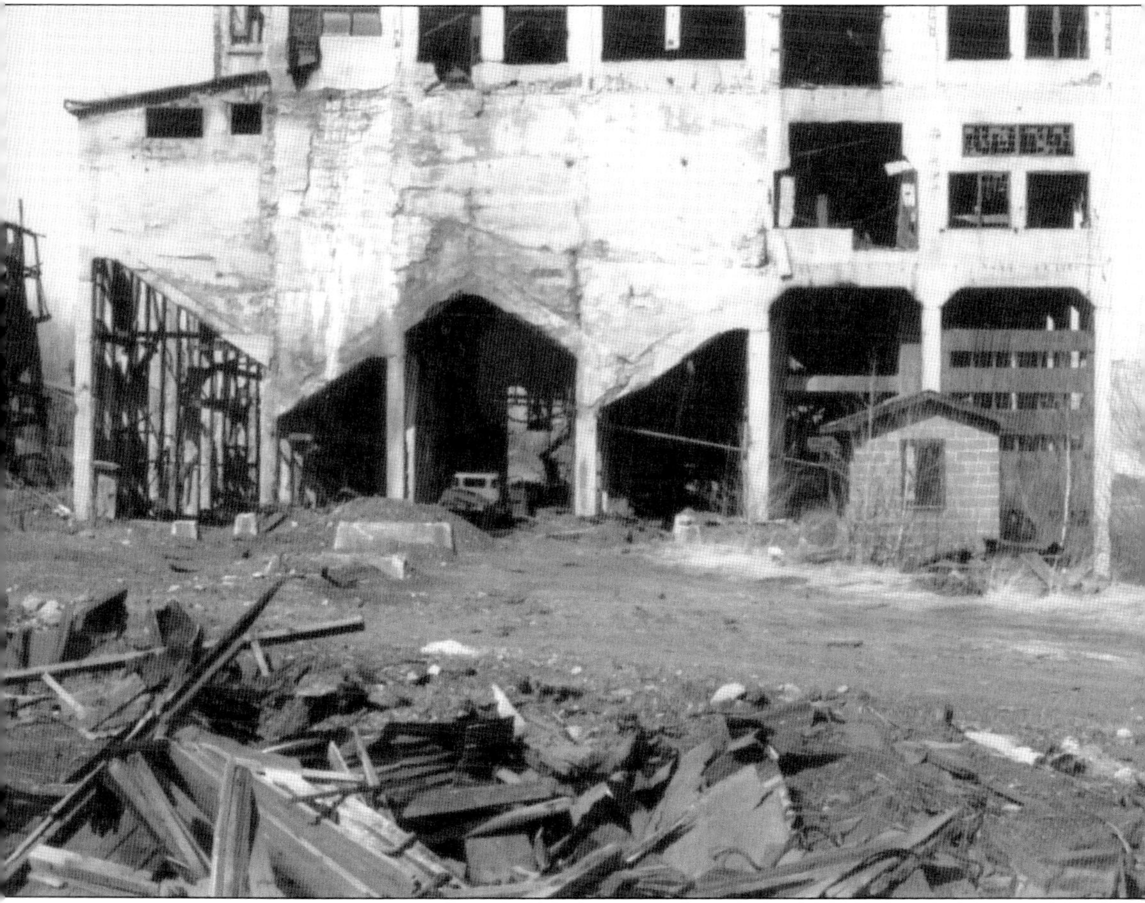

In Ruins. Portions of the Moffat Breaker's walls had to be wrecked in order to salvage the machinery inside, but the structure still remained standing. (Courtesy of Dan Zeleniak.)

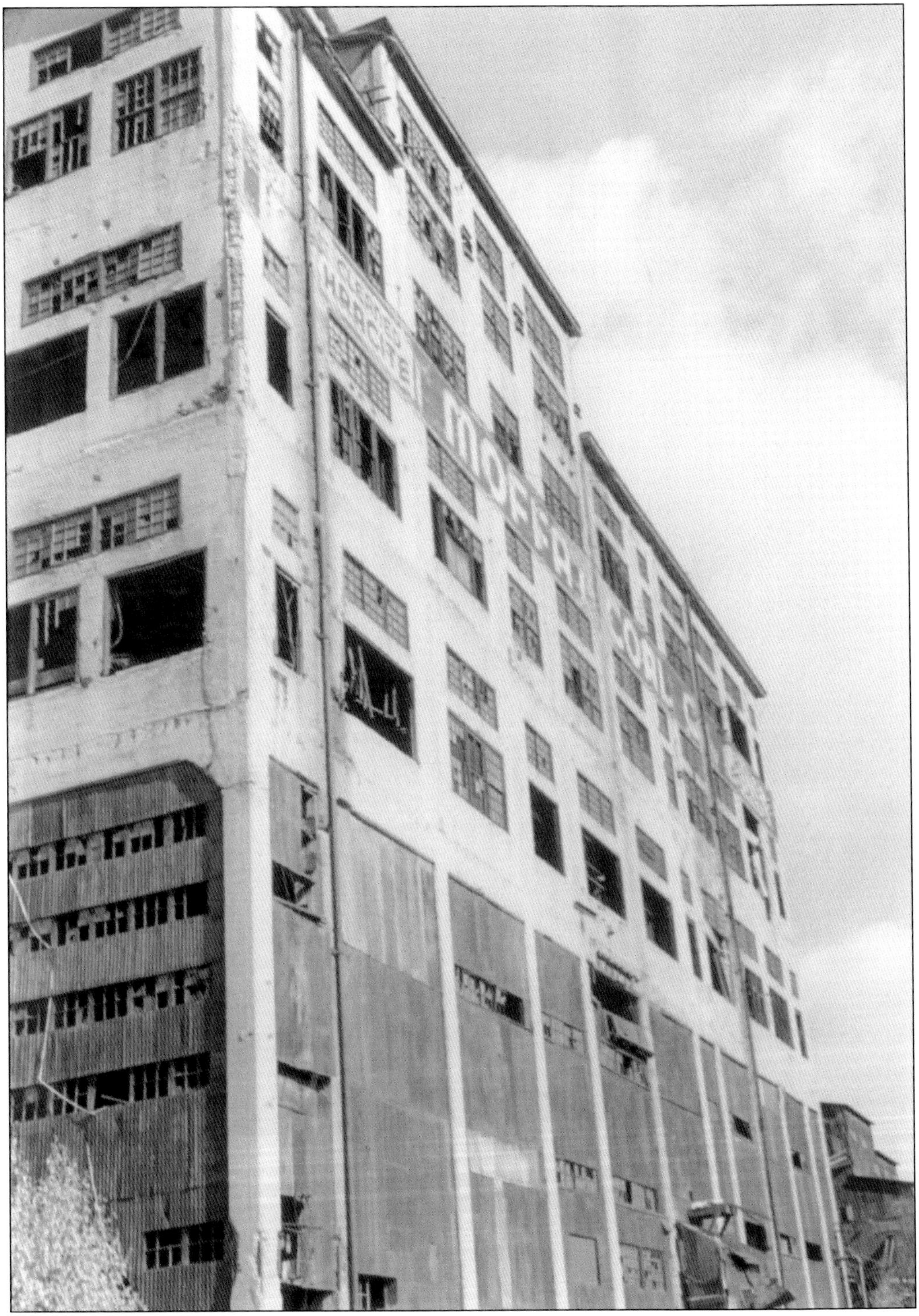

End of an Era. As time went on, some of the citizens deemed the structure an eyesore, and it was finally demolished in 1983. It was the last surviving coal breaker in Lackawanna County. (Courtesy of Dan Zeleniak.)

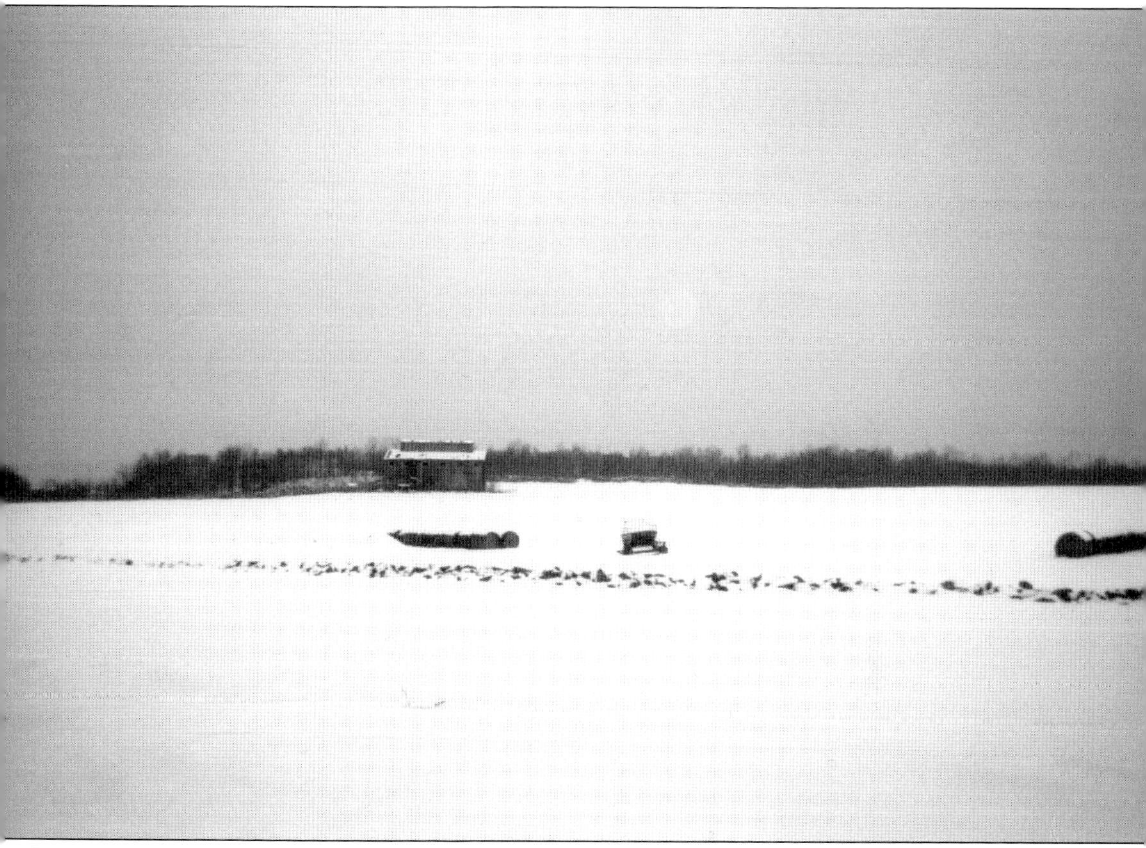

New Beginning. All that remains today of Taylor's anthracite heritage is the boiler house seen at the far end of the photograph. This area is currently under development, and efforts are being made for both commercial and residential homes to occupy this land as a new chapter begins in Taylor's history. (Author's collection.)